THE
CODE

DAVID DANIEL

In the early 2000s, while playing a word game, David Daniel and his family found a number of meaningful words hidden within famous names and places and other words. After taking the searches further—to a point where it no longer appeared random—David and his wife, Blythe, discussed the possibility of a secret code hidden in the English alphabet and in the English language. Blythe gave David a challenge: "Do you think you can find a code hidden in the English language?" David replied, "Yes. If there is a code, I will find it!" After reflecting a moment, she said, "If you can, you will do much more than find a code. You will prove there is a God!" That evening, David discovered the Code, its rules, and the evidence of its existence.

Just as suspected by Pythagoras, St. Augustine, Kabbalists, and numerous others, our world is built on numbers. As you are about to see, THERE IS A SECRET CODE HIDDEN IN THE ENGLISH LANGUAGE. Here lies the long-awaited proof!

THE MOST IMPORTANT DISCOVERY EVER MADE IN THE HISTORY OF THE WORLD

WINSTONLEONARDCHURCHILL

E**············R··D

S··T··O······L······O······A············C··H··U

D··E··R   H··O··L··O··C··A··U··S··T

All original material is Copyright © 2024, 2023, 2020, 2019, 2006 David Daniel

All Rights Reserved. No portion of this work may be reproduced or transmitted in any form or by any means, electronic or mechanical, including photocopying or recording, or by any information storage or retrieval system, without permission in writing from David Daniel or the respective copyright holder.

Library of Congress Control Number: 2202913056

Printed in the United States of America
First Paperback Edition, 2024

Edited by Blythe Daniel
Cover Art by David Daniel
Artwork by Roger Wong

Rajanata Publishing
3130 Balfour Rd.
Ste. D - 428
Brentwood, CA 94513-5516

www.thecodebreaker.org
email: david@thecodebreaker.org

ISBN-13-979-8-9866086-0-0

For Blythe—whose teachings cross the dimensions of time and space

For Rachel—whose truth lights up the darkness

For Jake—who carries the history of humanity in his soul

For Tanner—whose mind bends the light towards all that is good

For Natasha—who puts the word love in the word evolve

For Humanity—may we learn our lessons in time

ACKNOWLEDGMENTS

With praise and deep gratitude to:

Blythe Daniel for using her masterful editing skills to bring this book to fruition

David Kaczmarek for his genius in discovering statistical methods for measuring the unusual

Roger Wong, who is the most talented photo wizard on the planet

Grandma Inez, who taught me unconditional love

James Edward "Jimmy" Garrett, my best friend in elementary school, with whom I created many theories

Lela Alice Fairfield, my first-grade teacher, for recognizing something special in me

Majel Summer Siegrist Drake, my sixth-grade teacher, for her inspiring instruction and encouraging words

Richard Thompson, my junior high math teacher, who turned math into a life-long passion

Marjorie Leona Bolt, my senior high English teacher, who made words come alive

Robert Louis Kort, my psychology professor, friend, and mentor who encouraged me to ask questions and to delve into the improbable

Terence Roberts, my graduate school professor and member of the Little Rock Nine, who taught me that giving up is never an option

TABLE OF CONTENTS

SECTION I—INTRODUCTION AND INTRODUCTORY INFORMATION — 1

    Definitions of Terms — 4
    Exceptions — 7
    Words and Numbers—Background to the Code — 8
    My Story — 12
    The Discovery — 15
    The Alphabet Equality Hypothesis — 17
    The Code Revealed: The Alphanumeric Conversion Table — 19
    Rules of Substitution — 19

SECTION II—THE EVIDENCE — 21

    American War of Independence — 23
    The Findings of Three Major Wars Involving the United States that Support the Claim that there is a Secret Code Hidden in the English Language — 41
    The Civil War — 43
    World War One and the United States — 71
    WWI — 85
    World War I — 93
    First World War — 99
    World War Two and the United States — 107
    WWII — 123
    World War II — 133
    Second World War — 139
    The Findings of the Two World Wars and the Prime Ministers of the United Kingdom that Support the Claim that there is a Secret Code Hidden in the English Language — 147
    World War One — 149
    WWI — 153
    World War I — 157
    First World War — 169
    World War Two — 175
    WWII — 181
    World War II — 185
    Second World War — 189

The World Wars and the British Monarchs	195
Der Holocaust	209
Der Holocaust and the Prime Ministers of the United Kingdom	227
Der Holocaust and the British Monarchs	247

SECTION III—SUPPLEMENTAL EVIDENCE OF THE CODE — 255

Presentations in the Names of World Leaders Standing Alone and in Clusters — 257

Comparison of Name Length in the Names of World Leaders with Presentations or Incidental Displays — 271

SECTION IV—SUMMARY — 291

SECTION V—APPENDICES — 301

Appendix A: Legal and Historical Documents — 303
Appendix B: Exclusions from Tests — 309
Appendix C: Coolidge-Taft-Obama-Balfour Associations — 319
Appendix D: The Alternate Prediction: The Great War and Herbert Henry Asquith — 325
Appendix E: The 64-Year Phenomenon — 333

SECTION VI—STATISTICS — 337

NUMBERS ARE THE UNIVERSAL LANGUAGE
OFFERED BY THE DEITY
AS CONFIRMATION OF THE TRUTH

St. Augustine of Hippo

(A.D. 354 - 430)

CODE
(KOʊD) noun

a system of words, letters, numbers, and/or symbols for which there are rules for their association so that information can be communicated in secret and for which there are methods of translating or interpreting their meaning

FORMAT OF THE BOOK

This book examines the relationships between Historical Events and the Heads of State and Military Leaders who had a strong involvement in or association with the Events. It is written and designed in a reader-friendly format. The following is an outline of that format.

SECTIONS AND SUBSECTIONS: The six sections of the book are titled "Introduction and Introductory Information," "The Evidence," "Supplemental Evidence of the Code," "Summary," "Appendices," and "Statistics." There are also subsections for each of the Historical Events in relation to the leaders of a nation involved in the Event.

INTRODUCTION AND INTRODUCTORY INFORMATION: The first section serves as background to the book and includes information on such subjects as Pythagoras, Gematria, the Naming of Names and Etymology. Also included is a story about the author and his discovery of the Code. There is also a full description of how the Code works that will help with understanding how the author deciphers it.

HISTORIES: Each subsection has a brief history of the Historical Event that is the subject of discussion. The purpose of the history is to provide some background to the Event. The histories are printed in bold Palatino Linotype to differentiate them from the story of the discovery of the Code.

PICTURES OF HISTORICAL EVENTS: Each Historical Event is accompanied by one or more pictures.

BIOGRAPHIES: Each subsection has a brief biography of each Head of State and Military Leader strongly involved in or associated with the Historical Event that is the subject of discussion. There are two objectives for each biography. One is to give you some general background of the person. The other is to focus on why this person is important in relation to the Historical Event. This may mean that other important details regarding a Head of State or Military Leader are not included. In a few cases, a historical figure is a part of more than one section. In these cases, biographical information relating this individual to one Event and then to another will be seen. Therefore, these biographies differ. Like the histories, the biographies are printed in Bold Palatino Linotype to differentiate them from the story of the discovery of the Code.

PICTURES OF HEADS OF STATE AND MILITARY LEADERS: Each biography is accompanied by a picture.

STORY: The ongoing story of the discovery of the Code can be found throughout the book. The story is written to describe the moments of discovery as they happened. It is printed in Calibri Linotype to distinguish it from the histories and biographies.

TABLES: Tables throughout the book demonstrate the phenomenon being revealed. They are of two types. One type of table shows all the leaders of a nation (i.e., U.S., U.K. and Germany) with a leader (i.e., President, Prime Minister, Monarch, Chancellor) next to a listing of the letters in the Event their name contains or does not contain. The other type of table shows the actual letters and/or converted letters that are in a unique individual's name that are also found in the name of the Event. These tables provide visual evidence of the Code.

THE THREE CLAIMS: Three Claims are made in this book. The validity of the Claims is investigated and evaluated as the discovery of the Code is revealed.

SUMMARY: A summary is found at the end of each section and subsection. It is a summary of the evidence that supports each of the Three Claims.

AUTHOR'S STATEMENT: An author's statement is found at the end of each section and subsection. It describes the author's objective and subjective experience at each stage of discovery.

PROBABILITY PAGE: A probability page is found at the end of each subsection. A statistician calculated a Cumulative Probability, which shows what the chance would be of the findings in this book occurring randomly.

APPENDICES: The appendices provide supporting information that is relevant to the material in the book. The appendices can be found in Section V.

STATISTICAL TESTS: Statistical Tests were performed by a statistician to provide supporting statistical measures for the recurring phenomenon that is revealed in the book. These Statistical Tests are found in Section VI.

SECTION I

INTRODUCTION AND INTRODUCTORY INFORMATION

I have discovered that the English alphabet is a secret code hidden in the English language. I'm inviting you to join me on an exciting journey where you will experience the story of my discovery. Along the way, we'll explore history, linguistics, gematria, philosophy and my deciphering of the Code.

A code is a system used to encrypt a message for the purposes of secrecy. A code keeps information hidden until it reaches the designated recipient or until its due time. Depending on the complexity of the system, it can take many years before a code is interpreted or broken. There are codebreakers who are still trying to translate some codes from long ago.

To break a code, one must find the key or codebook that allows them to translate or interpret its meaning. This may involve studying the placement of letters in a word, examining the arrangement of numbers, or studying symbols which are used as a representation to convey messages. No matter what type of code is being investigated, the key must first be identified. In this book, I'll share with you how I discovered the key to the Code and how I found historical information hidden in names.

The book begins with introductory information on language and the origin of words, including Gematria, the Naming of Names and Etymology. I then describe and explain the way the Code works and how to use it. The essence of the book is the telling of the story of the discovery as the Code unfolds right before your very eyes. Tables demonstrate how particular Heads of State are related to certain Historical Events. The book contains brief histories of the Events and brief biographies of the characters involved as historical background. Evidence presented supports each of the Three Claims I make in this book, along with statistics that compare the frequency of words in the names of Heads of State with the general population and statistics that present the probability of what you see in this book occurring randomly.

I want you to know that after conducting extensive research and hiring a statistician to independently test all of my work, I conclude that the Code is not accidental nor random but intentional and irrefutable. The existence of the Code is nothing short of life-changing and the implications are limitless. It has the potential to change the way people think about themselves, their relationship to each other and the greater meaning and purpose of our lives.

It's astonishing that this deliberate but secret code has been etched into the English language to be discovered one day for all to see. So come with me now as we discover the secret code.

DEFINITIONS OF TERMS

Before we begin, we need to have a language to share in order for us to describe, explain and fully comprehend what we are seeing. Throughout this book, I use certain terms in a specific way. Some are familiar, such as *Display*, and some are unfamiliar but self-explanatory, such as *Overt Display*. These terms reflect a language I developed during my discovery of the Code. These terms and other terms important to the Claims I make in this book are capitalized.

Once you become familiar with the terms and learn how to use the Code, you'll be able to easily see the relationships between the Historical Events and the people discussed in this book. It will be as if you have put on 3D glasses, which will make what you are seeing self-evident and meaningful. The more you understand how the Code works, the more exciting the journey. The secret code that has been hidden in the English alphabet and English language will be revealed to you.

DISPLAY

A Display is any letters, words, names or initialisms found in a name or other word. Every letter in a name or word has many reasons for being there. As an example of a Display, you will find the words SOCKS—NO SHOES in JOSEPH JEFFERSON JACKSON (the given name of the baseball player known as Shoeless Joe Jackson) and SOCKS—SHOES ARE OFF.

OVERT DISPLAY

An Overt Display is a Display of the actual letters in a name or word without the use of Conversion or Substitution. Many actual letters are in a name or word for meaningful purposes. Many letters are there for multiple reasons—both Overt and Covert, as you will see in some of the names in this book. The previous example of SOCKS—NO SHOES is an Overt Display because the actual letters are found in JOSEPH JEFFERSON JACKSON.

COVERT DISPLAY

A Covert Display is a Display that is not the actual letters in a name or word, but one that appears in Code—using the Conversion Table and/or the Rules of Substitution as found in this book. Many findings include a mix of actual letters and converted or substituted letters. For example, the words WHITE SOX can be found covertly in the name JOSEPH JEFFERSON JACKSON. One O in Joseph can, in a way that will soon be explained, be converted to an X; the E can be a W; the K can be a

T; the R can be the letter I. The H and E and S and the other O are already there. We can also find a Covert Display of INNOCENT in his name. This is not proof that he was innocent of conspiring with other members of the Chicago White Sox to rig the 1919 World Series, a case which remains controversial to this day, so we do not know if this is just an Incidental Covert Display or if it is there for something more meaningful.

ABSENCE OF DISPLAY

Absence of Display is exactly that, the absence of a Display of a Historical Event. If a name has no Display of a particular Historical Event, it is said to have an Absence of Display. An Absence of Display is considered a "correct prediction" when the name of an Event is absent from the name of someone who has no strong involvement in or association with that Event. For example, JAMES MONROE has no association with THE CIVIL WAR and his name has no Display of THE CIVIL WAR. The Absence of Display is, then, a correct prediction that JAMES MONROE has no strong involvement in or association with THE CIVIL WAR.

INCIDENTAL DISPLAY

A Display that happens to be in a name but has no relationship with the name is called an Incidental Display. The letters or numerical values are there for other reasons—just not for the one being tested. Statistically, however, and only for statistical reasons, it is treated as a failure to predict no significant involvement or association when there is, indeed, none.

PRESENTATION

A Presentation is any Display—either Overt or Covert—that, by its appearance in a word or name, has a significant meaning or association within the name or word where it is found. The meaning and the rarity of SOCKS—NO SHOES as it is found in JOSEPH JEFFERSON JACKSON suggests this Display might be a Presentation. Be reminded that he also has SOCKS—SHOES OFF!

OVERT PRESENTATION

An Overt Presentation is an Overt Display in actual letters of a name or word(s) or an initialism found within a name or word(s) that has a perceived meaningful purpose for being there. For example, the Display of SOCKS—NO SHOES in the previous example is Overt. We don't need to convert any letters in Jackson's name to find SOCKS—NO SHOES or SOCKS—SHOES OFF.

COVERT PRESENTATION

A Covert Presentation is a Covert Display of a word or words or an initialism that has a perceived meaningful purpose for being in the name or word(s). The Code in this book uses Conversion and Substitution, as fully delineated below. Similar to the Overt Presentation, the finding of the word or words in a name or word does not make for a Presentation unless there is meaning or a significant association. To find WHITE SOX in the name of JOSEPH JEFFERSON JACKSON does require conversion, so it is Covert. Although to find SHOELESS JOE, we only change the C in JACKSON to an L for SHOELESS, it is still a Covert Presentation.

MIXED PRESENTATION

Sometimes, we find that part of a Presentation is Overt and part of it is Covert. There are four ways to express the Second World War—WORLD WAR TWO, WORLD WAR II, SECOND WORLD WAR, and WWII. A search for the actual letters in WWII is completely Overt. A search—using conversion—for WORLD WAR TWO or SECOND WORLD WAR in a name is Covert. But a search for WORLD WAR II includes a Covert search for WORLD WAR and an Overt Search for II. This is a Mixed Presentation.

LEVEL ZERO PRESENTATION

A Level Zero Presentation is the rare Overt or Covert Presentation found within only one of a person's names—often, but not always, the surname.

LEVEL ONE PRESENTATION

A Level One Presentation is an Overt or Covert Presentation in a name that is limited to only one given name and one surname.

LEVEL TWO PRESENTATION

A Level Two Presentation is an Overt or Covert Presentation in a name that contains *all* given names and the surname—even when the name has multiple given names. The search at Level Two is usually made after a search at Level One. We often find the names of more people associated with an Event than we do during a search for a Level One Presentation. Our finding of SOCKS—NO SHOES in JOSEPH JEFFERSON JACKSON requires the use of all three names, so our finding is a Level Two Presentation.

LEVEL THREE PRESENTATION

A Level Three Presentation includes more than given names and surnames—such as generational suffixes. These suffixes include Jr. and Sr., or I, II, III, IV, and so on. The inclusion of Roman numerals does not necessitate that the individual be named after one's parent; they can be named after another relative. Some Monarchs' names contain Roman numerals to identify them, e.g., GEORGE III, GEORGE IV, and GEORGE V. Other people may have the abbreviation JR or SR.

SUPERIOR PRESENTATION
We will consider an Overt Presentation as being Superior to a Covert Presentation because it is less common. In the research in this book, we find several examples in which the central Head of State has an Overt and/or a Covert Presentation, while others only have the Covert. We can also find a Level One Presentation to be Superior to a Level Two Presentation, as it is also much less common. In some cases, the leader who is most central to the Event has a Level One Presentation, while the names of others associated with the Event might also have a Level One or may only have a Level Two or Level Three Presentation.

RARE OR EXCLUSIVE DISPLAYS IN NAMES AND WORDS
It's not necessary for any Display (words or initialisms) to be totally exclusive in a name or word for it to be meaningful and to be accepted as an Overt or Covert Presentation. But the rarity or exclusivity is very strong evidence of the Code.

EXCEPTIONS

NAMESAKE EXCEPTION
When two people have the same given name(s) and surname, they are namesakes, even when they have name suffixes as generational designations, such as SR and JR or II. In these cases, all parties with the same name share Displays that could be meaningful to some and meaningless to others. U.S. President RUTHERFORD BIRCHARD HAYES was not in WORLD WAR I, but several namesakes were in the war. It's likely some of these Veterans have it in their names for a reason. President RUTHERFORD BIRCHARD HAYES does not. For this reason, HAYES and others in his situation are excluded from such investigations and tests.

EXCEPTIONS DUE TO SIMILARITIES OF NAMES OR EVENTS
The names of some of the wars in this book share many of their letters. WORLD WAR ONE and WORLD WAR TWO share all but two letters. WORLD WAR I and WORLD WAR II are nearly identical—as are WWI and WWII. SECOND contains all three of the letters in ONE, and FIRST contains I. There is a high probability, then, that a Head of State with a Presentation of one war will have an Incidental Display of another war. For this reason, some Heads of State must be excluded from the test of an Event when it appears to be an Incidental Display.

WORDS AND NUMBERS—BACKGROUND TO THE CODE

Before I share the story of my discovery of the Code, I thought it important to introduce you to several related subjects to provide background to the content of the book. I therefore invite you to learn more about Pythagoras, Gematria, the Naming of Names and Etymology.

PYTHAGORAS

Early history points to human fascination with numbers, letters, and language. Pythagoras and his early followers—known as Pythagoreans—have been widely credited with a pioneering influence on the idea that all things are made of numbers. They attributed meanings to all the numbers from one to nine. Numerous scholars credit Pythagoras as the founder of the theorem concerning right triangles given his name. He believed that numbers contained secrets about the universe.

GEMATRIA

Gematria is a Hebrew term for the practice of assigning numerical values to letters of an alphabet and then to words, names, and phrases based on those values. The term is believed to have derived either from the Greek *geōmetriā* (geometry) or the Greek *grammateia* (knowledge of writing) or from a combination of both. The term or variations of the term are used by many cultures (i.e., English, Greek), but some cultures use other terms (i.e., abjad in Arabic).

The most common ultimate purpose of Gematria is to find relationships between words or phrases or to find deeper meanings—sometimes hidden, often spiritual or mystical—in words or phrases.

Since the invention of written language, humans have sought secret meanings in letters, numbers, and words. The practice of Gematria as we know it originated with the Assyrians, Babylonians and Greeks and was passed to other cultures. The study and practice became important to Jewish culture. In Jewish culture, numbers are believed to be a pathway to an understanding of God and the Divine. It is especially of interest to some who are involved in studying the Kabbalah. Hebrew Gematria, in turn, has been a major influence on the practice of Gematria in other cultures. The practice involves assigning numerical values to letters using one of several systems—usually one of two related systems commonly known as Gematria and Small Gematria. To differentiate these two systems in this book, I refer to them as Large Gematria and Small Gematria.

For the English or Latin alphabet, this would mean either using the common or the large values of Large Gematria, which assigns values [1 - 9 for A to I, 10 - 90 for J to R, and 100 - 800 for S to Z] or Small Gematria, which uses the single-digit-value of the numbers in the first set [1 - 9 for A to I, 1 - 9 for J to R, 1 - 8 for S to Z]. The values of Small Gematria were calculated by adding the digits for each letter in the first set. For example, T=200. We add the digits: 2+ 0 + 0=2. Another method of finding Small Gematria can be described as the simple process of truncating the zeroes.

Large Gematria

A = 1	J = 10	S = 100
B = 2	K = 20	T = 200
C = 3	L = 30	U = 300
D = 4	M = 40	V = 400
E = 5	N = 50	W = 500
F = 6	O = 60	X = 600
G = 7	P = 70	Y = 700
H = 8	Q = 80	Z = 800
I = 9	R = 90	

Small Gematria

A = 1	J = 1	S = 1
B = 2	K = 2	T = 2
C = 3	L = 3	U = 3
D = 4	M = 4	V = 4
E = 5	N = 5	W = 5
F = 6	O = 6	X = 6
G = 7	P = 7	Y = 7
H = 8	Q = 8	Z = 8
I = 9	R = 9	

While these are the two most common methods of Gematria, some Kabbalists, mathematicians, clerics, mystics and hobbyists assign the letters their ordinal value from 1 to the number of the last letter. Still others assign a descending order from highest numerical value to lowest numerical value. This can be done with Large or Standard Gematria, Small Gematria or the ordinal form of Gematria. With whatever numerical values they use, it's common practice to find the numerical value of the word or phrase or reduce the value to a single digit.

Throughout time, many have searched for systems, ciphers or methodologies that might produce evidence or proof of a force or higher order we might call God or that could lead the way to a greater understanding of the universe.

There is also a history of Christian uses of Gematria. The most well-known is the Number of the Beast, which is stated as 666 in the Book of Revelation. This author finds it interesting to note that 666 is found in Revelation 13:18. The sum of three 6s is 18—the verse in Revelation 13 where it is found.

While many people restrict the study and practice of Gematria to the search for religious meanings and interpretations of such things as prayers or scripture or God, there are also many who search for meanings or relationships without any religious context. While the term Gematria is used for what is considered a study and practice of a long-studied and long-revered search for meaning, another term—Numerology—is also sometimes applied to similar practices of studying numbers. For some, the terms overlap. Gematria is often called "Jewish numerology."

Beyond the immediate scope of Gematria, many scientists and mathematicians have noticed patterns and coincidences between large numbers and have intuited meaning. The ratio of the age of the universe and the atomic unit of time is one of numerous examples of what could either be considered a numerical coincidence, a Godless cosmology or evidence of a Divine or Intelligent cosmology. Paul Dirac, considered one of the most important physicists of the 20th century, is known for his Large Number Hypothesis, which implies a cosmology with some unexplainable ratios. (In spite of a belief that this relationship was due to more than a coincidence, Dirac remained a committed atheist.)

There has been a recent revival of Gematria and Torah Codes and other numerological and number-related studies since the publication of *The Bible Code* by Michael Drosnin. This code uses Equidistant Letter Sequences to find predictions, usually in hindsight, of important events. The popular reception of the book has created a renewed interest in finding new discoveries and new methodologies in Gematria and Numerology and in finding "codes" on a grander scale.

THE NAMING OF NAMES

Another popular subject throughout history surrounds the question, "Where did we get the words and terms that we use in our everyday language that represent what we see, hear, and experience in our world?"

Plato was one of the first to discuss the naming of things. In his dialogue *Cratylus*, Hermogenes and Cratylus ask Socrates if the naming of names is conventional or natural. Without becoming involved in the debate over whether Socrates endorsed either school of thought, it's only important here for us to understand the conventional and natural positions on the origin of names. The conventionalist argues that names for things are random and arbitrary and "that any word will do," while the naturalist argues that names belong to things and that names are encoded descriptions of what they represent.

Philosophers and linguists have often discussed the appropriateness of names. An onomatopoeia is assumed to be appropriate because it is a word that imitates or suggests the sound it describes, like "splash" or "bang." But this is not the sole quality that makes a word suitable in its use to describe a person, place, thing or feeling. The ancient Greeks used onomatopoeia as evidence of the natural development of language. They believed that language arose from the natural sounds we hear. Some linguists theorize that onomatopoeia was the first human language. In the development of a language, natural sounds form the basis of words, which become the basis for building other words. Onomatopoeia does not explain all words, obviously, but it appears to have played an important role in the origin of language.

ETYMOLOGY

Etymology is the study of the origin of words through Philological Research (studying changes in forms using older texts), Dialectological Research (how dialectological variance may suggest earlier history), Comparative Methods (finding which words are derived from older languages and loan words "borrowed" from other languages) and Semantic Shift (making hypotheses about changes in the meaning of words). All these areas of study seek to understand if words are born with meaning.

Early in our history, humans began to make vocalizations and, obviously, these vocalizations expressed feelings and sought to identify things. As this continued, the vocalizations evolved into what we would call words and, eventually, language.

Certain sounds are consonant sounds, produced by complete or partial closure of the vocal tract, and they involve the lips, the front of the tongue, the back of the tongue, the teeth, the throat or any combination of two or more of these. Other sounds are vowel sounds, produced by an open vocal tract.

At some point, humans began to create symbols for these sounds. Some of the earliest alphabets omitted symbols for vowels and only had symbols for the consonant sounds.

Early humans developed arithmetic and alphabets. These alphabets were eventually sequenced in a special order, and then this order was numbered. Finally, at some point, some humans assigned numerical values to the letters based on those numbers. Some sought a meaning, usually spiritual or religious, of the numerical values ascribed to letters, words, phrases, sentences, gods and people. Over time, Gematria became a form of study and a practice of exploration of the relationship between numbers and words and phrases.

MY STORY

My story begins at Lafayette Elementary School in Jacksonville, Illinois. The wonderful schoolteachers we had there must have worked together as a team, because they all read to us from the same author—Laura Ingalls Wilder (*Little House on the Prairie* and *Little House in the Big Woods*)—and they all invited us to play the same word game.

They gave us a word like "*Thanksgiving*," or a word or name from history. Our task was to find as many words as we could using the letters from the given name or word. On one occasion, when we were looking for words in the name WASHINGTON, our teacher interrupted the game to ask how we were doing so far. She asked, "Has anyone found over one hundred words?" I raised my hand. To my astonishment, when I looked around the room, I was the only one who had raised a hand. I had found 161 words. I would always win that particular game.

Throughout elementary school, I had lots of fun with the alphabet. In second grade, I learned how to recite, sing, and pronounce the alphabet backwards, which I had fun doing for other kids and, sometimes, for their friends, siblings or parents. I was always aware of things that seemed to me to be in plain sight but that went unnoticed by others. For example, one day, a schoolmate named Harry approached me and recited a silly rhyme popular at the time, "If you want a nickel, go eat a pickle; if you want a dollar, go out in the street and holler." I immediately became aware that two coins rhymed with the names of our second-grade teacher, Mrs. Thelma Denney, and our principal, Ms. Lena Heim. So, I said, "If you want a penny, go ask Miss Denney; if you want a dime, go ask Miss Heim." He laughed hysterically and ran off joyfully to share it with others.

I was quite young, about eight years old, when I discovered that two of Lewis Carroll's poems were acrostics—that is, the first letters of the lines of the poems each spelled a name. One name is ALICE PLEASANCE LIDDELL. I soon found out this was the name of a real girl who inspired *Alice in Wonderland*. The other poem spelled out GERTRUDE CHATAWAY. These acrostics are known among aficionados of Lewis Carroll's works, but I noticed them while I was still a child.

I also had a penchant for numbers. When I was in fourth grade I discovered how to find if a number is divisible by 3, 6, or 9, and then I figured out how to find if a number is divisible by 11. Later, in junior high school, I discovered new ways of doing algebra. As a teenager, I figured out the Pythagorean theorem with a proof before I learned that it had already been discovered. Much later, as an adult taking a statistics class, I inadvertently figured out Pascal's triangle only to learn that it, too, had already been discovered. So, I always had a good eye for patterns in numbers and letters. They spoke to me.

But it was not only numbers and letters; patterns of many kinds spoke to me with the same fluidity. When I was in third grade, I was showing a few classmates something on a globe, and then on a map. Our teacher, Harriet Milburn, asked what we were looking at. One of the children told her that I was showing them how the borders of the continents used to fit together as one like the pieces of a puzzle. At some point, they had broken apart and moved far away from each other. Mrs. Milburn said, "David has such a wonderful imagination." (I was already quite used to this kind of reaction.) What I didn't know, of course, was that four centuries earlier, Abraham Ortelius imagined such a continental drift. Alfred Wegener received credit for the hypothesis in 1912. It was not until the 1960s that continental drift was confirmed and proven correct. I was showing my fellow students and explaining it pretty well for an eight-year-old.

Throughout my childhood, I often wondered if adults actually lived in a conscious world of pretend—that they pretended to believe in a lot more than just Santa

Claus and the tooth fairy. I honestly thought that adults pretended as if they did not see many of the things that I saw or noticed every day.

In 2002, while I was looking at the names of early cases and early suspected cases of death from complications due to AIDS, I saw that many names were given a first name and a last initial to hide their identities. I saw the names SADAYO F., ARDOUIN A., and DICK G. I was able to find the whole names of these individuals. One individual was given a whole name—ARVID DARRE NOE. I realized the name must be an anagram. So, I unscrambled the name several times, finding that the individual's real name was ARNE VIDAR ROED. I was then able to verify his name and the names of his wife and daughter through the Norwegian Death Index.

On another occasion, I looked at patterns in the locations of dump sites where the serial killer known as the Grim Sleeper had left the bodies of his victims and where he had left one victim still alive. I concluded, after some analysis, that he lived near the corner of 81st and Western in Los Angeles, California. As it turned out, he actually lived three houses from the corner of 81st and Western.

Several years ago, I published a book titled *The Mentalist Code and the Search for Red John* about secret codes found in the TV drama series *The Mentalist*. In this book, I share a great number of secret codes and patterns of events left by the brilliant creator of the series, Bruno Heller. The codes suggest the secret identity of Red John, a serial killer who is the main antagonist of the series. It became evident to me after the second episode and it was confirmed in many later episodes before the final reveal.

These are just a few examples of my fascination with words, numbers, and patterns. Searching for things hidden or unnoticed has been my passion. I have made the pursuit of studying and interpreting patterns my life's work. This is what has brought me to this moment of discovery.

THE DISCOVERY

Saturday night was family night at our home. Sitting in the living room with my wife and our four children was my time of delight. We had fun discussions, watched movies, and played games such as Charades, Monopoly and Scrabble. Some evenings we played the word game I had played at Lafayette Elementary School so many years before. All of us would put the chosen word or a person's name at the top of our paper and try to find as many words as we could using letters from that word or name. We played this game almost every Saturday night, and the children became very good at it. Our daughter, Natasha, was exceptional at finding long and meaningful words. One evening my son, Jake, suggested we call the game Scrubble, and so it came to pass that our game had a name.

As we played this game week by week, my wife, Blythe, and I began noticing that some of the words we found in names appeared to have a reason for being there. As we looked further, we kept finding what we considered meaningful or potentially meaningful words. For example, we found DIE IN ALLEY in Blythe's name. She was shocked to see this as she once had a life-threatening incident occur in an alley. We also found personal terms in our names that appeared meaningful.

We discussed the possibility that there was something more here than met the eye. What if there was a code? What if these seemingly coincidental constructions had hidden meanings and were not coincidental at all but somehow deliberately engineered into the language itself? Blythe mentioned *The Bible Code* by Michael Drosnin—a book that discusses a possible code in the Bible that purportedly predicts a great number of future events. We read it.

This book, along with our experiences with the word game, catalyzed and encouraged us to consider the possibility that there was a secret code hidden in the English alphabet and in the English language. Blythe asked, "What if there is a code in the English language that's right there in plain sight—in the letters and words and names we read every day—a secret code just waiting to be discovered?" She continued to ponder aloud for both of us, "What if there is a code that proves that nothing is random—but instead that there is a God—a Creator of all history who secretly, but deliberately, tells the story of the universe right there in the English language?"

Blythe went on, "Do you think you can find if there is a code hidden in the English language?

I replied, "Yes. If there is a code, I will definitely find it."

After reflecting a moment, she said, "If you can, you will do much more than discover a code. You will prove there is a God!"

That afternoon, I began.

My first thought was that if there is a code, it must begin with the alphabet. I read about Gematria and looked at the numerical values assigned to the letters in Small Gematria. The first thing I noticed was that each of the letters had other letters with the same numerical value. It was listed as such:

1 = A, J, S   6 = F, O, X
2 = B, K, T   7 = G, P, Y
3 = C, L, U   8 = H, Q, Z
4 = D, M, V   9 = I, R
5 = E, N, W

But I saw it like this:

1 = A = J = S   6 = F = O = X
2 = B = K = T   7 = G = P = Y
3 = C = L = U   8 = H = Q = Z
4 = D = M = V   9 = I = R
5 = E = N = W

I realized that each of the letters had other letters that were equal in value. I thought that this should be the first place to look for a code. If each of the letters is equal to other letters, maybe each letter can be converted to its numerical value and then to another letter of equal numerical value. This would mean that we can convert an A to 1 and then the 1 to an A, J or S, and so on. I experimented with this a bit, and I saw that this was working. I found several amazing Displays.

Then I made a discovery regarding the numerical values of the alphabet. I noticed that blends (digraphs and trigraphs) that are soundalikes of single letters were equal in numerical value. This is strong evidence that the numerical values of the letters in our alphabet are not random. Here I present this discovery.

THE ALPHABET EQUALITY HYPOTHESIS
(Numerical values are derived from SMALL GEMATRIA)

This is one of the discoveries I made while I was searching for a code. This heretofore undiscovered phenomenon is strong evidence that the numerical values of the letters in our alphabet are not random.

The Alphabet Equality Hypothesis is as follows:

Whenever a very common digraph or a trigraph is a soundalike (or homophone) of an individual letter, the sound-alike digraph or trigraph is equal in numerical value to that individual letter. This is evidence that the Code is as much about sounds as it is about letters and the numerical values we give them.

Here is a complete list of the digraphs and the trigraph that can be found:

CC = X = 6	as in accent, accidental (C+C=6)
CKS = X = 6	as in socks, tracks (C+K+S=6)
CH = K = 2	as in cholesterol, choir (C+H=3+8=11 and 1+1=2)
QU = K = 2	as in unique, clique (Q+U=8+3=11 and 1+1=2)
GH = F = 6	as in laugh, tough (G+H=7+8=15 and 1+5=6)
PH = F = 6	as in graph, phenomenon (P+H=7+8=15 and 1+ 5=6)

The sample size may only be six, but the sample size is the entire population of commonly used sound-alike blends (digraphs and the one trigraph). Therefore, the correlation coefficient is +1.

$$R = +1$$

In other words, there appears to be a perfect correlation between the commonly used sound-alike blends and the single letter the blend sounds like.

We have quite commonly used many of these equalities for many years. The Chicago and Boston Major League Baseball teams are called the WHITE SOX and RED SOX rather than White Socks and Red Socks. Many books and websites replace laugh with the colloquial LAFF, even though the F is doubled. Some parents name their child Chris while others name their child Kris.

One unique vowel sound, symbolized by /ə/, is called a schwa. It is described as the middle vowel sound or as one of four weak vowel sounds. It is the most common vowel sound in the English language. It occurs in most syllables that do not have a word stress. The sound can be represented by any of the five common vowels—by the A in about, the E in happen, the I in placid, the O in lemon, and the U in circus. The Y, which is sometimes a vowel, can also represent the same sound as in Brooklyn. Sometimes a digraph or trigraph represents this sound. In Lincoln (pronounced like LINKIN'), the OL is pronounced /ə/ and has a numeric value of 9 like I, therefore OL can be substituted with I, when we are in the process of deciphering. It is the same as in the name Malcolm.

I also found a unique blend that sounds as if it is composed of letters other than what it literally contains. To demonstrate, make the sound of a T with your tongue against the roof of your mouth. Say TUH as in TABLE. Now pronounce SH. Say SHUH as in the word SHOE. Now pronounce CH, as it is pronounced in the name CHARLES, by saying CHUH. To pronounce CH, one must pronounce T and SH at the same time. And we find that a more appropriate blend for the CH sound might have been TSH. (In fact, we do not really know why CH was chosen for that phoneme.) And what do you know? C+H=3+8=11 and 1+1=2; T+S+H=2+1+8=11 and 1+1=2. So, in this case, the blend CH is equal in numeric value to the more accurate letter combination that would produce the sound of TSH. Using substitution in the name CHARLES, BIRCHARD, or CHURCHILL, we would get TSHARLES, BIRTSHARD, and TSHURCHILL or CHURTSHILL.

Read the following sections ("The Code Revealed—The Alphanumeric Conversion Table" and "Rules of Substitution") carefully, because they are essential for understanding what comes afterward. Bear in mind that none of this is arbitrary. These values, their equivalencies, and their manipulations are derived from (a) the English alphabet as it has been delivered to Anglophone culture over the centuries, and (b) the fundamental digits and values 1 through 9.

THE CODE REVEALED—THE ALPHANUMERIC CONVERSION TABLE

1 = A = J = S   6 = F = O = X
2 = B = K = T   7 = G = P = Y
3 = C = L = U   8 = H = Q = Z
4 = D = M = V   9 = I = R
5 = E = N = W

In all cases, when deciphering the secret code hidden in a name, any letter in a set of equalities (i.e., D = M = V) can be converted to another letter of the same value. The letter J in a name can be converted to a 1 and then to an A or an S. The letter N can be converted to a 5 and then to an E or a W, because they have the same numerical value.

RULES OF SUBSTITUTION

Just as A can be converted to a 1 and then to a J or S, substitution can occur whenever there is an equality.

> X can substitute for CC when CC sounds like X
> X can substitute for CKS when CKS sounds like X
>
> K can substitute for CH when CH sounds like K
> K can substitute for QU when QU sounds like K
>
> F can substitute for GH when GH sounds like F
> F can substitute for PH when PH sounds like F
>
> TSH can substitute for CH when CH is pronounced like a T and SH simultaneously
>
> A blend, like a schwa as designated by /ə/, has the numeric value of a Vowel and can be substituted by the single vowel with the equal numeric value

The tests in this book will feature tables demonstrating the use of the Alphanumeric Conversion Table and the Rules of Substitution.

What follows is how I discovered that the English alphabet contains a secret code hidden in the English language. Names of Historical Events, Heads of State and Military Leaders contain secret relationships and references to each other that are beyond astounding and they are not mere coincidence. At first, you will not believe it; neither did I. But keep reading, and you will follow me as I moved from skepticism to clarity and conviction.

SECTION II

THE EVIDENCE

AMERICAN WAR OF INDEPENDENCE (AWOI)

The **AMERICAN WAR OF INDEPENDENCE (AWOI) (1775 - 1783)**, also known as the **AMERICAN REVOLUTIONARY WAR (ARW)**, was a war between Great Britain and the Thirteen Colonies that began as a conflict triggered by the colonists' opposition to taxation without representation—i.e., the colonists were being taxed by the Crown without any representation in Parliament. The conflict grew into boycotts, the Boston Tea Party, and other events, and the two nations developed strong political differences that eventually detonated into war. Twelve colonies formed a Continental Congress to organize their resistance. The Second Continental Congress appointed George Washington Commander of the Continental Army. Both sides found allies in other nations, and some Native American tribes fought in the war—some for the colonies and others for Britain. During the war, the colonies declared their independence from Britain and became the United States of America. A formal Declaration of Independence was written. Its principal author was Thomas Jefferson, but it contained revisions by John Adams and Benjamin Franklin. Years later, after the deaths of between 120,000 and 160,000, the war came to an end. General Cornwallis surrendered October 19, 1781, to George Washington at the Siege of Yorktown. Britain continued its war with France and Spain for another two years and its war with America was limited mostly to harbors and forts until Britain finally accepted America's independence with the Treaty of Paris on September 3, 1783.

Before I share with you the exciting story of my discovery of the Code, I want to show you what the code looks like in practice. Let's say, as an example, we were examining the names of all the U.S. Presidents, and we were looking for the initialism of the American War of Independence—AWOI—in their names. It would be interesting if we found it in the name of GEORGE WASHINGTON, as he was the Commander of the Continental Army during the war.

Indeed, what if we found that among all the Kings and Queens of Great Britain and Ireland and the later Kings and Queens of the United Kingdom (three centuries of monarchs), GEORGE WILLIAM FREDERICK, who reigned during the AWOI, was the only Monarch with AWOI in his name? Then we might begin to think that this was no longer just a coincidence. We might even consider a nearly exclusive Level One Presentation of AWOI in GEORGE WASHINGTON and an exclusive Presentation of AWOI in GEORGE WILLIAM FREDERICK interesting enough to contribute to a book—but, quite likely, the book would just be a book of oddities, at this stage. That is, of course, until we looked further.

GEORGE WASHINGTON—COMMANDER-IN-CHIEF OF THE CONTINENTAL ARMY

GEORGE WASHINGTON had grown increasingly opposed to British rule because of taxation without representation. He had acquired experience in military leadership during his command of the Virginia regiment on the side of the British in the French and Indian War. So, he was easily nominated and unanimously elected Commander-in-Chief of the Continental Army against the British. Even as he was challenged by legendary obstacles, Washington's brilliant military strategies, his strong command, his development of the army, his development and use of an outstanding espionage network and an alliance with the French, all worked together to defeat British forces, climaxing with the Allied victory at the Siege of Yorktown. On October 19, 1781, General Cornwallis surrendered to General Washington. Britain continued its war with France and Spain for another two years and its war with America was limited mostly to harbors and forts until they finally accepted America's independence with the Treaty of Paris on September 3, 1783.

GEORGE WASHINGTON—FOUNDING FATHER OF HIS COUNTRY

GEORGE WASHINGTON (1732 - 1799) was a soldier, farmer, and statesman and Founding Father who served as the first President of the United States. Appointed Commander-in-Chief of the Continental Army during the American War of Independence, he led America to victory. Largely because of this, he was considered the best choice to preside over the 1787 Constitutional Convention which created and ratified the Constitution of the United States. Washington was chief among the nation's Founding Fathers. As the 1st President of the United States, he created and defined the office of the Presidency. He set a precedent of two terms of office, which was followed by the majority of Presidents thereafter. In his Farewell Address, Washington warned the nation of the dangers of political partisanship. Because of his defeat of the British as the Commander-in-Chief of the Continental Army, his presiding over the Constitutional Convention and him being the first President of the United States, the Citizens of the United States call George Washington the Father of their Country.

LEVEL ZERO: OVERT PRESENTATION OF **AWOI** IN THE NAME **WASHINGTON**	
W—W	W
A—A	A
S	
H	
I—I	I
N	
G	
T	
O—O	O
N	
	AWOI

For the purpose of understanding the phenomenon revealed in this book, let us examine the name of GEORGE WASHINGTON in search of the initialism for the AMERICAN WAR OF INDEPENDENCE, which is AWOI.

First, we do find AWOI in his name. In fact, it is in his surname. No other U.S. President has AWOI in their surname. We call finding a Historical Event in just one of a person's names a Level Zero Display, and if the Event appears to belong in a person's name because the person has a strong involvement in or a strong association with the Event, we then call it a Level Zero Presentation.

As this is an Overt Presentation (the actual letters as opposed to using conversion), we just go down the left column and search for the letters A-W-O-I in the name WASHINGTON. We repeat the letters and place them in the middle of the table to show that the letters of AWOI are, in fact, there in his name.

LEVEL ONE: OVERT PRESENTATION OF **AWOI** IN THE NAME **GEORGE WASHINGTON**

G	
E	
O—O	O
R	
G	
E	
W—W	W
A—A	A
S	
H	
I—I	I
N	
G	
T	
O	
N	
AWOI	

Obviously, if we find AWOI in WASHINGTON's surname, we will find it in his full name. And there it is.

LEVEL ONE: OVERT PRESENTATION OF **AWOI HERO GEN** IN **GEORGE WASHINGTON**

	AWOI	HERO	GEN
G—G			G
E—E			E
O—O	O		
R—R		R	
G			
E—E		E	
W—W	W		
A—A	A		
S			
H—H		H	
I—I	I		
N			
G			
T			
O—O		O	
N			N
AWOI	**HERO**	**GEN**	

We also find AWOI HERO GEN in WASHINGTON's whole name in this table. GEN is the common abbreviation for General. This is, indeed, very interesting!

THE 64-YEAR PHENOMENON

LEVEL ONE: OVERT PRESENTATION OF **AWOI** IN **WILLIAM HARRISON**

W—W	W
I — I	I
L	
L	
I	
A—A	A
M	
H	
A	
R	
R	
I	
S	
O—O	O
N	
AWOI	

During my studies of the leaders in this book, I came across what I call the 64-Year Phenomenon. The leader who serves approximately 64 years after a major turning point in an Historical Event also contains the name of the Event. In the case of the AMERICAN WAR OF INDEPENDENCE (AWOI), the most definitive moment during the war that we still celebrate today is the Declaration of Independence—which was signed on July 4, 1776. Sixty-four years after the signing of the Declaration of Independence was July 4, 1840. The next person to become President after the 64th celebration of the 4th of July was WILLIAM HARRISON. This makes him the 64-Year Phenomenon for the AWOI. A complete explanation of the 64-Year Phenomenon can be found in Appendix E.

Examinations of the U.S. Presidents at Level Two find AWOI in some other names of U.S. Presidents, but for other reasons. Tables and explanations can be found in Appendix B.

LEVEL ONE: THE SEARCH FOR **AWOI** IN THE NAMES OF THE U.S. PRESIDENTS

	(PRESENT)	(MISSING)
GEORGE WASHINGTON	***AWOI***	
JOHN ADAMS	AO	WI
THOMAS JEFFERSON	AO	WI
JAMES MADISON	AOI	W
JAMES MONROE	AO	WI
JOHN ADAMS	AO	WI
ANDREW JACKSON	AWO	I
MARTIN VAN BUREN	AI	OW
WILLIAM HARRISON	***AWOI***	64-YEAR PHEN
JOHN TYLER	O	AWI
JAMES POLK	AO	WI
ZACHARY TAYLOR	AO	WI
MILLARD FILLMORE	AOI	W
FRANKLIN PIERCE	AI	WO
JAMES BUCHANAN	A	WOI
ABRAHAM LINCOLN	AOI	W
ANDREW JOHNSON	AWO	I
ULYSSES GRANT	A	WOI
RUTHERFORD HAYES	AO	WI
JAMES GARFIELD	AI	WO
CHESTER ARTHUR	A	WOI
GROVER CLEVELAND	AO	WI

As George Washington and most of the early Presidents have no middle name, it is logical for us to first examine the names of all the U.S. Presidents at Level One—most commonly used given name and their surname before we examine their names at Level Two. (Level Two Display and Level Two Presentation are demonstrated and explained in the "Definition of Terms" section). As I am testing to see if the Code predicts both—those with a strong involvement in or association with AWOI and those without—this table provides the names of all U.S. Presidents and demonstrates the process of determining the category to which they belong.

Special Note: Heads of State who have a strong involvement in or strong association with an Event and also have the Event in their name, will be in bold and have two sets of three asterisks

LEVEL ONE: THE SEARCH FOR **AWOI** IN THE NAMES OF THE U.S. PRESIDENTS

	(PRESENT)	(MISSING)
BENJAMIN HARRISON	AOI	W
WILLIAM MCKINLEY	AWI	O
THEODORE ROOSEVELT	O	AWI
WILLIAM TAFT	AWI	O
WOODROW WILSON	WI	AO
WARREN HARDING	AWI	O
CALVIN COOLIDGE	AOI	W
HERBERT HOOVER	O	AWI
FRANKLIN ROOSEVELT	AOI	W
HARRY TRUMAN	A	WOI
DWIGHT EISENHOWER	WOI	A
JOHN KENNEDY	O	AWI
LYNDON JOHNSON	O	AWI
RICHARD NIXON	AOI	W
LESLIE KING	I	AWO
JAMES CARTER	A	WOI
RONALD REAGAN	AO	WI
GEORGE BUSH	O	AWI
WILLIAM BLYTHE	AWI	O
GEORGE BUSH	O	AWI
BARACK OBAMA	AO	WI
DONALD TRUMP	AO	WI
JOSEPH BIDEN	OI	AW

As we note here in a list of U.S. Presidents at Level One, only two have the Presentation of AWOI. One is GEORGE WASHINGTON, the Commander of the Continental Army during the AWOI. The other is WILLIAM HARRISON whose Presentation was just discussed.

Special Note: For these tests I chose to use the originally assigned names of the U.S. Presidents in the tables and the tests. Gerald Rudolf Ford, Jr. was originally named LESLIE LYNCH KING, JR. William Jefferson Clinton was originally named WILLIAM JEFFERSON BLYTHE III. I do this to alleviate confusion over including the same person twice. However, I have tested their other names, as well, and the later assumed names do not affect any of the final results.

KING GEORGE III

> **GEORGE III WILLIAM FREDERICK (1738 - 1820)** is the full name of King George III, who served as King for 59 years. He was first known as the King of Great Britain and the King of Ireland, and later as the King of the United Kingdom of Great Britain and Ireland (when they were united). This is the King whom the colonists protested, the King who is the accused tyrant mentioned in the Declaration of Independence: "He has abdicated government here. He has plundered our seas, burnt our towns, and destroyed the lives of our people." George III never acknowledged the United States as a free nation and was accused of trying to keep the war going for an unnecessarily long time. Historians debate his legacy as either a cruel tyrant or a victim of circumstances.

Let's follow up on the Monarch mentioned earlier, GEORGE III WILLIAM FREDERICK, who served as King George III. He does contain a Presentation of AWOI in his name. But let's examine the names of the Kings and Queens of the United Kingdom of Great Britain and Ireland just to see if this is unique.

Special Note: In this book, a monarch will be listed with his or her whole name and the suffix will immediately follow the name he or she is known by. Since he is known as GEORGE III, GEORGE WILLIAM FREDERICK is listed in this book as GEORGE III WILLIAM FREDERICK.

EXAMINATION OF NAMES OF KINGS AND QUEENS OF GREAT BRITAIN AND IRELAND/UNITED KINGDOM

	(PRESENT)	(MISSING)
WILLIAM III HENRY	AWI	O
(ANNE)	A	WOI
GEORGE I LOUIS	OI	AW
GEORGE II AUGUSTUS	AOI	W
GEORGE III WILLIAM FREDERICK	***AWOI***	
GEORGE IV AUGUSTUS FREDERICK	AOI	W
WILLIAM IV HENRY	AWI	O
ALEXANDRINA VICTORIA	AOI	W
ALBERT EDWARD VII	AWI	O
GEORGE V FREDERICK ERNEST ALBERT	AOI	W
EDWARD VIII ALBERT CHRISTIAN GEORGE ANDREW PATRICK DAVID	<<<AWOI>>><<<49 LETTERS>>>	
ALBERT FREDERICK ARTHUR GEORGE VI	AOI	W
ELIZABETH II ALEXANDRA MARY WINDSOR	<<<AWOI>>><<<31 LETTERS>>>	

Using this sample table that charts names and presentations, we can see that the name ANNE is too small. ANNE is four letters, the same as AWOI. A name would have to be an anagram of AWOI. At the other end is EDWARD ALBERT CHRISTIAN GEORGE ANDREW PATRICK DAVID. His name is forty-nine letters. Statistically, he is almost guaranteed of having the four letters AWOI in his name. For these reasons, it is not reasonable or logical to include ANNE or EDWARD DAVID in this study. ELIZABETH II ALEXANDRINA MARY WINDSOR has 31 letters, which also surpasses the rest. Excluding these names, we have a fair test of ten names. Of these ten Kings and Queens, only GEORGE III WILLIAM FREDERICK (George III) has AWOI in his name, and he was the King during the AMERICAN WAR OF INDEPENDENCE. And it was he who was recognized by the colonies as the enemy.

LEVEL ONE: OVERT PRESENTATION OF AWOI IN GEORGE III WILLIAM FREDERICK

G		
E		
O—O	O	
R		
G		
E		
I—I	I	
I		
I		
W—W	W	
I		
L		
L		
I		
A—A	A	
M		
F		
R		
E		
D		
E		
R		
I		
C		
K		
AWOI		

THE OTHER INITIALISM

During the investigations of Heads of State for the Code, I realized that there are two possible initialisms for the war we call the American War of Independence and the American Revolutionary War. They are AWOI and ARW. After completing my work on the other three great American wars and scrutinizing the results for WWI and WWII, I decided to search for AWOI and ARW. I was fully aware that there is a problem with ARW. It is an anagram of WAR. There is no way to differentiate the two in the appropriate names—GEORGE WASHINGTON, ANDREW JACKSON, and WILLIAM HENRY HARRISON. How do we know which is presenting—ARW or WAR? Or are they both presenting? For the other Presidents who have WAR in their names, it is obvious that WAR fits perfectly as a Presentation.

At Level One, the following Presidents have the letters of WAR/ARW in their name:

1. GEORGE WASHINGTON (ARW)
2. ANDREW JACKSON (War of 1812)
3. WILLIAM HARRISON (War of 1812)
4. ANDREW JOHNSON (The Civil War)
5. WARREN HARDING (WWI—Aftermath of the war)

At Level Two and Level Three the list is longer. All the U.S. Presidents with ARW/WAR were involved in or associated with one or more wars:

1. GEORGE WASHINGTON (ARW)
2. ANDREW JACKSON (War of 1812)
3. WILLIAM HARRISON (War of 1812)
4. ANDREW JOHNSON (The Civil War)
5. WILLIAM MCKINLEY JR (The Civil War, Spanish-American War)
6. WILLIAM HOWARD TAFT (WWI)
7. THOMAS WOODROW WILSON (WWI)
8. WARREN GAMALIEL HARDING (WWI—Aftermath of the war)
9. DWIGHT DAVID EISENHOWER (WWII)
10. RONALD WILSON REAGAN (WWII)
11. GEORGE HERBERT WALKER BUSH (WWII, Gulf War)
12. WILLIAM JEFFERSON BLYTHE III (WWII—Presentation belongs to his father)
13. GEORGE WALKER BUSH (Iraq War, War in Afghanistan)

THE PROBABILITY OF GEORGE WASHINGTON AND WILLIAM HARRISON AND KING GEORGE III WILLIAM FREDERICK HAVING THE QUITE EXCLUSIVE AND THE CORRECT PRESENTATION OF AWOI IN THEIR NAMES IS:

1
IN
218,526

(ONE IN OVER 218 THOUSAND)*

*See Section VI for Statistical Tests

PREVIEW OF THINGS TO COME

This summary of findings from a search for AWOI, an initialism for the American War of Independence, in the names of the U.S. Presidents, offers an excellent preparation for what follows in this study. While the AWOI preceded the other wars and events addressed in this book, it was the subject of investigation only after I completed my studies of THE CIVIL WAR, WORLD WAR ONE, and WORLD WAR TWO.

What I have just presented are the first results you see in this book. The demonstrations in the tables are quite amazing. You may already be asking yourself how this can be possible. But this is only a preview of what's to come. What if this phenomenon repeats itself—again and again?

THE FINDINGS
OF
THREE MAJOR WARS
INVOLVING THE
UNITED STATES
THAT SUPPORT
THE CLAIM
THAT THERE IS A
SECRET CODE
HIDDEN IN THE
ENGLISH LANGUAGE

THE CIVIL WAR

THE CIVIL WAR is the most common American name for the American Civil War, fought in the United States between 1861 and 1865. The belligerents in the war were the Union (northern United States) and the Confederacy (states in the southern United States that had seceded from the Union). The war had its roots in the great divide over the issue of the enslavement of Africans and African Americans. The Civil War took more American lives than all the other wars combined until the Vietnam War. The number of deaths may have been as high as a million. The election of Abraham Lincoln triggered the conflict. His opposition to the expansion of slavery and Southerners' fear that this would lead to the prohibition of slavery led the Southern states to form the Confederacy. Even before Lincoln's election, many Southern leaders threatened secession if Lincoln was elected, and when he was elected, they carried out that threat. War was imminent, but Lincoln waited for the South to draw first blood. Confederate forces attacked Fort Sumter in South Carolina in April 1861. The Confederacy eventually grew to 11 "'slave states."' In April 1865, Robert E. Lee, commander of the Confederate forces, surrendered to Ulysses Grant at the Battle of Appomattox Court House—leading to the end of the Civil War. This meant an end to the Confederacy, an end to the enslavement and freedom for over four million enslaved people. Reconstruction began in the middle of the war and continued until 1877, working toward restoring national unity and giving civil rights to African Americans.

As stated earlier, my study of Heads of State during the American War of Independence came after my studies of THE CIVIL WAR and the world wars. Initially, I had been searching for meaningful words in the names of people who are well-known (artists, entertainers, sports figures, world leaders, etc.). One of the most interesting and most lengthy discoveries (11 letters) was of a Covert Presentation of THE CIVIL WAR encoded in the name ABRAHAM LINCOLN. This was the finding that launched the research in this book.

But finding words in names, as interesting as it was, still left something missing. One could argue that these findings were all well and good, but they did not provide any support for a claim or for hypothesis testing. They did not constitute what we could consider worthy evidence.

Re-examining my list of famous and infamous people, I took a second look at my findings of THE CIVIL WAR encoded in the name of the 16th President of the United States. To give the discovery significance, I would have to make claims I could investigate and hypothesis tests that I could perform. I realized that to do that I would have to search all of the U.S. Presidents' names for THE CIVIL WAR—those who were strongly involved in or associated with the war and those who were not.

I then decided that I would expand my investigation to include the two world wars, as well. I would look for Covert (encoded) Presentations of THE CIVIL WAR, WORLD WAR ONE, and WORLD WAR TWO in the names of the U.S. Presidents. These are full names—in code—of the three largest wars that involved the United States. THE CIVIL WAR is known in other nations as the AMERICAN CIVIL WAR, but in the United States as THE CIVIL WAR. I realized I should also look for Overt Presentations (the actual letters) of WWI and WWII—common expressions for the two world wars. I would also look for Mixed Presentations of WORLD WAR I and WORLD WAR II and Covert Presentations of FIRST WORLD WAR and SECOND WORLD WAR—as they are expressions of the same wars.

I had remained confident that I would find something significant, because of the findings I had made in the names of other well-known people. But I certainly had no idea of what was to come.

Can we choose to be born?
Or are we fitted to the times
we are born into?

Abraham Lincoln

ABRAHAM LINCOLN II

ABRAHAM LINCOLN (1809 - 1865) was the 16th President of the United States. His name—above all others—is the name most associated with The Civil War and with the end of slavery in the United States. Raised by parents who were Separatist Baptists—a religious group that opposed, among other things, slavery—he denounced slavery throughout his life. Still, he married a woman whose parents enslaved human beings, but she soon supported his beliefs and encouraged the direction he was taking in law and in politics. During his days as a lawyer, he often defended people over the issue of slavery, including helping a woman and her children, who had already been legally freed, to return to their freedom. Lincoln served as a State Representative in Illinois from 1834 to 1842, and later as a U.S. Representative from Illinois from 1847 until 1849. In 1849, Lincoln retired from government to return to his law practice. But the 1854 passage of the Kansas-Nebraska Act, which mandated popular sovereignty—the right of settlers in a new territory to decide if their new state would be a slave state or a free state—angered Lincoln and motivated him to return to politics with a passion. He ran against Stephen Douglas for U.S. Senator from Illinois. At the time, senators were chosen by the state legislature. The districts were drawn up in favor of the Democrats, and, in addition, an October surprise in the shape of an endorsement by John Crittenden, a former Whig, all but handed the election to Douglas. But the coverage of the Lincoln-Douglas debates gave Lincoln a chance to make a name for himself—which he did indeed—giving him a boost to become the 1860 Republican candidate for the Presidency. In the 1860 U.S. Presidential election, Lincoln had three opponents. Lincoln's strongest opponent was the same Stephen Douglas who had defeated him in the Senate Race. (The other two candidates were John Breckinridge and John Bell.) Lincoln won the election, and his election triggered The Civil War.

I first examined the names of the Presidents for Level One Presentations. "Level One," as defined earlier, refers to the most used given name—often the first name, but sometimes a middle name—and the surname. In this study, we are searching for Covert Presentations. In other words, we are converting the letters in their names to numbers and then back to letters. We are doing this to see if within the letters that appear in the name of President LINCOLN, we can find the letters that spell THE CIVIL WAR.

LEVEL ONE: COVERT PRESENTATION OF **THE CIVIL WAR** IN **ABRAHAM LINCOLN**

	THE	CIVIL	WAR
A—A			A
B = T	T		
R—R			R
A			
H—H	H		
A			
M = V		V	
L— L		L	
I — I		I	
N = E	E		
C—C		C	
OL = I		I	
N = W			W
	THE	**CIVIL**	**WAR**

As is evident, by using the Conversion Table and Rules of Substitution, ABRAHAM LINCOLN has encoded in his name the words—THE CIVIL WAR.

As LINCOLN does not have a middle name, his name doesn't change at Level Two. His name remains ABRAHAM LINCOLN. Using the Code, I searched the names of all the Presidents who served before Lincoln. None of them had coded THE CIVIL WAR. I continued looking at the Presidents who served after Lincoln and found no others at Level One.

So, at Level One, the only U.S. President with THE CIVIL WAR in his name is ABRAHAM LINCOLN. This was, indeed, LINCOLN's War. It was a war that ended slavery and preserved the Union.

LEVEL ONE: COVERT PRESENTATIONS OF **THE CIVIL WAR** IN THE NAME OF U.S. PRESIDENTS

	(PRESENT)	(MISSING)
GEORGE WASHINGTON	THEIWAR	CVIL
JOHN ADAMS	HEVA	TCIILWR
THOMAS JEFFERSON	THEVWAR	CIIL
JAMES MADISON	EIVWA	THCILR
JAMES MONROE	EVWAR	THCIIL
JOHN ADAMS	HEVA	TCIILWR
ANDREW JA**CKS**ON	TECVWAR	HIIL
ANDREW JA**X**ON	EVWAR	THCIIL
MARTIN VAN BUREN	TECIVIWAR	HL
WILLIAM HARRISON	HECIVILWAR	T
JOHN TYLER	THELWAR	CIVI
JAMES POLK	TEVLA	HCIIWR
ZA**CH**ARY TAYLOR	THCILAR	EVIW
ZA**K**ARY TAYLOR	TILAR	HECVIW
MILLARD FILLMORE	ECIVILAR	THW
FRANKLIN PIERCE	TECIILWAR	HV
JAMES BU**CH**ANAN	THECVLWA	IIR
JAMES BU**K**ANAN	TECVWA	HIILR
ABRAHAM LINC**OL**N	THECIVLWAR	I
+**ABRAHAM LINCIN**	***THE CIVIL WAR***	
ANDREW JOHNSON	HEVWAR	TCIIL
ULYSSES GRANT	TECLWAR	HIVI
RUTHERFORD HAYES	THECIVIWAR	L
JAMES GARFIELD	EIVLWAR	THCI
CHESTER ARTHUR	THECIILWAR	V

+ THE LETTER "I" SUBSTITUTES FOR THE "OL" WHICH IS A "SCHWA" EQUAL TO THE "I"

Special Note: For 'THE CIVIL WAR', the tables show all the substitutions possible among the U.S. Presidents. The blend (group of letters that sound like a single letter) and the single letter the blend sounds like, are highlighted in black. You will find the Rules of Substitution on page 19. Such rigorous examinations have been done for all the other wars, but these are not included in this book.

LEVEL ONE: COVERT PRESENTATIONS OF **THE CIVIL WAR** IN THE NAME OF U.S. PRESIDENTS

	(PRESENT)	(MISSING)
GROVER CLEVELAND	ECIVLWAR	THI
BENJAMIN HARRISON	THEIVIWAR	CL
WILLIAM MCKINLEY	TECIVILWAR	H
THEODORE ROOSEVELT	THEIVLWR	CI
WILLIAM TAFT	TCIVILWA	HER
WOODROW WILSON	EIVLWAR	THCI
WARREN HARDING	HEIVIWAR	TCL
CALVIN COOLIDGE	ECIVILWA	THR
HERBERT HOOVER	THEIVIWR	CLA
FRANKLIN ROOSEVELT	TECIVILWAR	H
HARRY TRUMAN	THECIVIAR	LW
DWIGHT EISENHOWER	THEIVIWAR	CL
JOHN KENNEDY	THEVWA	CIILR
LYNDON JOHNSON	HEVLWA	TCIIR
RICHARD NIXON	HECIVIWAR	TL
LESLIE KING	TECIILWA	HVR
JAMES CARTER	TECIVWAR	HIL
RONALD REAGAN	EVILWAR	THCI
GEORGE BUSH	THECWAR	IVIL
WILLIAM BLYTHE	THECIVILWA	R
GEORGE BUSH	THECWAR	IVIL
BARACK OBAMA	TCVAR	HEIILW
DONALD TRUMP	TECVLAR	HIIW
JOSE**PH** BIDEN	THEIVWA	CILR
JOSE**F** BIDEN	TEIVWA	HCILR

Because it was, indeed, in so many ways, LINCOLN's war, it is no wonder that LINCOLN stands alone at Level One, and that after taking THE CIVIL WAR from the name ABRAHAM LINCOLN, there are only two letters remaining—and both are the letter "A." This phenomenon strongly connects THE CIVIL WAR and ABRAHAM LINCOLN.

LEVEL TWO: COVERT PRESENTATION OF **THE CIVIL WAR** IN **HIRAM ULYSSES GRANT**

H—H	H		
I—I		I	
R = I		I	
A			
M = V		V	
U = C		C	
L—L		L	
Y			
S			
S			
E—E		E	
S			
G			
R—R			R
A—A			A
N = W			W
T—T	T		
	THE	**CIVIL**	**WAR**

At Level Two (using the whole name), Lincoln is no longer alone. Of the Presidents preceding Lincoln, only three have middle names, so I only had to look at Level Two for three names. But I did begin to see some names *after* Lincoln in a chronological list of the Presidents. I looked with some excitement and suspense at the name HIRAM ULYSSES GRANT (the birth name of the General and President who became more commonly known as Ulysses S. Grant). As I completed a search for THE CIVIL WAR in his name, I was astonished. There it was. Right in front of me. How could this confirmation of the Code be unfolding right before my very eyes?

OVERT PRESENTATION OF U.S. GEN IN HIRAM ULYSSES GRANT

H		
I		
R		
A		
M		
U—U	U	
L		
Y		
S—S	S	
S		
E—E		E
S		
G—G		G
R		
A		
N—N		N
T		
	U.S.	**GEN**

Just as we see that GEORGE WASHINGTON contains the words HERO GEN in his name, we find U.S. GEN in the name HIRAM ULYSSES GRANT. In fact, he is the only U.S. President with U.S. GEN in his name.

HIRAM ULYSSES GRANT — COMMANDING GENERAL OF THE UNION ARMY

HIRAM ULYSSES GRANT, known as Ulysses S. Grant, was an American soldier and President who served as Commanding General of the Union Army and President of the United States. His military genius became noticeable to Lincoln after his many successes — winning control of Tennessee and most of Kentucky, winning the battle at Shiloh, seizing Vicksburg, succeeding in the Chattanooga campaign and gaining control of the Mississippi River, brilliantly dividing the Confederacy. Lincoln considered Grant the obvious best choice to command the Union armies. He promoted him to Lieutenant General, a rank that had previously been reserved for George Washington. After many more battles, Grant's army trapped the Confederates in Richmond. In April of 1865, Robert E. Lee surrendered to General Grant at Appomattox. Not only was Grant the most acclaimed General of The Civil War and the only General during The Civil War to receive the surrender of three Confederate Armies, but Grant is considered one of the greatest military geniuses and strategists of all time. His winning strategies are the subject of numerous war histories and military textbooks.

ULYSSES S. GRANT—BORN HIRAM ULYSSES GRANT

HIRAM ULYSSES GRANT (1822 - 1885) was the 18th President of the United States. After The Civil War and the assassination of Abraham Lincoln, Grant strongly opposed the policies of President Andrew Johnson and joined the Radical Republicans. He was easily nominated and elected President in 1868 and served two terms. He was a very effective and forceful advocate as President for Reconstruction and civil rights. He stabilized the economy, utilized the military to strictly enforce laws in the South and aggressively prosecuted the Ku Klux Klan. Furthermore, Grant supported the 15th Amendment which gave African Americans the right to vote, signed the Civil Rights Act and the Enforcement Acts and created the Department of Justice to protect the basic rights of African Americans. He was the first President to appoint African Americans and Jewish Americans to prominent federal offices. His civil rights record is one of the most progressive of all presidents. He sought but did not win the nomination for President in 1880. Because of this and because of some poor investments he had made, Grant worried about leaving his wife with no money until his good friend, Mark Twain, came to his aid and published his memoirs.

RUTHERFORD BIRCHARD HAYES I

RUTHERFORD BIRCHARD HAYES (1822 - 1903) was the 19th President of the United States. He had eight very distinct relationships with The Civil War. (1) He was a very strong abolitionist. (2) Before the war, as a lawyer, he defended refugee slaves in court. (3) He was wounded five times in the war. (4) His leadership and gallantry had a real impact on the war. (5) He was praised by General Grant. (6) He rose in the ranks during The Civil War to Brigadier General and Breveted Major General. (7) The disputed 1876 election of Rutherford Hayes had an impact on the aftermath of The Civil War. He ran as a Republican against Democrat Samuel Tilden. Tilden won the popular vote, but the electoral votes were disputed. Grant appointed a commission to decide the votes. The electoral votes were in Hayes's favor. To avoid filibustering to prevent the vote, the two sides negotiated a compromise. Hayes would be the new President, but he would withdraw troops from the South and would accept the Democratic governments in the South. Although Hayes was a strong Republican Reconstructionist, he, nonetheless, had to acquiesce to the promises he had made to enter the Oval Office—to allow the South to rule itself. In addition, Congress was controlled by Democrats. They refused to supply funds to oversee the South. Hayes made attempts to protect African Americans, but every effort was stymied or limited by the Democrats. They passed a bill that appropriated money for the Army but that repealed the Enforcement Act. In spite of all his efforts, Hayes could not get the South to accept equality or Congress to appropriate the necessary funds to enforce civil rights laws. (8) As President, he attempted to heal the division between the North and South caused by The Civil War and Reconstruction.

LEVEL TWO: COVERT PRESENTATION OF THE CIVIL WAR IN RUTHERFORD BIRCHARD HAYES

R—R			R
U = L		L	
T—T	T		
H—H	H		
E—E	E		
R—I		I	
F			
O			
R			
D			
B			
I—I		I	
R			
C—C		C	
H			
A			
R			
D = V		V	
H			
A—A			A
Y			
E = W			W
S			
	THE	**CIVIL**	**WAR**

I decided to look again at the table of Covert Presentations of THE CIVIL WAR in the name of U.S. Presidents at Level Two. The next name after GRANT was RUTHERFORD BIRCHARD HAYES. His strong relationship with THE CIVIL WAR is told in his biography. The history of his service as a Breveted Major General in the Union Army and the compromise that put him in office as President of the United States are just two of his many relationships with THE CIVIL WAR.

WILLIAM HOWARD TAFT I

WILLIAM HOWARD TAFT (1857 - 1930) was the 27th President of the United States. Taft has seven relationships with the war, even though it took place during his childhood. (1) He was the first openly racist Republican in the White House (Stephen Grover Cleveland, a Democrat who had served earlier, was the first openly racist post-Civil War President). (2) He chose not to honor the Post-Civil War Republicans' humanitarian mission toward civil rights. (3) He appointed a second Confederate soldier to the Supreme Court—Horace H. Lurton of Georgia (Benjamin Harrison had appointed an ex-Confederate who had held a civil, not military, post; Grover Cleveland, a Democrat, had appointed the first Confederate Soldier). (4) Taft also promoted Edward Douglass White, a Lieutenant in the Confederate Army, and a former member of the Ku Klux Klan, from Associate Justice to Chief Justice of the Supreme Court. (5) Taft's racism also revealed itself during the Negro Rebellion in Cuba in 1912. Taft sent a total of 2,789 U.S. Marines, officers and enlisted men, to Guantanamo Naval Base to help the Cuban government end the rebellion of former slaves. The Afro-Cuban casualties were between 3,000 and 6,000. (6) Because of his overt racism, he caused the beginning of the mass exodus of African Americans from the Republican Party—the very party that had freed them. (7) As Chief Justice of the U.S. Supreme Court, his appointee, Edward White, decided in *Lum v Rice* in 1927 that exclusion of minorities from schools reserved for whites did not violate the Fourteenth Amendment, as there were segregated schools that minority children could attend. (This decision was overruled in 1954 by *Brown v Board of Education*.)

LEVEL TWO: COVERT PRESENTATION OF **THE CIVIL WAR** IN **WILLIAM HOWARD TAFT**

W—W			W
I—I	I		
L—L	L		
L = C	C		
I —I	I		
A—A			A
M = V	V		
H—H	H		
O			
W = E	E		
A			
R—R			R
D			
T—T	T		
A			
F			
T			
	THE	**CIVIL**	**WAR**

As history tells us, a war doesn't just begin with the first shot at Fort Sumter or an attack on Pearl Harbor. Events often known as causes or precursors to a war, "events leading up to a war," are also part and parcel to the war. Similarly, tensions, dissatisfaction, treaties yet to sign, problems left to resolve, border disputes, cold wars and the like are waiting in the wings in the aftermath of a war. All of these are also essential and, often, integral to the true history of a war. WILLIAM HOWARD TAFT, who served as president long after THE CIVIL WAR, turned against the humanitarian efforts of his party and everything the Republican Party had stood for—thereby placing him in the history of the long aftermath of THE CIVIL WAR. So, it's no surprise that the first Republican President to turn against the rights of African Americans—a President who would promote an ex-Confederate—ex-Klansman to Chief Justice of the Supreme Court—and appoint another ex-Confederate as a Supreme Court Justice—also has THE CIVIL WAR in his name.

THE 64-YEAR PHENOMENA
LEVEL TWO: COVERT PRESENTATION OF **THE CIVIL WAR** IN **HERBERT CLARK HOOVER**

H—H	H		
E—E	E		
R = I		I	
B			
E			
R = I		I	
T—T	T		
C—C		C	
L—L		L	
A—A			A
R—R			R
K			
H			
O			
O			
V—V		V	
E = W			W
R			
	THE	**CIVIL**	**WAR**

As I previously mentioned, throughout my studies of the leaders in this book, I came across what I call the 64-Year Phenomenon. The leader who serves approximately 64 years after a major turning point in a Historical Event also contains the name of the Event. THE CIVIL WAR ended in 1865. If we add 64 to the year 1865, we get the year 1929. That was the year that HERBERT CLARK HOOVER became President, making him the 64-Year Phenomenon for THE CIVIL WAR.

LEVEL TWO: COVERT PRESENTATION OF THE CIVIL WAR IN WILLIAM JEFFERSON BLYTHE

W—W	W		
I—I	I		
L—L	L		
L = C	C		
I—I	I		
A—A		A	
M = V	V		
J			
E			
F			
F			
E			
R—R		R	
S			
O			
N			
B			
L			
Y			
T—T	T		
H—H	H		
E—E	E		
	THE	**CIVIL**	**WAR**

I was surprised to see that WILLIAM JEFFERSON BLYTHE, better known as Bill Clinton, also contains the words THE CIVIL WAR. Indeed, an extension of the 64-Year Phenomenon is at work. Approximately 64 years after Hoover became President in 1929, Clinton (Blythe) became President in 1993. This makes WILLIAM JEFFERSON BLYTHE the second 64-Year Phenomenon for THE CIVIL WAR.

LEVEL TWO: COVERT PRESENTATIONS OF **THE CIVIL WAR** IN THE NAMES OF U.S. PRESIDENTS

	(PRESENT)	(MISSING)
GEORGE WASHINGTON	THEIWAR	CVIL
JOHN ADAMS	HEVA	TCIILWR
THOMAS JEFFERSON	THEVWAR	CIIL
JAMES MADISON	EIVWA	THCILR
JAMES MONROE	EVWAR	THCIIL
JOHN QUINCY ADAMS	HECIVLWA	TIR
ANDREW JA**CKS**ON	TECVWAR	HIIL
ANDREW JA**X**ON	EVWAR	THCIIL
MARTIN VAN BUREN	TECIVIWAR	HL
WILLIAM HENRY HARRISON	HECIVILWAR	T
JOHN TYLER	THELWAR	CIVI
JAMES KNOX POLK	TEVLWA	HCIIR
ZA**CH**ARY TAYLOR	THCILAR	EVIW
ZA**K**ARY TAYLOR	THILAR	ECVIW
MILLARD FILLMORE	ECIVILAR	THW
FRANKLIN PIERCE	TECIILWAR	HV
JAMES BU**CH**ANAN	THECVLWA	IIR
JAMES BU**K**ANAN	THEVLWA	CIIR
ABRAHAM LINCOLN	THE CIVLWAR	I
ABRAHAM LINCIN	***THE CIVIL WAR***	
ANDREW JOHNSON	HEVWAR	TCIIL
HIRAM ULYSSES GRANT	***THE CIVIL WAR***	
RUTHERFORD BIRCHARD HAYES	***THE CIVIL WAR***	
JAMES ABRAM GARFIELD	TEIVILWAR	HC
CHESTER ALAN ARTHUR	THECIILWAR	V
STEPHEN GROVER CLEVELAND	THECIVLWAR	I

LEVEL TWO: COVERT PRESENTATIONS OF **THE CIVIL WAR** IN THE NAMES OF U.S. PRESIDENTS

	(PRESENT)	(MISSING)
STE**F**EN GROVER CLEVELAND	TECIVLWAR	HI
BENJAMIN HARRISON	THEIVIWAR	CL
WILLIAM MCKINLEY	TECIVILWAR	H
THEODORE ROOSEVELT	THEIVLWAR	CI
WILLIAM HOWARD TAFT	***THE CIVIL WAR***	
THOMAS WOODROW WILSON	THEIVLWAR	CI
WARREN GAMALIEL HARDING	HECIVILWAR	T
JOHN CALVIN COOLIDGE	HECIVILWA	TR
HERBERT CLARK HOOVER	***THE CIVIL WAR***	**64-YEAR PHEN**
FRANKLIN DELANO ROOSEVELT	TECIVILWAR	H
HARRY S TRUMAN	THECIVIAR	LW
DWIGHT DAVID EISENHOWER	THEIVIWAR	CL
JOHN FITZGERALD KENNEDY	THEIVLWAR	CI
LYNDON BAINES JOHNSON	THEIVLWA	CIR
RICHARD MILHAUS NIXON	HECIVILWAR	T
LESLIE LYNCH KING	THECIILWA	VR
JAMES EARL CARTER	TECIVILWAR	H
RONALD WILSON REAGAN	ECIILWAR	TH
GEORGE HERBERT WALKER BUSH	THECIILWAR	V
WILLIAM JEFFERSON BLYTHE	***THE CIVIL WAR***	**64-YEAR PHEN (64 X 2)**
GEORGE WALKER BUSH	THECILWAR	VI
BARACK HUSSEIN OBAMA	THECIVLWAR	I
DONALD JOHN TRUMP	THECVLWAR	II
JOSE**PH** ROBINETTE BIDEN	THEIVIWAR	CL
JOSE**F** ROBINETTE BIDEN	TEIVIWAR	HCL

BARACK HUSSEIN OBAMA II

BARACK HUSSEIN OBAMA (born 1961) was elected the 44th President of the United States in 2008. First a State Senator in Illinois, then a U.S. Senator for Illinois, he became the first African American President. Unlike other African Americans who have run for the nomination of a major party (i.e., Jesse Jackson, Ben Carson) or have run for President for another political party (i.e., Frederick Douglass, the Equal Rights Party), Obama's only known roots at the time of his election were through his Africa-born father and his America-born white mother, and it did not appear at the time that he was descended from enslaved people in the United States. It was only after he became President that it was discovered by Ancestry.com that Obama was the likely eleventh great-grandson (twelfth-generation grandson) of John Punch, America's first "slave." So, Obama has three very unique, strong and pertinent relationships with the war that began one hundred years before his birth: (1) He was the first African American to run for election as President from a major political party. (2) He was the first African American President of the United States. (3) He was likely a direct descendant of the nation's first slave, John Punch.

LEVEL THREE: COVERT PRESENTATION OF **THE CIVIL WAR** IN **BARACK HUSSEIN OBAMA II**

B = T	T		
A—A			A
R—R			R
A			
C—C		C	
K			
H—H	H		
U = L		L	
S			
S			
E—E	E		
I—I		I	
N = W			W
O			
B			
A			
M = V		V	
A			
I—I		I	
I			
	THE	**CIVIL**	**WAR**

During an examination of U.S. Presidents at Level Three (with suffixes now included), I was quite stunned to see one additional name only. It is none other than BARACK HUSSEIN OBAMA II, the first African American President. His election delivered on the promise made to all Americans by the Constitution, and reaffirmed by The Civil War, Reconstruction, the Freedom Amendments, the Civil Rights movement and the American dream, that one day an African American—not only could be but would be—President of the United States. It was slow in coming, but it was never a question of "if"— only a question of "when." And this was predicted with the presence of THE CIVIL WAR in the name of BARACK HUSSEIN OBAMA II.

LEVEL THREE: COVERT PRESENTATIONS OF **THE CIVIL WAR** IN PRESIDENTS WITH SUFFIXES

	(PRESENT)	(MISSING)
JOHN ADAMS JR	HEVAR	TCIILW
THOMAS JEFFERSON II	THEIVIWAR	CL
JAMES MADISON JR	EIVWAR	THCIL
ANDREW JACKSON JR	TECIVWAR	HIL
MARTIN VAN BUREN SR	TECIVIWAR	HL
WILLIAM HENRY HARRISON SR	HECIVILWAR	T
JOHN TYLER JR	THEILWAR	CVI
ZACHARY TAYLOR II	THCIIAR	EVW
FRANKLIN PIERCE SR	TECIILWAR	HV
JAMES BUCHANAN JR	THECVWAR	IIL
ABRAHAM LINCOLN II	***THE CIVIL WAR***	
ANDREW JOHNSON SR	HEVWAR	TCIIL
RUTHERFORD BIRCHARD HAYES I	***THE CIVIL WAR***	
JAMES ABRAM GARFIELD I	TEIVILWAR	HC
CHESTER ALAN ARTHUR I	THECILWAR	V
WILLIAM MCKINLEY JR	TECIVILWAR	H
THEODORE ROOSEVELT JR	THEIVILWAR	C
WILLIAM HOWARD TAFT I	***THE CIVIL WAR***	
JOHN CALVIN COOLIDGE JR	HECIVILWAR	T
HERBERT CLARK HOOVER SR	***THE CIVIL WAR***	
FRANKLIN DELANO ROOSVELT SR	TECIVILWAR	H
DWIGHT DAVID EISENHOWER I	THEIVIWAR	CL
JOHN FITZGERALD KENNEDY SR	THEIVILWAR	C
LESLIE LYNCH KING JR	THECIILWAR	V
JAMES EARL CARTER JR	TECIVILWAR	H
WILLIAM JEFFERSON BLYTHE III	***THE CIVIL WAR***	64-YEAR PHEN (64 X 2)
BARACK HUSSEIN OBAMA II	***THE CIVIL WAR***	
DONALD JOHN TRUMP SR	THECIVLWAR	I
JOSEPH ROBINETTE BIDEN JR	THEIVIWAR	CL

This is the table for Level Three Presentations of THE CIVIL WAR in the names of the U.S. Presidents. Level Three is the full name plus any name suffix that may appear after their name at birth, such as JR, JNR, II or III, to denote a descendant with the same name or, a name suffix to denote they have descendants such as SR, SNR or I. Histories and biographies typically exclude these suffixes. For example, we are not taught that Thomas Jefferson and Abraham Lincoln were named for their grandfathers. In some cases, families have confused the issue. All suffixes are included in this book.

The Three Claims Tested For Historical Events and World Leaders

The purpose of this book is to disseminate a pattern that I discovered between the names of Historical Events and the names of Heads of State and Military Leaders strongly involved in or strongly associated with the Events. My research into the scope of possibilities in this regard led me to focus on the following Three Claims.

1. The Head of State or Military Leader most central to a war or other Historical Event has a Superior Presentation of the Event in his or her name.

2. A Head of State who serves approximately 64 years after a major turning point in the Historical Event under examination has a Presentation of the Historical Event in his or her name. This major turning point is a defining moment in the Event—one that typifies or determines all subsequent related occurrences.

3. Heads of State and/or Military Leaders who were strongly involved in or highly associated with the Historical Event have a Presentation of the Event in their name.

The validity of these Claims will be further explored and evaluated using evidence, statistical inquiry and probability estimation. Evidence will be provided in each case for the Three Claims throughout this book.

Statistical Analysis, found in Section VI, will be used to determine whether the observed results for Heads of State are different from that for random names from the general population.

We will also estimate the probabilities that the observed results would happen by chance. These will also be found in Section VI of the book.

Summary of Evidence Supporting the Claims:
THE CIVIL WAR
in the Names of U.S. Presidents

Claim 1—
ABRAHAM LINCOLN, the Head of State of the United States most central to THE CIVIL WAR, has a Superior Presentation of THE CIVIL WAR in his name—a Level One Presentation with Substitution.

Claim 2—
The 64-Year Phenomenon: HERBERT CLARK HOOVER, the President who began his term approximately 64 years after the end of THE CIVIL WAR, and WILLIAM JEFFERSON BLYTHE III (better known as Bill Clinton), who began his term approximately 64 years after HOOVER began his, both have THE CIVIL WAR in their name.

Claim 3—
ABRAHAM LINCOLN, the U.S. President who served during THE CIVIL WAR, HIRAM ULYSSES GRANT, the Military Leader of the Union during the war, and RUTHERFORD BIRCHARD HAYES, the other U.S. President with the strongest involvement in and association with the war, all have THE CIVIL WAR in their names.

THE PROBABILITY OF GEORGE WASHINGTON AND KING GEORGE III WILLIAM FREDERICK HAVING EXCLUSIVE AND CORRECT DISPLAYS OF AWOI IN THEIR NAMES
AND
ABRAHAM LINCOLN, HIRAM ULYSSES GRANT, RUTHERFORD BIRCHARD HAYES, WILLIAM HOWARD TAFT, BARACK HUSSEIN OBAMA II, HERBERT CLARK HOOVER SR AND WILLIAM JEFFERSON BLYTHE III HAVING EXCLUSIVE AND CORRECT DISPLAYS OF THE CIVIL WAR IN THEIR NAMES IS

1
IN
825,600,000,000,000
(ONE IN 825 TRILLION, 600 BILLION)

THE CIVIL WAR was the first extensive investigation I performed in search of the Code. I was, of course, very surprised by the results. ABRAHAM LINCOLN, whose life's purpose was the abolition of slavery, and whose very life was at the center of THE CIVIL WAR, is the only U.S. President to have THE CIVIL WAR in his name at Level One (most common given name and last name). This was quite a shock. After all, I had chosen to review the Presidents because of finding THE CIVIL WAR in LINCOLN's name. So, this was an exciting start.

At Level Two, LINCOLN was joined by HIRAM ULYSSES GRANT. My eyes lit up at this finding. The words THE CIVIL WAR belong in GRANT's name every bit as much as they belong in LINCOLN's. GRANT was not only the Commanding General of the U.S. Army during THE CIVIL WAR, but he also served as President during the Reconstruction Era. Then I found RUTHERFORD BIRCHARD HAYES to have THE CIVIL WAR in his name—at Level Two. His service in the war, during which he was wounded multiple times, and the sacrificing of Reconstruction in exchange for his Presidency over Samuel Tilden to resolve a controversial election, gives meaning to the Presentation of THE CIVIL WAR in his name. WILLIAM HOWARD TAFT also had a Presentation of the war. This appears to be due to his standing as the first racist Republican in the White House. BARACK HUSSEIN OBAMA II, who was the first African American President of the United States, has THE CIVIL WAR in his name at Level Three. As I have stated, the fact of his election to the Presidency is highly important historically and in the context of the new possibilities for African Americans after THE CIVIL WAR.

I was already intrigued by these findings after only carefully examining the Presidents' names for THE CIVIL WAR. If this first inquiry had not produced promising results, I would have stopped. In fact, as I first approached this test, I considered, "What if Lincoln is only joined by Presidents James Knox Polk and Theodore Roosevelt?" Both would have been "incorrect" (i.e., not indicative of a Code), and such results would not have been intriguing. Or what if he were joined by eleven others? My work would have ended there.

But what I found was that the Presidents who had a strong relationship with THE CIVIL WAR had these words in their name and those without did not have these words in their names. This made my whole search more than intriguing.

So, I had to know. I had to know what was next.

WORLD WAR ONE AND THE UNITED STATES

WORLD WAR ONE, commonly known as WORLD WAR I (especially in the United States) or the FIRST WORLD WAR (popular in the British Empire) or abbreviated WWI, is considered to have officially begun on July 28, 1914 (the United States did not get involved until April 2, 1917), and to have officially ended on November 11, 1918. It was one of the largest wars in history—involving over 70 million military personnel—and, also, one of the deadliest wars—killing over 9 million military and over 7 million civilians. Associated genocides and the 1918 influenza pandemic killed millions of others. The assassination of Archduke Ferdinand of Austria triggered a series of events that resulted in global war. The original belligerents were the Triple Entente (Britain, France and Russia) and the Dual Alliance (Germany, Austria-Hungary). But the Allied victory of the Entente in the war once called "the war to end all wars," the Treaty of Versailles and even the newly created League of Nations could not prevent a Second World War that would come in just 20 years and 10 months.

At the start of my investigation, I had begun to fill up notebooks with my searches of all the Presidents' names. The notebooks contained charts, tables and other significant findings. At this point, I realized that I would need many more notebooks in which I could document my ongoing discoveries.

Now it was time for me to examine the U.S. Presidents for Presentations of WORLD WAR ONE. I held no specific expectations, but I admit the interesting surprises from examining THE CIVIL WAR had given me some indication that this was not a fluke. I jokingly said to myself, "Now I wonder what I will find in the name THOMAS 'WORLD WAR' WILSON?" This was, of course, a play on the name of THOMAS WOODROW WILSON. I first examined the names of the Presidents at Level One. So, at this level, WILSON's name was simply WOODROW WILSON. I started with GEORGE WASHINGTON and, as I went down the chronological list of U.S. Presidents, I found nothing before the 20th century. Finally, as the suspense began to mount, and shortly before I reached the name of WILSON, I found WORLD WAR ONE encoded in the name THEODORE ROOSEVELT. As an ex-President, he became the co-leader of the Preparedness Movement. It was named exactly for what it was, a movement to prepare the United States for entry into the war. He also had a number of other relationships with WORLD WAR ONE.

THOMAS WOODROW WILSON

THOMAS WOODROW WILSON (1856 - 1924) was the 28th President of the United States, serving as President during World War One. He was commonly known as Woodrow Wilson. He served from 1913 to 1921. He kept the United States out of the war for several years. He believed that a League of Nations could put an end to the war or that the United Sates could play the role of peacemaker and negotiate peace. Wilson did not declare war until Germany sank U.S. ships. Because of Wilson's delay in entering WORLD WAR I, the United States was only involved in the war for the last year-and-a-half of a nearly four-and-a-half-year war. In spite of the late entrance of the United Sates into the war, it is considered a turning point in the war that led to the victory of the Allies. Wilson was the chief architect of the aforementioned League of Nations that was founded January 10, 1920, by the Paris Peace Conference. It operated until April 20, 1946. Some components of the League of Nations were moved to the United Nations which had been founded in 1945.

Just two names later I came to WOODROW WILSON. I thought of the near pun—THOMAS WORLD WAR WILSON. The suspense was overwhelming. Would he have WORLD WAR ONE encoded in his name? I did the work—and, yes, I found WORLD WAR ONE encoded in WOODROW WILSON at Level One. There was no need to use his first name Thomas. I asked myself, "How is this happening?"

LEVEL ONE: COVERT PRESENTATION OF WORLD WAR ONE IN WOODROW WILSON

W—W	W		
O—O	O		
O			
D—D	D		
R—R	R		
O			
W—W		W	
W = E			E
I = R		R	
L—L	L		
S = A		A	
O—O			O
N—N			N
	WORLD	**WAR**	**ONE**

It was amazing to find that, just as with ABRAHAM LINCOLN and THE CIVIL WAR, WOODROW WILSON has a rare Covert Presentation of WORLD WAR ONE at Level One. Also, like Lincoln, Wilson only has two letters left after the conversion and decoding of WORLD WAR ONE in the name WOODROW WILSON. And very similar to Lincoln, who has two displays of an "A" left after the Covert Presentation of THE CIVIL WAR, WOODROW WILSON is also left with two displays of the same letter—this time it is two displays of the letter "O."

75

FRANKLIN DELANO ROOSEVELT SR

Long before he became 32nd President of the United States, a younger Franklin Roosevelt served as the Assistant Secretary of the Navy during World War One. Unlike Wilson, Roosevelt supported the Preparedness Movement, which advocated a military buildup after World War One began. The campaign was led by his fifth cousin, Theodore Roosevelt, and General Leonard Wood. They differed in political parties: Franklin's side of the family were Democrats, while Teddy's side of the Roosevelt family were Republicans. However, they both agreed on military preparedness as the best protection for the United States and Democracy. When the United States entered the war, Franklin asked Woodrow Wilson to appoint him as a naval officer, but Wilson insisted he was needed more in his current position. Franklin took on that position with enthusiasm and focus. He held an important role in the mobilization of the Navy during the early days of the war, and when the war was over, in the demobilization of the Navy. His seven years as Assistant Secretary of the Navy gave him experience in issues related to labor, the Navy, and logistics and he acquired a great deal of experience in managing government during wartime—all valuable to him when he was President during the next World War. So, Franklin Roosevelt has five good reasons for having World War One in his name: (1) He served as Assistant Secretary of the Navy during the war. (2) This position gave him experience at running a government during a world war. (3) He played a role in the mobilization of the Navy. (4) Before the U.S. got involved in the war, he supported military preparedness. (5) His position was part of his journey in politics to New York Governor and, finally, President of the United States.

LEVEL ONE: COVERT PRESENTATION OF **WORLD WAR ONE** IN **FRANKLIN ROOSEVELT**

F			
R—R		R	
A—A		A	
N = W		W	
K			
L			
I			
N = W	W		
R—R	R		
O—O	O		
O—O			O
S			
E = N			N
V = D	D		
E—E			E
L—L	L		
T			
	WORLD	**WAR**	**ONE**

At Level One, I also found WORLD WAR ONE in the name of FRANKLIN ROOSEVELT. He was Assistant Secretary of the Navy during WORLD WAR ONE. He was well-focused on his job. Franklin oversaw the business of operations, personnel and contracting. The impact of this experience on Franklin was immeasurable. As you see in his brief biography, it made him prominent enough to be chosen to run for Vice President—which, in turn, gave him enough recognition to run for Governor, which, in turn, put him in position to run for President. And it gave Franklin an education in managing a government during wartime—something very important to the man who would be President during WORLD WAR TWO.

THEODORE ROOSEVELT JR

THEODORE ROOSEVELT (1858 - 1919) was the 26th President of the United States, a job he inherited when William McKinley was assassinated during the first year of his second term. He was then elected to a second term. "Teddy" was the fifth cousin of future president Franklin Roosevelt. They were members of different parties, but they were both progressive. Theodore had his Square Deal; Franklin had his New Deal. And although Theodore was a Republican and Franklin a Democrat, after World War One began they agreed that the United States had to build toward military readiness should the country be attacked and forced into the war. In fact, Theodore Roosevelt and General Leonard Wood led the Preparedness Movement—a campaign toward that very goal. In addition, Roosevelt was authorized by Congress to form four divisions to fight in France, somewhat similar to the Rough Riders that Roosevelt had led during the Spanish-American War. But Wilson refused to comply with the offer and the authorization. Roosevelt was greatly disappointed. So, Theodore Roosevelt has five relationships with World War One: (1) He championed the Preparedness Movement. (2) He was authorized by Congress to lead four divisions in France, but Wilson refused to comply. (3) Five of his six children served in World War One. (4) His son, Quentin, was shot down over France. (5) His namesake, Theodore Roosevelt III, served in World War I.

COVERT PRESENTATION OF **WORLD WAR ONE** IN **THEODORE ROOSEVELT**

T			
H			
E—E			E
O—O			O
D			
O—O	O		
R—R	R		
E = W	W		
R—R		R	
O			
O			
S = A		A	
E = W		W	
V = D	D		
E = N			N
L—L	L		
T			
	WORLD	**WAR**	**ONE**

As mentioned earlier, Wilson is joined by not just one Roosevelt but two. THEODORE ROOSEVELT was one of the two leaders—with Leonard Wood—of the Preparedness Movement that began shortly after the beginning of WORLD WAR ONE before the United States entered the war. The organization promoted the idea that the United States should be militarily ready in every way possible for entry into the war. Theodore Roosevelt also had five children who participated in WORLD WAR ONE. One of them was a namesake, Theodore Roosevelt III. These are just a few of THEODORE ROOSEVELT's relationships with WORLD WAR ONE.

LEVEL ONE: COVERT PRESENTATIONS OF **WORLD WAR ONE** IN THE NAMES OF U.S. PRESIDENTS

	(PRESENT)	(MISSING)
GEORGE WASHINGTON	WORWARONE	LD
JOHN ADAMS	ODAN	WRLWROE
THOMAS JEFFERSON	WORDAONE	LWR
JAMES MADISON	ORDANE	WLWRO
JAMES MONROE	WORDAONE	LWR
JOHN ADAMS	ODAN	WRLWROE
ANDREW JACKSON	WORLDWANE	RO
MARTIN VAN BUREN	WRLDWARNE	OO
JOHN TYLER	ORLANE	WDWRO
JAMES POLK	OLDAE	WRWRON
ZACHARY TAYLOR	ORLAR	WDWONE
MILLARD FILLMORE	ORLDAROE	WWN
FRANKLIN PIERCE	WORLWARNE	DO
JAMES BUCHANAN	WLDANE	ORWRO
ABRAHAM LINCOLN	WORLDAR	WOE
ANDREW JOHNSON	WORDWAONE	LR
ULYSSES GRANT	RLANE	WODWRO
CHESTER ARTHUR	WRLARE	ODWON
GROVER CLEVELAND	WORLDWARNE	O
BENJAMIN HARRISON	WORDWARNE	LO
WILLIAM MCKINLEY	WRLDARNE	OWO
THEODORE ROOSEVELT	***WORLD WAR ONE***	
WILLIAM TAFT	WORLDAR	WONE
WOODROW WILSON	***WORLD WAR ONE***	

LEVEL ONE: COVERT PRESENTATIONS OF **WORLD WAR ONE** IN THE NAMES OF U.S. PRESIDENTS

	(PRESENT)	(MISSING)
WARREN HARDING	WRDWARNE	OLO
CALVIN COOLIDGE	ORLDARONE	WW
HERBERT HOOVER	WORDWROE	LAN
FRANKLIN ROOSEVELT	***WORLD WAR ONE***	
HARRY TRUMAN	RLDARN	WOWOE
DWIGHT EISENHOWER	WORDWARNE	LO
JOHN KENNEDY	WODWANE	RLRO
LYNDON JOHNSON	WOLDWAONE	RR
RICHARD NIXON	ORLDWARON	WE
LESLIE KING	WRLARNE	ODWO
JAMES CARTER	WRLDARE	OWON
RONALD REAGAN	WORLDARNE	WO
GEORGE BUSH	WORLAE	DWRON
GEORGE BUSH	WORLAE	DWRON
BARACK OBAMA	ORLDA	WWRONE
DONALD TRUMP	ORLDAN	WWROE
JOSEPH BIDEN	WORDANE	LWRO

It is important to note the rarity—in fact, the exclusivity—of the Level One Covert Presentations of WORLD WAR ONE in the names of the U.S. Presidents. Here we see the names of Presidents with anywhere from two to seven letters missing. In fact, in only one name is there only one letter missing.

Special Note: Some names have been excluded from the claim investigations and the statistical tests of WORLD WAR ONE/WORLD WAR I and FIRST WORLD WAR. This is for statistical reasons. For example, some names are excluded because of the strong similarity between the terms WORLD WAR ONE and WORLD WAR TWO, WORLD WAR I and WORLD WAR II, and WWI and WWII. Having a Presentation of one of the wars in one's name greatly increases the probability of having a Display of the other world war in one's name. Being the namesake of someone associated with a war is another reason for an exclusion. Exclusions are fully explained in Appendix B.

LEVEL TWO: COVERT PRESENTATIONS OF **WORLD WAR ONE** IN THE NAMES OF U.S. PRESIDENTS

	(PRESENT)	(MISSING)
GEORGE WASHINGTON	WORWARONE	LD
JOHN ADAMS	ODAN	WRLWROE
THOMAS JEFFERSON	WORDAONE	LWR
JAMES MADISON	ORDANE	WLWRO
JAMES MONROE	WORDAONE	LWR
JOHN QUINCY ADAMS	WORLDAN	WROE
ANDREW JACKSON	WORLDWANE	RO
MARTIN VAN BUREN	WRLDWARNE	OO
JOHN TYLER	ORLANE	WDWRO
JAMES KNOX POLK	OLDAONE	WRWR
ZACHARY TAYLOR	ORLAR	WDWONE
MILLARD FILLMORE	ORLDAROE	WWN
FRANKLIN PIERCE	WORLWARNE	DO
JAMES BUCHANAN	WLDANE	ORWRO
ABRAHAM LINCOLN	WORLDARN	WOE
ANDREW JOHNSON	WORDWAONE	LR
HIRAM ULYSSES GRANT	RLDRNE	WOWO
CHESTER ALAN ARTHUR	WRLARE	ODWO
STEPHEN GROVER CLEVELAND	WORLDWARNE	O
BENJAMIN HARRISON	WORDWARNE	LO
WILLIAM MCKINLEY	WRLDARNE	OWO

LEVEL TWO: COVERT PRESENTATIONS OF **WORLD WAR ONE** IN THE NAMES OF U.S. PRESIDENTS

	(PRESENT)	(MISSING)
THEODORE ROOSEVELT	***WORLD WAR ONE***	
WILLIAM HOWARD TAFT	WORLDWARO	NE
THOMAS WOODROW WILSON	***WORLD WAR ONE***	
WARREN GAMALIEL HARDING	WRLDWARNE	OO
JOHN CALVIN COOLIDGE	WORLDARONE	W
HERBERT CLARK HOOVER	WORLDWAROE	N
HARRY S TRUMAN	RLDARN	WOWOE
FRANKLIN DELANO ROOSEVELT	***WORLD WAR ONE***	
DWIGHT DAVID EISENHOWER	WORDWARNE	LO
LYNDON BAINES JOHNSON	WORLDWAONE	R
RICHARD MILHAUS NIXON	WORLDAR	WE
LESLIE LYNCH KING	WRLWARNE	ODO
JAMES EARL CARTER	WRLDWARE	OON
RONALD WILSON REAGAN	***WORLD WAR ONE***	64-YEAR PHEN
GEORGE HERBERT WALKER BUSH	WORLWARNE	DO
GEORGE WALKER BUSH	WORLWARNE	DO
BARACK HUSSEIN OBAMA	ORLDARNE	WWO
DONALD JOHN TRUMP	WORLDAON	WRE
JOSEPH ROBINETTE BIDEN	WORDWARONE	L

A few Presidents are excluded from the tests because of the similarity of the terms WORLD WAR ONE and WORLD WAR TWO. Having one of the wars in one's name creates a high probability of having the other war because of this similarity. This is fully explained in Appendix B.

64-YEAR PHENOMENON

LEVEL TWO: COVERT PRESENTATION OF WORLD WAR ONE IN RONALD WILSON REAGAN

R—R	R		
O—O	O		
N = W		W	
A—A		A	
L— L	L		
D—D	D		
W—W	W		
I			
L			
S			
O—O			O
N—N			N
R—R		R	
E—E			E
A			
G			
A			
N			
	WORLD	**WAR**	**ONE**

We were introduced to the 64-Year Phenomenon when we found AWOI in the name WILLIAM HARRISON. Approximately sixty-four years after the signing of the Declaration of Independence, Harrison became President. We also found THE CIVIL WAR in the names of HERBERT CLARK HOOVER and WILLIAM JEFFERSON BLYTHE. Their terms as President began approximately 64 years and 128 years (64 X 2) after the declared end of THE CIVIL WAR. In our examination of WORLD WAR ONE, we find that RONALD WILSON REAGAN was President at the time of the 64th anniversary of the end of WORLD WAR ONE. This makes RONALD WILSON REAGAN the 64-Year Phenomenon for WORLD WAR ONE.

WWI

A COMMON EXPRESSION FOR WORLD WAR ONE

LEVEL ONE: OVERT PRESENTATIONS OF **WWI** IN THE NAMES OF U.S. PRESIDENTS

	(PRESENT)	(MISSING)
GEORGE WASHINGTON	WI	W
JOHN ADAMS		WWI
THOMAS JEFFERSON		WWI
JAMES MADISON	I	WW
JAMES MONROE		WWI
JOHN ADAMS		WWI
ANDREW JACKSON	W	WI
MARTIN VAN BUREN	I	WW
JOHN TYLER		WWI
JAMES POLK		WWI
ZACHARY TAYLOR		WWI
MILLARD FILLMORE	I	WW
FRANKLIN PIERCE	I	WW
JAMES BUCHANAN		WWI
ABRAHAM LINCOLN	I	WW
ANDREW JOHNSON	W	WI
ULYSSES GRANT		WWI
CHESTER ARTHUR		WWI

Another common expression of WORLD WAR ONE is WWI, just as WWII is a common expression for WORLD WAR TWO. It was time for me to explore the names of the Presidents for Overt Level One Presentations of WWI and WWII. It was amazing to see that there were no Presidents that served before the 20th century, the century when the two world wars were fought, that contained a Display of WWI or WWII.

LEVEL ONE: OVERT PRESENTATIONS OF **WWI** IN THE NAMES OF U.S. PRESIDENTS

	(PRESENT)	(MISSING)
CHESTER ARTHUR		WWI
GROVER CLEVELAND		WWI
BENJAMIN HARRISON	I	WW
WILLIAM MCKINLEY	WI	W
WILLIAM TAFT	WI	W
WOODROW WILSON	***WWI***	
WARREN HARDING	WI	W
CALVIN COOLIDGE	I	WW
HERBERT HOOVER		WWI
HARRY TRUMAN		WWI
LYNDON JOHNSON		WWI
LESLIE KING	I	WW
JAMES CARTER		WWI
GEORGE BUSH		WWI
GEORGE BUSH		WWI
BARACK OBAMA		WWI
DONALD TRUMP		WWI
JOSEPH BIDEN	I	WW

One President in the 20th century does have WWI at Level One. Not only that, but he is also the correct one! WOODROW WILSON contains WWI. He was the President of the United States during WORLD WAR I.

LEVEL THREE: OVERT PRESENTATIONS OF **WWI** IN THE NAMES OF U.S. PRESIDENTS

	(PRESENT)	(MISSING)
GEORGE WASHINGTON	WI	W
JOHN ADAMS JR		WWI
THOMAS JEFFERSON II	I	WW
JAMES MADISON JR	I	WW
JAMES MONROE		WWI
JOHN QUINCY ADAMS	I	WW
ANDREW JACKSON JR	W	WI
MARTIN VAN BUREN SR	I	WW
JOHN TYLER JR		WWI
JAMES KNOX POLK		WWI
ZACHARY TAYLOR II	I	WW
MILLARD FILLMORE	I	WW
FRANKLIN PIERCE I	I	WW
JAMES BUCHANAN JR		WWI
ABRAHAM LINCOLN II	I	WW
ANDREW JOHNSON SR	W	WI
HIRAM ULYSSES GRANT	I	WW
CHESTER ALAN ARTHUR I	I	WW

I conducted a search for Level Three Presentations of WWI in the U.S. Presidents. Again, as I mentioned before, suffixes have been largely ignored in biographies and histories. Some leaders never used the suffix while some did not want the suffix. Nevertheless, the suffixes are a part of the Code. In some cases, families have confused the issue. Lincoln's grandson was named Abraham Lincoln II after his famous grandfather—ignoring his great-great-grandfather, Captain Abraham Lincoln. The suffixes for the namesake descendants of Theodore Roosevelt Jr. have also been the cause of some confusion—as his son was also often known as Theodore Roosevelt Jr.

LEVEL THREE: OVERT PRESENTATIONS OF **WWI** IN THE NAMES OF U.S. PRESIDENTS

	(PRESENT)	(MISSING)
STEPHEN GROVER CLEVELAND		WWI
BENJAMIN HARRISON	I	WW
WILLIAM MCKINLEY JR	WI	W
WILLIAM HOWARD TAFT I	*****WWI*****	
THOMAS WOODROW WILSON	*****WWI*****	
WARREN GAMALIEL HARDING	WI	W
JOHN CALVIN COOLIDGE JR	I	WW
HARRY S TRUMAN		WWI
LYNDON BAINES JOHNSON	I	WW
RICHARD MILHAUS NIXON	I	WW
LESLIE LYNCH KING JR	I	WW
JAMES EARL CARTER JR		WWI
GEORGE HERBERT WALKER BUSH	W	WI
GEORGE WALKER BUSH	W	WI
BARACK HUSSEIN OBAMA II	I	WW
DONALD JOHN TRUMP SR		WWI
JOSEPH ROBINETTE BIDEN JR	I	WW

So, here I was, seeing even more of the Code unfold right before my very eyes. Searching for Overt Presentations of WWI at Level Three, I still found that no President before the 20th century contained more than one "W" in their name, even now using their whole names. In the 20th century, two Presidents, WILLIAM HOWARD TAFT I and THOMAS WOODROW WILSON, have Level Two and Level Three Overt Presentations of WWI in their names, and, as we will see, there will be one more with WWII.

WILLIAM HOWARD TAFT I

> **WILLIAM HOWARD TAFT (1857 - 1930)** was the 27th President of the United States. He served one term and was succeeded by Woodrow Wilson. During the early years of World War I, both Taft and Wilson hoped that a League of Nations could prevent war. In fact, Taft was the president of the League to Enforce Peace. But when Germany sank two U.S. ships, Wilson declared war on Germany and Taft became an enthusiastic supporter. Wilson assigned him to be the Chairman of the Executive Committee of the American Red Cross. This was a huge job. To make it possible for executives of the Red Cross to carry out their duties, Wilson gave them high military ranks. Ex-President William Taft was given the rank of Major General.

As we see in this brief biography, President Wilson appointed ex-President William Howard Taft as Chairman of the American Red Cross during WORLD WAR ONE with the military rank Major General. He contains WWI in his name. He is one of only two Presidents with this abbreviation of the war in his name at Level Two.

LEVEL ONE: OVERT PRESENTATION OF WWI IN WOODROW WILSON

W—W	W
O	
O	
D	
R	
O	
W—W	W
W	
I—I	I
L	
S	
O	
N	
WWI	

LEVEL TWO: OVERT PRESENTATION OF WWI IN WILLIAM HOWARD TAFT

W—W	W
I—I	I
L	
L	
I	
A	
M	
H	
O	
W—W	W
A	
R	
D	
T	
A	
F	
T	
WWI	

WORLD WAR I

A COMMON EXPRESSION FOR WORLD WAR ONE

LEVEL THREE: MIXED PRESENTATIONS OF **WORLD WAR I** IN THE NAMES OF U.S. PRESIDENTS

	(PRESENT)	(MISSING)
GEORGE WASHINGTON	WORWARI	LDR
JOHN ADAMS JR	WORDA	LWRI
THOMAS JEFFERSON II	WORDWAI	LR
JAMES MADISON JR	WORDWAI	LR
JAMES MONROE	WORDWA	LRI
JOHN QUINCY ADAMS	WOLDWAI	RR
ANDREW JACKSON JR	WORLDWAR	I
MARTIN VAN BUREN SR	WRLDWARI	O
JOHN TYLER JR	WORLWAR	DI
JAMES KNOX POLK	WOLDWA	RRI
ZACHARY TAYLOR II	ORLARI	WDW
MILLARD FILLMORE	WORLDARI	W
FRANKLIN PIERCE SR	WORLWARI	D
JAMES BUCHANAN JR	WRLDWA	ORI
ANDREW JOHNSON SR	WORDWAR	LI
HIRAM ULYSSES GRANT	WRLDWARI	O
CHESTER ALAN ARTHUR I	WRLWARI	OD

This is the first appearance of the MIXED PRESENTATION which is when a Presentation includes both Overt and Covert Presentations. In the Presentations of WORLD WAR I and WORLD WAR II, WORLD WAR is a Covert Presentation as it involves Conversion. The I and II are Overt, meaning the actual letters are found in the name.

This is also the first appearance of the Namesake Exception. Some names have been excluded due to Exceptions as explained in Appendix B.

LEVEL THREE: MIXED PRESENTATIONS OF **WORLD WAR I** IN THE NAMES OF U.S. PRESIDENTS

	(PRESENT)	(MISSING)
STEPHEN GROVER CLEVELAND	WORLDWAR	I
BENJAMIN HARRISON	WORDWARI	L
WILLIAM MCKINLEY JR	WRLDWARI	O
WILLIAM HOWARD TAFT I	***WORLD WAR I***	
WARREN GAMALIEL HARDING	WRLDWARI	O
JOHN CALVIN COOLIDGE JR	***WORLD WAR I***	
FRANKLIN DELANO ROOSEVELT SR	***WORLD WAR I***	
HARRY S TRUMAN	WRLDAR	OWI
LYNDON BAINES JOHNSON	WOLDWAI	RR
LESLIE LYNCH KING JR	WRLWARI	OD
JAMES EARL CARTER JR	WRLDWAR	OI
RONALD WILSON REAGAN	***WORLD WAR I***	**64-YEAR PHEN**
GEORGE HERBERT WALKER BUSH	WORLWAR	DI
GEORGE WALKER BUSH	WORLWAR	DI
DONALD JOHN TRUMP SR	WORLDWAR	I
JOSEPH ROBINETTE BIDEN JR	WORDWARI	L

Three of the Presidents with WORLD WAR I also have other expressions for the war in their names. WILLIAM HOWARD TAFT has an Overt Presentation of WWI while RONALD WILSON REAGAN (the 64-Year Phenomenon) has a Presentation of WORLD WAR ONE. At Level One, FRANKLIN ROOSEVELT has WORLD WAR ONE, and, as we will soon see, he has still another Presentation in his name at Level Three. JOHN CALVIN COOLIDGE JR has this expression—WORLD WAR I.

JOHN CALVIN COOLIDGE JR

JOHN CALVIN COOLIDGE (1872 - 1933) was the 30th President of the United States. (1) He was Vice President during the aftermath of World War I. (2) His highest office before President was Governor of Massachusetts. He first ran successfully for that office on strong positions, including support for U.S. involvement in World War I, and was elected by a very small margin just one week before the war ended! (3) After the war was over, Coolidge asked the state legislature to give a bonus of $100 for all citizens of Massachusetts who were Veterans of World War I; $100 in 1919 was equal to approximately $1500 in 2020—larger than the first COVID-19-related stimulus check. (4) Ironically, on May 15, 1924, as President of the United States, Coolidge refused to sign the World War Adjusted Compensation Act, arguing that patriotism rewarded is not patriotism, even though he had as Governor given a bonus to World War I Veterans. The bill was passed into law over his veto. (5) The most important and historic association between John Calvin Coolidge Jr. and World War I, was his authorization of the Dawes Plan, a plan authored by a committee chaired by his Vice President, Charles Dawes. The Dawes Plan ended the Allied Occupation and resolved Germany's reparation plan. The plan ended a major crisis and led to Dawes winning a Nobel Prize in 1929.

LEVEL THREE: MIXED PRESENTATION OF WORLD WAR I IN JOHN CALVIN COOLIDGE JR

J			
O—O	O		
H			
N = W	W		
C			
A—A		A	
L—L	L		
V			
I—I			I
N = W		W	
C			
O			
O			
L			
I = R		R	
D—D	D		
G			
E			
J			
R—R	R		
	WORLD	**WAR**	**I**

JOHN CALVIN COOLIDGE JR has a strong association with WORLD WAR I as described in his biography. As we see here, he has a Level Three Presentation of WORLD WAR I.

FIRST WORLD WAR

A COMMON EXPRESSION FOR WORLD WAR ONE

LEVEL THREE: COVERT PRESENTATIONS OF **FIRST WORLD WAR** IN THE NAMES OF U.S. PRESIDENTS

	(PRESENT)	(MISSING)
GEORGE WASHINGTON	FIRSTWOWA	RLDR
JOHN ADAMS JR	RSWODA	FITRLWR
THOMAS JEFFERSON II	FIRSTWODWA	RLR
JAMES MADISON JR	IRSWODWA	FTRLR
JAMES MONROE	FRSWODWA	ITRLR
JOHN QUINCY ADAMS	ISWOLDQA	FRTRR
ANDREW JACKSON JR	RSTWORLDWA	FIR
MARTIN VAN BUREN SR	IRSTWRLDWAR	FO
JOHN TYLER JR	RSTWORLWA	FIDR
JAMES KNOX POLK	FSTWOLDWA	IRRR
ZACHARY TAYLOR II	IRSTORLA	FWDWR
MILLARD FILLMORE	FIRWORLDAR	STW
FRANKLIN PIERCE SR	FRSTRLWAR	OD
JAMES BUCHANAN JR	RSTWLDWA	FIORR
ABRAHAM LINCOLN II	IRSTWORLDWAR	F
ANDREW JOHNSON SR	FRSWORDWA	ITLR
HIRAM ULYSSES GRANT	IRSTWRLDWA	FOR
CHESTER ALAN ARTHUR I	IRSTWRLWAR	FOD
STEPHEN GROVER CLEVELAND	RSTWORLDWA	FIR

LEVEL THREE: COVERT PRESENTATIONS OF **FIRST WORLD WAR** IN THE NAMES OF U.S. PRESIDENTS

	(PRESENT)	(MISSING)
BENJAMIN HARRISON	IRSTWORDWAR	FL
WILLIM MCKINLEY JR	IRSTWRLDW	FO
WARREN GAMALIEL HARDING	IRSWRLDWAR	FTO
JOHN CALVIN COOLIDGE JR	FIRSWORLDWA	TR
HERBERT CLARK HOOVER SR	***FIRST WORLD WAR***	
FRANKLIN DELANO ROOSEVELT SR	***FIRST WORLD WAR***	
HARRY S TRUMAN	RSTWRLDAR	FIOW
DWIGHT DAVID EISENHOWER I	IRSTWORDWAR	FL
JOHN FITZGERALD KENNEDY SR	FIRSTWORLDWA	R
LYNDON BAINES JOHNSON	FISTWOLDWA	RRR
RICHARD MILHAUS NIXON	FIRSWORLDWAR	T
LESLIE LYNCH KING JR	IRSTWRLWA	FODR
JAMES EARL CARTER JR	IRSTWRLDWAR	FO
RONALD WILSON REAGAN	FIRSWORLDWA	TR
GEORGE HERBERT WALKER BUSH	IRSTWORLWAR	FD
GEORGE WALKER BUSH	RSTWORLWA	FIDR
BARACK HUSSEIN OBAMA II	IRSTWORLDWAR	F
DONALD JOHN TRUMP SR	FRSTWOLRDWA	IR
JOSEPH ROBINETTE BIDEN JR	FIRSTWORDWAR	L

We have already seen the expressions WORLD WAR ONE and WORLD WAR I in the name of FRANKLIN DELANO ROOSEVELT, but now that we are including his name suffix, SR, in Level Three, we also find FIRST WORLD WAR in his name. HERBERT CLARK HOOVER SR also has FIRST WORLD WAR at Level Three.

HERBERT CLARK HOOVER SR

HERBERT CLARK HOOVER (1874 - 1964) was considered a great humanitarian for his wartime and post-war work during and after both of the world wars. Before the involvement of the United States in the First World War, Hoover established the Commission for Relief in Belgium. During the First World War, he headed the U.S. Food Administration and, postwar, he headed the American Relief Administration, which provided food on a mass scale for those in need in Central and Eastern Europe. His humanitarianism during and following both world wars could be said to outshine his years in the Presidency.

HERBERT CLARK HOOVER presents with FIRST WORLD WAR for his wartime and post-war work during and after WORLD WAR ONE. His great humanitarian work was essential to prevent starvation on a mass scale in Belgium during the war and in Central and Eastern Europe after the war.

COVERT PRESENTATION OF **FIRST WORLD WAR** IN **HERBERT CLARK HOOVER SR**

H			
E = W		W	
R—R	R		
B			
E = W			W
R—R		R	
T—T	T		
C			
L—L		L	
A—A			A
R—R			R
K			
H			
O—O		O	
O = F	F		
V = D		D	
E			
R = I	I		
S—S	S		
R			
	FIRST	**WORLD**	**WAR**

We have seen that many U.S. Presidents have served their nation after their Presidency—some during a time of war. This was the case for WILLIAM HOWARD TAFT and for HERBERT CLARK HOOVER. Not only did Hoover lead the relief funds, but after the war, as we see in his biography, he provided meals for millions of schoolchildren in the Allied Zones of Germany.

Summary of Evidence Supporting the Claims:
WORLD WAR ONE, WORLD WAR I, WWI, FIRST WORLD WAR
in the names of U.S. Presidents

Claim 1—
WOODROW WILSON, the U.S. President most central to WORLD WAR ONE/WORLD WAR I/WWI/FIRST WORLD WAR, has two Superior Presentations—a Level One Presentation of WORLD WAR ONE and a Level One Overt Presentation of WWI in his name.

Claim 2—
The 64-Year Phenomenon: RONALD WILSON REAGAN, the President who began his term approximately 64 years after the beginning of U.S. involvement in WORLD WAR ONE and who was still President 64 years after the end of the war, has both WORLD WAR ONE and WORLD WAR I in his name.

Claim 3—
The U.S. Presidents with the strongest involvement in or association with the war have one or more Presentations. In addition to the two Superior Presentations in the name of WOODROW WILSON, WILLIAM HOWARD TAFT has Level Two Presentations of WORLD WAR II and WWII; FRANKLIN DELANO ROOSEVELT has Level One Presentations of WORLD WAR ONE and WORLD WAR I, and a Level Two Presentation of FIRST WORLD WAR; THEODORE ROOSEVELT has a Level Two Presentation for WORLD WAR ONE; HERBERT CLARK HOOVER has a Level Three Presentation of FIRST WORLD WAR; and JOHN CALVIN COOLIDGE JR has a Level Three Presentation of WORLD WAR I.

THE PROBABILITY OF GEORGE WASHINGTON, WILLIAM HARRISON, AND GEORGE III WILLIAM FREDERICK HAVING EXCLUSIVE AND CORRECT DISPLAYS OF AWOI IN THEIR NAMES

AND

ABRAHAM LINCOLN, HIRAM ULYSSES GRANT, RUTHERFORD BIRCHARD HAYES, WILLIAM HOWARD TAFT, BARACK HUSSEIN OBAMA, HERBERT CLARK HOOVER AND WILLIAM JEFFERSON BLYTHE HAVING EXCLUSIVE AND CORRECT DISPLAYS OF THE CIVIL WAR IN THEIR NAMES

AND

WOODROW WILSON, THEODORE ROOSEVELT, FRANKLIN ROOSEVELT, WILLIAM HOWARD TAFT, JOHN CALVIN COOLIDGE, HERBERT CLARK HOOVER AND RONALD WILSON REAGAN HAVING EXCLUSIVE AND CORRECT DISPLAYS OF WORLD WAR ONE/WWI/WORLD WAR I/FIRST WORLD WAR IN THEIR NAMES IS

1
IN
914,800,000,000,000

(ONE IN OVER 941 TRILLION, 800 BILLION)

The findings of my study of WORLD WAR ONE/WORLD WAR I/WW I/FIRST WORLD WAR replicated the earlier findings of my study of THE CIVIL WAR. Thus, I was met with the same kind of results. These results strongly suggested to me that what I had been seeing could not be relegated to mere coincidence. I was witnessing the unveiling of a Code with very strong evidence.

Just as ABRAHAM LINCOLN's name contained THE CIVIL WAR, WOODROW WILSON's name contained WORLD WAR ONE and WWI, two common expressions for the same war. And there were other Presidents with the expressions.

One amazing aspect of this rigorous investigation was that I was reviewing four expressions. And, of those who have a Presentation, many have two of the four expressions. WOODROW WILSON is the only President at Level One to have WWI, but he also has a Level One WORLD WAR ONE. WILLIAM HOWARD TAFT has WWI at Level Two and, also, has WORLD WAR I. FRANKLIN ROOSEVELT SR has WORLD WAR ONE, WORLD WAR I and FIRST WORLD WAR. RONALD WILSON REAGAN, the 64-Year Phenomenon, has WORLD WAR ONE and WORLD WAR I. THEODORE ROOSEVELT, JOHN CALVIN COOLIDGE JR and HERBERT CLARK HOOVER SR have just one of the expressions.

The work I had conducted, so far, fully supported all my claims. But I could not define, with absolute confidence, exactly what I was witnessing. The Three Claims were fully investigated and, indeed, all Three Claims were supported by the evidence. But I knew my claims needed to be investigated further. I had one more war to examine. What if the test of WORLD WAR TWO/WORLD WAR II/WWII/SECOND WORLD WAR failed to support my claims? The suspense now became overwhelming. The next test was crucial to determine if the Code is real. Indeed, what if my investigation of this war supported my earlier findings?

WORLD WAR TWO AND THE UNITED STATES

WORLD WAR TWO, often known as WORLD WAR II or the SECOND WORLD WAR or abbreviated WWII, was fought from 1939 to 1945. Many of the antecedents, precursors and causes of the war can also be considered the aftermath, consequences and unresolved tensions and conditions of World War One. This was the second of two global wars, this time fought—for the most part—along ideological lines. Most of the major belligerents were nations with alliances. The two sides became members of the Allies or the Axis. World War Two was the deadliest war in history, killing between fifty million and eighty-five million people, the majority being civilians. There were massacres, bombings and deaths from disease and starvation. The Holocaust killed between five million and seven million Jews, but the Nazis were also responsible for killing millions of others. The major causes of the war were the aggression of Hitler's Nazi Germany and Hirohito's Japan. Hitler wanted to build an empire; Hirohito's Japan wanted to dominate the Pacific. Germany's attack on Poland began the war. The most powerful saving grace may have been Winston Churchill's resistance to Hitler. Ultimately, General Dwight David Eisenhower, as Supreme Allied Commander in Europe, brought Germany to surrender on May 7, 1945. One of the greatest atrocities in history, the dropping of atomic bombs on Hiroshima and Nagasaki, also occurred during the war in August 1945. On September 2, 1945, Japan surrendered, officially ending World War Two.

"I have seen war. I have seen war on land and sea. I have seen blood running from the wounded…I have seen the dead in the mud. I have seen cities destroyed…I have seen children starving. I have seen the agony of mothers and wives. I hate war."

"This generation of Americans has a rendezvous with destiny."

Franklin Roosevelt

FRANKLIN DELANO ROOSEVELT SR

FRANKLIN DELANO ROOSEVELT (1882 - 1945), popularly known as FDR, was the 32nd President of the United States from 1933 until 1945. He was elected four times and was the only President to be elected more than two times. Roosevelt directed the federal government during most of the Great Depression. His third term and his very brief fourth term (eighty-two days) were dominated by World War Two. His rise in politics included election to the New York Senate in 1910, serving as Assistant Secretary of the Navy during World War One, an unsuccessful bid for the Vice Presidency in 1920, and serving as Governor of New York from 1929 to 1933. Toward the end of his second term, Roosevelt had no plans for an unprecedented run for a third term in the nation's highest office. But the growing threat of Hitler's Nazi Germany made him reverse his decision. He ran and won a third term. He had already been giving growing support to the United Kingdom, China and the Soviet Union for the war effort. He had been maintaining secret communication with Winston Churchill, and he had been overseeing a military buildup and the passage of a bill for a peacetime draft in anticipation of war. Finally, in response to Japan's attack on Pearl Harbor on December 7, 1941, Roosevelt had no problem getting Congress to declare war on Japan and, soon after, on Germany and Italy. Roosevelt worked closely with British Prime Minister Winston Churchill, Soviet leader Joseph Stalin and the Chinese leader Chiang Kai-shek. His death was announced shortly before the surrender of Germany and a few months before the surrender of Japan.

Now it was time to examine WORLD WAR TWO. If ABRAHAM LINCOLN had THE CIVIL WAR, and WOODROW WILSON had WORLD WAR ONE, I wondered if FRANKLIN ROOSEVELT had WORLD WAR TWO in his name.

LEVEL ONE: COVERT PRESENTATION OF WORLD WAR TWO IN FRANKLIN ROOSEVELT

F			
R—R		R	
A—A		A	
N = W	W		
K			
L			
I			
N = W			W
R—R	R		
O—O	O		
O—O			O
S			
E = W		W	
V = D	D		
E			
L—L		L	
T			T
	WORLD	**WAR**	**TWO**

As I completed the table, there it was! There was WORLD WAR TWO in the name FRANKLIN ROOSEVELT at Level One. And, at Level One, he was alone—after excluding necessary Exceptions.* This definitely provided further support for the Code. It was just incredible. It still, somehow, did not make sense that this was all happening. This whole process of discovery was beyond belief. I mean, to find the names of the wars in the names given to future Presidents when they were born was incomprehensible. Perplexed, I continued with my search. But now I was beginning to suspect what was coming next. I assumed that at Level Two—among the various expressions for the war—Roosevelt would be joined by others. I wondered if I would see Dwight Eisenhower and John Kennedy. Or, if I would see a man like Herbert Hoover again.

*See Appendix B for Exclusions from Tests

HERBERT CLARK HOOVER SR

HERBERT CLARK HOOVER (1874 - 1964), as mentioned earlier, was considered a great humanitarian for his wartime work during and his postwar work immediately following World War One and World War Two. Early on in World War Two, before the United States joined the war, Hoover created the Commission of Polish Relief and the Finnish Relief Fund. However, because of his opposition to U.S. involvement in World War Two and his strong opposition to FDR's New Deal, Hoover was not appointed by Roosevelt to a position he anticipated during World War Two. But after the war, in April 1947, Hoover established a food program for schoolchildren aged 6 through 18 in the Allied Zones of Germany, where over three-and-a-half million children were fed.

COVERT PRESENTATION OF **WORLD WAR TWO** IN **HERBERT CLARK HOOVER**

H			
E = W	W		
R—R	R		
B			
E = W		W	
R—R		R	
T—T			T
C			
L—L	L		
A—A		A	
R			
K			
H			
O—O	O		
O—O			O
V = D	D		
E = W			W
R			
	WORLD	**WAR**	**TWO**

I knew that HERBERT HOOVER had made a major impact on the world during the war. He was a great humanitarian in his work after WORLD WAR ONE and during the early days of and after WORLD WAR TWO. In fact, as we see in his biography, he helped a great number of people in Poland and Finland, leading the Poland Relief Fund and Finnish Relief Fund—even before the United States had officially entered WORLD WAR TWO.

JOHN FITZGERALD KENNEDY SR

JOHN FITZGERALD KENNEDY (1917 - 1963), the 35th President of the United States, was born May 17, 1917, into a wealthy family in Brookline, Massachusetts, just 53 days after the United States entered World War One. John and his older brother, Joe, were Navy Lieutenants in World War Two. His brother was killed in action. John Kennedy has six important relationships with World War Two. (1) He was an early supporter of U.S. intervention into World War Two. (2) He wrote a book before the U.S. entered the war. It was his senior thesis at Harvard called *Why England Slept*. (3) He was a lieutenant in the Navy. (4) He became a war hero when his PT boat was destroyed, and he led ten other survivors to safety. (5) One of the reasons for Kennedy's nomination and election as U.S. Representative from Massachusetts was his being a World War Two Veteran. (6) Kennedy's father had plans for his eldest son, Joseph Jr., to run for President, but when Joseph was killed in World War Two, their father's aspirations fell on John. Thus, the war was Kennedy's reason for his political journey to the U.S. Presidency. He was elected to represent Massachusetts in the U.S. House of Representatives for three terms and the U.S. Senate for a term before being elected to his nation's highest office.

COVERT PRESENTATION OF **WORLD WAR TWO** IN **JOHN FITZGERALD KENNEDY**

J			
O—O	O		
H			
N = W	W		
F = O			O
I = R		R	
T—T			T
Z			
G			
E = W		W	
R—R	R		
A—A		A	
L—L	L		
D—D	D		
K			
E = W			W
N			
N			
E			
D			
Y			
	WORLD	**WAR**	**TWO**

I was, indeed, expecting to find a Covert Presentation of WORLD WAR TWO in the name of JOHN FITZGERALD KENNEDY. He was a hero in this war, and his being a WORLD WAR TWO hero helped him in his rapid rise in politics. But expecting to find a Presentation made it no less suspenseful as I looked in his name. As each letter appeared, I experienced the anticipation of the next.

LEVEL ONE: COVERT PRESENTATIONS OF **WORLD WAR TWO** IN THE NAMES of U.S. PRESIDENTS

	(PRESENT)	(MISSING)
GEORGE WASHINGTON	WORWARTWO	LD
JOHN ADAMS	WODA	RLWRTWO
THOMAS JEFFERSON	WORDWATWO	LR
JAMES MADISON	WORDWA	LRTWO
JAMES MONROE	WORDWAWO	LRT
JOHN ADAMS	WODA	RLWRTWO
ANDREW JACKSON	WORLDWATW	RO
MARTIN VAN BUREN	WRLDWARTW	OO
JOHN TYLER	WORLWAT	DRWO
JAMES POLK	WOLDAT	RWRWO
ZACHARY TAYLOR	ORLART	WDWWO
MILLARD FILLMORE	ORLDWARO	WTW
FRANKLIN PIERCE	WORLWARTW	DO
JAMES BUCHANAN	WLDWATW	ORRO
ABRAHAM LINCOLN	WORLDWART	WO
ANDREW JOHNSON	WORDWAWO	LRT
ULYSSES GRANT	WRLWAT	ODRWO
CHESTER ARTHUR	WRLWART	ODWO
GROVER CLEVELAND	WORLDWARN	TO

LEVEL ONE: COVERT PRESENTATIONS OF **WORLD WAR TWO** IN THE NAMES OF U.S. PRESIDENTS

	(PRESENT)	(MISSING)
BENJAMIN HARRISON	WORDWARTW	LO
WILLIAM MCKINLEY	WRLDWARTW	OO
WILLIAM TAFT	WORLDART	WWO
WARREN HARDING	WRDWARTW	OLTO
CALVIN COOLIDGE	WORLDWARO	TW
HERBERT HOOVER	WORDWRTWO	LA
FRANKLIN ROOSEVELT	***WORLD WAR TWO***	
HARRY TRUMAN	WRLDART	OWWO
DWIGHT EISENHOWER	WORDWARTW	LO
LYNDON JOHNSON	WOLDWAWO	RRT
RICHARD NIXON	WORLDWARO	TW
LESLIE KING	WRLWARTW	ODO
JAMES CARTER	WRLDWART	OWO
RONALD REAGAN	WORLDWARW	TO
GEORGE BUSH	WORLWAT	DRWO
GEORGE BUSH	WORLWAT	DRWO
BARACK OBAMA	ORLDAT	WWRWO
DONALD TRUMP	WORLDAT	WRWO
JOSEPH BIDEN	WORDWATW	LRO

I marveled as I looked through the names of the Presidents without WORLD WAR TWO in their names at Level One. Many were missing two or three or four or five letters. In fact, a few were missing six or seven. After exclusions, only one President's name contains WORLD WAR TWO and that is FRANKLIN ROOSEVELT who was at the very center of the war.

Special Note: Some names have been excluded from some of the tests of WORLD WAR TWO, WORLD WAR II and SECOND WORLD WAR. This is for statistical reasons. Some names are excluded because of the strong similarity between the terms WORLD WAR ONE and WORLD WAR TWO. Having one of the wars in one's name greatly increases the probability of having the other world war in one's name. Being the namesake of someone associated with a war is another reason for an exclusion. Exclusions are explained in Appendix B.

LEVEL TWO: COVERT PRESENTATIONS OF **WORLD WAR TWO** IN THE NAMES OF U.S. PRESIDENTS

	(PRESENT)	(MISSING)
GEORGE WASHINGTON	WORWARTWO	LD
JOHN ADAMS	WODA	RLWRTWO
THOMAS JEFFERSON	WORDWATWO	LR
JAMES MADISON	WORDWA	LRTWO
JAMES MONROE	WORDWAWO	LRT
JOHN QUINCY ADAMS	WORLDWA	RTWO
ANDREW JACKSON	WORLDWATW	RO
MARTIN VAN BUREN	WRLDWRTW	OO
JOHN TYLER	WORLWAT	DRWO
JAMES KNOX POLK	WOLDWATO	RRW
ZACHARY TAYLOR	ORLART	WDWWO
MILLARD FILLMORE	ORLDWARO	WTW
FRANKLIN PIERCE	WORLWARTO	DO
JAMES BUCHANAN	WLDWATW	ORRO
ABRAHAM LINCOLN	WORLDWART	WO
ANDREW JOHNSON	WORDWAWO	LRT
HIRAM ULYSSES GRANT	WRLDWART	OWO
CHESTER ALAN ARTHUR	WRLWARTW	ODO
STEPHEN GROVER CLEVELAND	WORLDWARTW	O

LEVEL TWO: COVERT PRESENTATIONS OF **WORLD WAR TWO** IN THE NAMES OF U.S. PRESIDENTS

	(PRESENT)	(MISSING)
BENJAMIN HARRISON	WORDWARTW	LO
WILLIAM MCKINLEY	WRLDWARTW	OO
WARREN GAMALIEL HARDING	WRLDWARW	OTO
JOHN CALVIN COOLIDGE	WORLDWARWO	T
HERBERT CLARK HOOVER	*****WORLD WAR TWO*****	
FRANKLIN DELANO ROOSEVELT	*****WORLD WAR TWO*****	
HARRY S TRUMAN	WRLDART	OWWO
DWIGHT DAVID EISENHOWER	WORDWARTW	LO
JOHN FITZGERALD KENNEDY	*****WORLD WAR TWO*****	
LYNDON BAINES JOHNSON	WORLDWATWO	R
RICHARD MILHAUS NIXON	WORLDWARO	TW
LESLIE LYNCH KING	WRLWARTW	ODO
JAMES EARL CARTER	WRLDWARTW	OO
RONALD WILSON REAGAN	WORLDWARWO	T
GEORGE HERBERT WALKER BUSH	WORLWARTW	DO
GEORGE WALKER BUSH	WORLWARTW	DO
BARACK HUSSEIN OBAMA	WORLDWART	WO
DONALD JOHN TRUMP	WORLDWATO	RW
JOSEPH ROBINETTE BIDEN	WORDWARTWO	L

Even at Level Two, some names were missing as many as three or four letters, while others were missing only one or two. Whatever force was at work here, the Presidents who had a strong involvement in the war were expressing the names of their Historical Events, and those not involved were not.

WWII

A COMMON EXPRESSION FOR WORLD WAR TWO

DWIGHT DAVID EISENHOWER 1—U.S. ARMY GENERAL

DWIGHT DAVID "Ike" EISENHOWER was a U.S. Army General who would later serve as the 34th President of the United States. Named David Dwight Eisenhower at birth, his mother switched his two given names to Dwight David, because there was already another David in the family. Growing up, Dwight developed an interest in military history. He entered West Point in 1911 and graduated in 1915 and reported to the 19th Infantry Regiment. In 1917, when the U.S. declared war on Germany, Eisenhower requested an assignment overseas, but he was denied his request. He was, however, promoted to Captain and he was given the assignment of training officers. During World War I, he was promoted to Major and then Lieutenant Colonel. After the war, he received a loss of rank to Captain but would soon return to Major. During the Depression, most of his work was in preparation for another war. In 1936, he returned to the rank of Lieutenant Colonel. During World War II, he was promoted to General and was given many important assignments. He was responsible for orchestrating the invasion of North Africa in Operation Torch in 1942 - 1943. In December of 1943, Eisenhower was promoted to Supreme Commander of the Allied Expeditionary Forces in Europe. On May 7, 1945, he accepted the unconditional surrender of Germany. Anticipating future attempts at propaganda and Holocaust denial, he ordered extensive photo stills and film documentation of all the Nazi death camps.

DWIGHT DAVID EISENHOWER 1

DWIGHT DAVID "Ike" EISENHOWER (born David Dwight Eisenhower) (1890 - 1969) was the 34th President of the United States, serving from 1953 to 1961. In 1947, Truman asked him to run for President for the Democratic Party, stating that he (Truman) would run as his Vice President. But Ike stated he was not interested in politics. Four years later, in 1952, he ran for President for the Republican Party and won the election. In 1956, he was re-elected. Just as George Washington, who had been the Commander of the Continental Army during the American War of Independence, had been the one who accepted the surrender of the United Kingdom, and Ulysses Grant, who had been the Commander of the Union Army during the Civil War, had accepted the surrender of the Confederate Army, Eisenhower, who had been the Commander of the Allied Forces—accepted the unconditional surrender of Germany. And just as George Washington went on to become the first President of the United States, and Ulysses Grant went on to become the first President elected after the end of the Civil War, Eisenhower went on to become President several years after the end of World War II. So, all three of these great military leaders went on to take the highest office in the United States. And like George Washington, Eisenhower gave the nation a stern warning. Washington had warned of the dangers of political partisanship; Eisenhower warned the nation of the dangers of the growing power of the military-industrial complex.

LEVEL ONE: OVERT PRESENTATION OF **WWII** IN **DWIGHT EISENHOWER**

D	
W—W	W
I—I	I
G	
H	
T	
E	
I—I	I
S	
E	
N	
H	
O	
W—W	W
E	
R	
	WWII

It is interesting that just as GEORGE WASHINGTON is one of only two U.S. Presidents, along with WILLIAM HARRISON, to have the initialism of the AMERICAN WAR OF INDEPENDENCE—AWOI—in his name at Level One, DWIGHT EISENHOWER is the only U.S. President with an Overt Presentation of WWII in his name at Level One, and, with one exclusion explained in the appendix, also at Level Two. They were both Commanders of major wars, but neither of them served as President during these wars.

LEVEL ONE: OVERT PRESENTATION OF THE WWII HERO GEN IN DWIGHT EISENHOWER

	THE	WWII	HERO	GEN
D				
W—W		W		
I—I		I		
G—G				G
H—H			H	
T—T	T			
E—E			E	
I—I		I		
S				
E—E				E
N—N				N
H—H	H			
O—O			O	
W—W		W		
E—E	E			
R—R			R	
	THE	WWII	HERO	GEN

Going a step farther, I found WWII HERO in the name of DWIGHT DAVID EISENHOWER. It was only after these findings that I decided to study the acronym for the AMERICAN WAR OF INDEPENDENCE—AWOI. I was amazed to find something similar in the name of GEORGE WASHINGTON—AWOI HERO GEN, just as we find in DWIGHT DAVID EISENHOWER—WWII HERO GEN.

LEVEL ONE: OVERT PRESENTATIONS OF **WWII** IN THE NAMES OF U.S. PRESIDENTS

	(PRESENT)	(MISSING)
GEORGE WASHINGTON	WI	WI
JOHN ADAMS		WWII
THOMAS JEFFERSON		WWII
JAMES MADISON	I	WWI
JAMES MONROE		WWII
JOHN ADAMS		WWII
ANDREW JACKSON	W	WII
MARTIN VAN BUREN	I	WWI
JOHN TYLER		WWII
JAMES POLK		WWII
ZACHARY TAYLOR		WWII
MILLARD FILLMORE	II	WW
FRANKLIN PIERCE	II	WW
JAMES BUCHANAN		WWII
ABRAHAM LINCOLN	I	WWI
ANDREW JOHNSON	W	WII
ULYSSES GRANT		WWII
CHESTER ARTHUR		WWII
GROVER CLEVELAND		WWII
BENJAMIN HARRISON	I	WWI
WILLIAM MCKINLEY	WII	W
THEODORE ROOSEVELT		WWII
WILLIAM TAFT	WII	W

LEVEL ONE: OVERT PRESENTATIONS OF **WWII** IN THE NAMES OF U.S. PRESIDENTS

	(PRESENT)	(MISSING)
WOODROW WILSON	***WWI***	
WARREN HARDING	WI	WI
CALVIN COOLIDGE	II	WW
HERBERT HOOVER		WWII
FRANKLIN ROOSEVELT	I	WWI
HARRY TRUMAN		WWII
DWIGHT EISENHOWER	***WWII***	
JOHN KENNEDY		WWII
LYNDON JOHNSON		WWII
LESLIE KING	II	WW
JAMES CARTER		WWII
RONALD REAGAN		WWII
GEORGE BUSH		WWII
WILLIAM BLYTHE	WII	W
GEORGE BUSH		WWII
BARACK OBAMA		WWII
DONALD TRUMP		WWII
JOSEPH BIDEN	I	WWI

We see at Level One that DWIGHT EISENHOWER is alone with WWII just as WOODROW WILSON is alone at Level One with WWI.

LEVEL THREE: OVERT PRESENTATIONS OF **WWII** IN THE NAMES OF U.S. PRESIDENTS

	(PRESENT)	(MISSING)
GEORGE WASHINGTON	WI	WI
JOHN ADAMS JR		WWII
THOMAS JEFFERSON II	II	WW
JAMES MADISON JR	I	WWI
JAMES MONROE		WWII
JOHN QUINCY ADAMS	I	WW
ANDREW JACKSON JR	W	WII
MARTIN VAN BUREN SR	I	WWI
WILLIAM HENRY HARRISON SR	WII	W
JOHN TYLER JR		WWII
JAMES KNOX POLK		WWII
ZACHARY TAYLOR II	II	WWII
MILLARD FILLMORE	II	WW
FRANKLIN PIERCE SR	II	WW
JAMES BUCHANAN JR		WWII
ABRAHAM LINCOLN II	II	WW
ANDREW JOHNSON SR	W	WII
HIRAM ULYSSES GRANT	I	WWI
CHESTER ALAN ARTHUR I	I	WWI
STEPHEN GROVER CLEVELAND		WWII
BENJAMIN HARRISON	II	WW
WILLIAM MCKINLEY JR	WII	I

LEVEL THREE: OVERT PRESENTATIONS OF **WWII** IN THE NAMES OF U.S. PRESIDENTS

	(PRESENT)	(MISSING)
THEODORE ROOSEVELT JR		WWII
WARREN GAMALIEL HARDING	WII	W
JOHN CALVIN COOLIDGE JR	II	WW
HARRY S TRUMAN		WWII
DWIGHT DAVID EISENHOWER I	***WWII***	
LYNDON BAINES JOHNSON	I	WWI
LESLIE LYNCH KING JR	II	WW
JAMES EARL CARTER JR		WWII
RONALD WILSON REAGAN	WI	WI
GEORGE HERBERT WALKER BUSH	W	WII
GEORGE WALKER BUSH	W	WII
BARACK HUSSEIN OBAMA II	II	WW
DONALD JOHN TRUMP SR		WWII
JOSEPH ROBINETTE BIDEN JR	II	WW

We now look for Overt Presentations of WWII in the names of the U.S. Presidents at Level Three—full names with suffixes—and we still find only one name, DWIGHT DAVID EISENHOWER I.

WORLD WAR II

A COMMON EXPRESSION FOR WORLD WAR TWO

LEVEL THREE: MIXED PRESENTATIONS OF **WORLD WAR II** IN THE NAMES OF U.S. PRESIDENTS

	(PRESENT)	(MISSING)
GEORGE WASHINGTON	WORWAI	LDRI
JOHN ADAMS JR	WORDA	LWRII
THOMAS JEFFERSON II	WORDWAII	LR
JAMES MADISON JR	WORDWAI	LRI
JAMES MONROE	WORDWA	LRII
JOHN QUINCY ADAMS	WOLDWAI	RRI
ANDREW JACKSON JR	WORLDWAR	II
MARTIN VAN BUREN SR	WRLDWARI	OI
JOHN TYLER JR	WORLWAR	DII
JAMES KNOX POLK	WOLDWA	RRII
ZACHARY TAYLOR II	ORLARII	WDW
MILLARD FILLMORE	WORLDARII	W
FRANKLIN PIERCE SR	WORLWARII	D
JAMES BUCHANAN JR	WRLDWA	ORII
ABRAHAM LINCOLN II	(((WORLD WAR II)))	
ANDREW JOHNSON SR	WORDWAR	LII
HIRAM ULYSSES GRANT	WRLDWARI	OI
RUTHERFORD BIRCHARD HAYES I	WORLDWARI	I
CHESTER ALAN ARTHUR I	WRLWARI	ODI
STEPHEN GROVER CLEVELAND	WORLDWAR	II

Testing for Level Three Presentations increases the chances of Incidental Displays—those that occur because the letters are there for other reasons. But what is very interesting here is that with just one failure to predict we otherwise only find Presidents associated with the war or the 64-Year Phenomenon.

Special Note: Heads of State without a strong involvement in or strong association with an Historical Event but who have a Display of the Event in their name, will have three parentheses in bold to signify an incorrect prediction.

LEVEL THREE: MIXED PRESENTATIONS OF **WORLD WAR II** IN THE NAMES OF U.S. PRESIDENTS

	(PRESENT)	(MISSING)
BENJAMIN HARRISON	WORDWARII	L
WILLIAM MCKINLEY JR	WRLDWARII	O
WARREN GAMALIEL HARDING	WRDWARII	O
JOHN CALVIN COOLIDGE JR	WOLDWAII	R
HARRY S TRUMAN	WRLDAR	OWII
LYNDON BAINES JOHNSON	WOLDWAI	RRI
RICHARD MILHAUS NIXON	***WORLD WAR II***	
LESLIE LYNCH KING JR	WRLWAII	ODR
JAMES EARL CARTER JR	WRLDWAR	OII
RONALD WILSON REAGAN	WORLDWARI	I
GEORGE HERBERT WALKER BUSH	WORLWAR	DII
GEORGE WALKER BUSH	WORLWAR	DII
BARACK HUSSEIN OBAMA II	***WORLD WAR II***	**64-YEAR PHEN**
DONALD JOHN TRUMP SR	WORLDWAR	II
JOSEPH ROBINETTE BIDEN JR	WORDWARII	L

In this WORLD WAR II table, there is a Display that is meaningful and is, therefore, a Presentation. It is of RICHARD MILHAUS NIXON who did participate in WORLD WAR II. In fact, as we see in his biography, he didn't even have to serve, as he was exempted from service—both as a Quaker and as a government employee.

And, again, we see the 64-Year Phenomenon as we saw it for THE CIVIL WAR and WORLD WAR I. BARACK HUSSEIN OBAMA II is the President of the United States who fulfills the role of the 64-Year Phenomenon for WORLD WAR II. He became President approximately 64 years after the end of WORLD WAR II.

We are already witnessing the prediction of these wars and who will be the leaders during these wars. But with the 64-Year Phenomenon, we are also witnessing the prediction of who will be the leader 64 years later.

RICHARD MILHAUS NIXON

RICHARD MILHAUS NIXON (1913 - 1994) was the 37th President of the United States. Nixon has several relationships with World War II. (1) He served in the Office of Price Administration early on during the war. (2) He eventually served in World War II even though he could have claimed conscientious objector status as a Quaker. (3) He chose to serve in the war even though he was already exempt from service because of his work for the government in the Office of Price Administration. (4) He sought and received a commission in the Navy. (5) In his political campaign, he stated that his first response to Pearl Harbor was working in the Office of Price Administration and, later, by seeking and receiving a commission in the Navy. (6) He was saved from being dropped from the 1952 Eisenhower-Nixon ticket after accusations of misuse of campaign funds due to his Checkers Speech, during which he spoke of being a patriot who had served in World War II.

LEVEL THREE: MIXED PRESENTATION OF **WORLD WAR II** IN **RICHARD MILHAUS NIXON**

R—R	R		
I—I			I
C			
H			
A—A		A	
R—R		R	
D—D	D		
M			
I—I			I
L—L	L		
H			
A			
U			
S			
N = W	W		
I			
X			
O—O	O		
N = W		W	
	WORLD	**WAR**	**II**

We see a Mixed Presentation of WORLD WAR II in the name RICHARD MILHAUS NIXON. The first reason this war was meaningful in his life is that he served in the war even when, as stated in his brief biography, he had two reasons for being exempt. Also stated in his biography, Nixon's patriotic service to his country in WORLD WAR II helped preserve his status as Ike's running mate when Nixon became the subject of a major controversy regarding possible misuse of political funds that reimbursed him for political expenses. Nixon's speech in his own defense, along with his record as a loyal, patriotic WORLD WAR II Veteran, saved the Eisenhower-Nixon ticket.

SECOND WORLD WAR

A COMMON EXPRESSION FOR WORLD WAR TWO

LEVEL THREE: COVERT PRESENTATIONS OF **SECOND WORLD WAR** IN THE NAMES OF U.S. PRESIDENTS

	(PRESENT)	(MISSING)
GEORGE WASHINGTON	SEONWORWAR	CDLD
JOHN ADAMS JR	SONDRDA	ECWOLWR
THOMAS JEFFERSON II	SEONDWORA	CLDWR
JAMES MADISON JR	SEONDRDAR	CWOLW
JAMES MONROE	SEONDWORDA	CLWR
JOHN QUINCY ADAMS	SECONDRLDA	WOWR
ANDREW JACKSON JR	SECONDWRWAR	OLD
MARTIN VAN BUREN SR	SECNDWRDWAR	OOL
WILLIAM HENRY HARRISON SR	SECONDWRLWAR	OD
JOHN TYLER JR	SEONRLAR	CDWODW
JAMES KNOX POLK	SEONDOLA	CWRDWR
ZACHARY TAYLOR II	SCORLAR	ENDWODW
MILLARD FILLMORE	ECODORLDAR	SNWW
FRANKLIN PIERCE SR	SECONWRLWAR	DOD
JAMES BUCHANAN JR	SECNDWRLA	OODWR
ABRAHAM LINCOLN II	SECONDRLAR	WODW
ANDREW JOHNSON SR	SEONDWORWAR	CLD
HIRAM ULYSSES GRANT	SECNDRLAR	OWODW
RUTHERFORD BIRCHARD HAYES I	SECONDORLDAR	WW
JAMES ABRAM GARFIELD I	SEONDRLDAR	CWOW
CHESTER ALAN ARTHUR I	SECNWRLAR	ODODW
STEPHEN GROVER CLEVELAND	SECONDWRLDWAR	O
BENJAMIN HARRISON	SEONDWRWAR	COLD
WILLIAM MCKINLEY JR	SECNDWRLDAR	OOW
THEODORE ROOSEVELT JR	SEONDWORLDWAR	C
WILLIAM HOWARD TAFT I	SCONDWORLDWAR	EN

LEVEL THREE: COVERT PRESENTATIONS OF **SECOND WORLD WAR** IN THE NAMES OF U.S. PRESIDENTS

	(PRESENT)	(MISSING)
THOMAS WOODROW WILSON	SEONDWORLDWAR	C
WARREN GAMALIEL HARDING	SECNDWRLDWAR	OO
JOHN CALVIN COOLIDGE JR	SECONDWORLDAR	W
HERBERT CLARK HOOVER SR	ECONDWORLW	DW
FRANKLIN DELANO ROOSEVELT SR ***SECOND WORLD WAR***		
HARRY S TRUMAN	SCNDRAR	EOWOLDW
DWIGHT DAVID EISENHOWER I	SEONDWRDWAR	COL
JOHN FITZGERALD KENNEDY SR	SEONDWORLDWAR	C
LYNDON BAINES JOHNSON	SEONDWORLWA	CDR
RICHARD MILHAUS NIXON	SECONDORLDAR	WW
LESLIE LYNCH KING JR	SECNWRLWAR	ODOD
JAMES EARL CARTER JR	SECNDWRLAR	OODW
RONALD WILSON REAGAN	SECONDWORLWAR	D
GEORGE HERBERT WALKER BUSH	SECONWRLWAR	DOD
WILLIAM JEFFERSON BLYTHE III	SECONDWORLWAR	D
GEORGE WALKER BUSH	SECONWRLWAR	DOD
BARACK HUSSEIN OBAMA II	SECONDRLAR	WODW
DONALD JOHN TRUMP SR	SECONDORLDAR	WW
JOSEPH ROBINETTE BIDEN JR	SEONDWORWAR	CLD

I have already shared my amazement at finding WORLD WAR TWO in the name FRANKLIN ROOSEVELT at Level One and at discovering that—after exclusions—he is the only one with a Presentation at Level One. But I was completely and utterly astonished when I discovered that—even without exclusions—he is the only U. S. President with SECOND WORLD WAR in his name at any level. In fact, in the variation of his name—FRANKLIN D ROOSEVELT—a name with only eighteen letters—he has the fourteen-letter expression—SECOND WORLD WAR. With a complete examination of all the other U.S. Presidents at Level Three—complete name with suffix—no other President has SECOND WORLD WAR. His full name with suffix—FRANKLIN DELANO ROOSVELT SR—is listed here as this is an examination of all U.S. Presidents at Level Three.

COVERT PRESENTATION OF **SECOND WORLD WAR** IN **FRANKLIN DELANO ROOSEVELT**

F			
R—R		R	
A—A			A
N—N	N		
L—L		L	
I			
N = W		W	
D—D	D		
E—E	E		
L = C	C		
A			
N = W			W
O—O	O		
R—R			R
O—O		O	
O			
S—S	S		
E			
V = D		D	
E			
L			
T			
	SECOND	**WORLD**	**WAR**

Summary of Evidence Supporting the Claims: WORLD WAR TWO, WORLD WAR II, WWII, SECOND WORLD WAR in the names of U.S. Presidents

Claim 1_
FRANKLIN DELANO ROOSEVELT, the Head of State of the United States most central to WORLD WAR TWO/WORLD WAR II/WWII/SECOND WORLD WAR, has the only Presentation of SECOND WORLD WAR and also has a Level One Presentation of WORLD WAR TWO. DWIGHT DAVID EISENHOWER, the Supreme Commander of the Allied Expeditionary Force in Europe, has the exclusive Level One Presentation of WWII.

Claim 2_
The 64-Year Phenomenon: BARACK HUSSEIN OBAMA II, the President who began his term approximately 64 years after the end of the war, has WORLD WAR II in his name.

Claim 3_
The U.S. Presidents with the strongest involvement in or association with the war contain one or more Presentations. In addition to the aforementioned Presentations of ROOSEVELT and EISENHOWER, HERBERT CLARK HOOVER JR and JOHN FITZGERALD KENNEDY SR have WORLD WAR TWO in their names; and RICHARD MILHAUS NIXON has WORLD WAR II in his name.

THE PROBABILITY OF GEORGE WASHINGTON, WILLIAM HARRISON, AND GEORGE III WILLIAM FREDERICK HAVING EXCLUSIVE AND CORRECT DISPLAYS OF AWOI IN THEIR NAMES

AND

ABRAHAM LINCOLN, HIRAM ULYSSES GRANT, RUTHERFORD HAYES, HERBERT CLARK HOOVER, WILLIAM JEFFERSON BLYTHE III, BARACK HUSSEIN OBAMA II AND WILLIAM HOWARD TAFT, AT LEVEL TWO, HAVING EXCLUSIVE AND CORRECT DISPLAYS OF THE CIVIL WAR IN THEIR NAMES

AND

WOODROW WILSON, THEODORE ROOSEVELT, FRANKLIN ROOSEVELT, WILLIAM HOWARD TAFT, JOHN CALVIN COOLIDGE, HERBERT CLARK HOOVER AND RONALD WILSON REAGAN HAVING EXCLUSIVE AND CORRECT DISPLAYS OF WORLD WAR ONE/WWI IN THEIR NAMES

AND

FRANKLIN ROOSEVELT, HERBERT CLARK HOOVER, DWIGHT DAVID EISENHOWER, JOHN FITZGERALD KENNEDY, RICHARD MILHAUS NIXON AND BARACK HUSSEIN OBAMA II HAVING EXCLUSIVE AND CORRECT DISPLAYS OF WORLD WAR TWO/WWII/WORLD WAR II/SECOND WORLD WAR IN THEIR NAMES IS

1
IN

1,663,000,000,000,000

(ONE IN OVER 1 QUADRILLION, 663 TRILLION)

Someone who solves a crime or unravels a scientific mystery must feel a bit like I did when I once again found support for each of the Three Claims. In fact, as I began my final investigation of this series of tests, I felt as though I were approaching the definitive result, one that would finally confirm that the English alphabet is a secret code hidden in the English language. The excitement as I made this inquiry was overwhelming.

Upon re-examining the results of my investigations of the three major American Wars—THE CIVIL WAR, WORLD WAR ONE/WORLD WAR I/WWI/FIRST WORLD WAR, and WORLD WAR TWO/WORLD WAR II/WWII/SECOND WORLD WAR, I can say that they all support all Three Claims.

Furthermore, my investigations of WORLD WAR TWO/WORLD WAR II/WWII/SECOND WORLD WAR fully support my claim that the English alphabet is a secret code hidden in the English language.

Although I had been seeing this phenomenon unfold as it confirmed itself with every Historical Event, the full magnitude of this revelation suddenly hit me. I was stunned. It took me quite some time to comprehend the full dimensions of this new discovery. How could this be? Not only are the involvements and associations with the wars predicted, but the wars themselves were predicted long before they took place. These predictions told us there was going to be THE CIVIL WAR, WORLD WAR ONE, and WORLD WAR TWO. They also told us who would be President 64 years later. In other words, not only is there a Code, but the past, present, and future exist in the Code. Of course, it is only in retrospect that we see the predictions.

At this point my mind was racing, looking for explanations. The future is in the Code. Once again, the idea of some kind of force behind this phenomenon emerged, and I was overcome with emotions. Amazement, shock, disbelief, unreality and a sense of a great realization overcame me.

Now it was time to bring my discoveries to Blythe. As I presented my findings, she stared in astonishment and said, "The Code is real. There really is a Code." We looked at each other and wondered out loud, "How is this possible?"

Soon after, we shared the Code with our children. Tanner marveled at the tables as I showed them to him one by one. Rachel was very surprised and really liked the discovery. Natasha caught on to the system right away. As I did my work, she would look over my shoulder—anxiously awaiting the results. Jake asked, "Does this mean everything is predestined and that there is such a thing as fate?" From this day forward, throughout the writing of the book, Jake, who is a history buff, would go on to add valuable information to the histories and biographies of Heads of State and Military Leaders.

We were all amazed at what was unfolding before our eyes. As a family, we now shared a secret—the secret of the Code. It may have been the only thing we talked about for many months.

I had already performed the series of investigations for evidence that included the U.S. wars known as THE CIVIL WAR, WORLD WAR ONE/WORLD WAR I/WWI/FIRST WORLD WAR, and WORLD WAR TWO/WORLD WAR II/WWII/SECOND WORLD WAR, and I had seen the astounding results of those tests.

The American War of Independence (AWOI) appears first in this book—before the other U.S. wars—to keep them in chronological order and to avoid confusion. But it wasn't until I had completed the investigations of the other wars that I studied the American War of Independence.

I had not made this inquiry earlier than the others because I was thinking of the names of the war as either the American War of Independence or the American Revolutionary War. It wasn't until my findings of WWI and WWII as expressions of the world wars that I realized I could investigate the initialisms for the American War of Independence—the AWOI, as well. These results did also support my claim of a Code in the English language.

With all this work completed, I was now beckoned by another country and another list of Heads of State. The suspense returned very quickly.

THE FINDINGS
OF THE
TWO WORLD WARS
AND THE
PRIME MINISTERS
OF THE
UNITED KINGDOM
THAT SUPPORT
THE CLAIM
THAT THERE IS A
SECRET CODE
HIDDEN IN THE
ENGLISH LANGUAGE

WORLD WAR ONE

COVERT PRESENTATIONS OF **WORLD WAR ONE** IN THE PRIME MINISTERS OF THE U.K.

	(PRESENT)	(MISSING)
WILLIAM PITT II (the Younger)	WRLDAR	OWONE
HENRY ADDINGTON	WORDWARNE	LO
SPENCER PERCEVAL I	WRLDWARNE	OO
ROBERT BANKS JENKINSON	WORWARONE	LD
GEORGE CANNING JNR	WORLWARNE	DO
ARTHUR WELLESLEY	WRLWARNE	ODO
CHARLES GREY II	WRLARE	ODWON
HENRY WILLIAM LAMB	WRLDWARNE	OO
ROBERT PEEL II	WORLWRE	DAON
JOHN RUSSELL II	ORLANE	WDWRO
HENRY JOHN TEMPLE	WORLDWANE	RO
BENJAMIN DISRAELI	WRLDWARNE	OO
ARCHIBALD PHILIP PRIMROSE	ORLDARE	WWON
ROBERT ARTHUR TALBOT GASCOYNE-CECIL	WORLWARONE	D
ARTHUR JAMES BALFOUR	ORLDAROE	WWN
HENRY CAMPBELL-BANNERMAN	WRLDWARNE	OO

COVERT PRESENTATIONS OF **WORLD WAR ONE** IN THE PRIME MINISTERS OF THE U.K.

	(PRESENT)	(MISSING)
HERBERT HENRY ASQUITH	WRLWARNE	ODO
STANLEY BALDWIN	WRLDWANE	ORO
JAMES RAMSAY MACDONALD	ORLDANE	WWRO
ARTHUR NEVILLE CHAMBERLAIN	WRLDWARNE	OO
WINSTON LEONARD CHURCHILL	***WORLD WAR ONE***	
CLEMENT RICHARD ATTLEE	WRLDWARNE	OO
ROBERT ANTHONY EDEN	WORDWARONE	L
MAURICE HAROLD MACMILLAN	ORLDARNE	WWO
JAMES HAROLD WILSON	WORLDARONE	W
LEONARD JAMES CALLAGHAN	WORLDWANE	RO
MARGARET HILDA ROBERTS THATCHER	WORLDWARE	ON
JOHN ROY MAJOR	ORDARON	WLWE
ANTHONY CHARLES LYNTON BLAIR	WORLWARONE	D
JAMES GORDON BROWN	WORDWARONE	L
THERESA MARY BRASIER MAY	WRDWARE	OLON
ALEXANDER BORIS DE PFEFFEL JOHNSON	(((WORLD WAR ONE)))	

Looking at this Presentation of WORLD WAR ONE, we do not as yet find any of the wartime Prime Ministers. We do have WINSTON LEONARD CHURCHILL who was at that time the Lord of the Admiralty.

We also find an Incidental Display of WORLD WAR ONE in the name of ALEXANDER BORIS DE PFEFFEL JOHNSON, who has no known relationship with the world wars.

Special Note: Some names have been excluded from some of the tests of the world wars. This is for statistical reasons. For example, some names are excluded because of the strong similarity between the terms WORLD WAR ONE and WORLD WAR TWO. Having one of the wars in one's name greatly increases the probability of having the other world war in one's name. There are also exclusions due to the number of letters in a name or because namesakes served in the war. Exclusions are fully explained in Appendix B.

WWI

A COMMON EXPRESSION FOR WORLD WAR ONE

OVERT PRESENTATIONS OF WWI IN THE PRIME MINISTERS OF THE U.K.

	(PRESENT)	(MISSING)
WILLIAM PITT II	WI	W
HENRY ADDINGTON	I	WW
SPENCER PERCEVAL I	I	WW
ROBERT BANKS JENKINSON	I	WW
GEORGE CANNING JNR	I	WW
ARTHUR WELLESLEY	W	WI
CHARLES GREY II	I	WW
HENRY WILLIAM LAMB	WI	W
ROBERT PEEL II	I	WW
JOHN RUSSELL II	I	WW
HENRY JOHN TEMPLE		WWI
BENJAMIN DISRAELI	I	WW
ARCHIBALD PHILIP PRIMROSE	I	WW
ROBERT ARTHUR TALBOT GASCOYNE-CECIL	I	WW
ARTHUR JAMES BALFOUR		WWI
HENRY CAMPBELL-BANNERMAN		WWI
HERBERT HENRY ASQUITH	I	WW

OVERT PRESENTATIONS OF **WWI** IN THE PRIME MINISTERS OF THE U.K.

	(PRESENT)	(MISSING)
ANDREW BONAR LAW I	***WWI***	
STANLEY BALDWIN	WI	I
JAMES RAMSAY MACDONALD		WWI
ARTHUR NEVILLE CHAMBERLAIN	I	WW
WINSTON LEONARD CHURCHILL	WI	W
CLEMENT RICHARD ATTLEE	I	WW
ROBERT ANTHONY EDEN		WWI
MAURICE HAROLD MACMILLAN	I	WW
JAMES HAROLD WILSON	WI	W
LEONARD JAMES CALLAGHAN		WWI
MARGARET HILDA ROBERTS THATCHER	I	WW
JOHN ROY MAJOR		WWI
ANTHONY CHARLES LYNTON BLAIR	I	WW
JAMES GORDON BROWN		WWI
THERESA MARY BRASIER MAY	I	WW
ALEXANDER BORIS DE PFEFFEL JOHNSON	I	WW

ANDREW BONAR LAW was leader of the Conservative Party in Britain during WWI. He was a part of Henry Herbert Asquith's coalition government and played a major role in David Lloyd George becoming Prime Minister. For the rest of the war, he was an important member of the British War Cabinet. He has several relationships with WORLD WAR I.

WORLD WAR I

A COMMON EXPRESSION FOR WORLD WAR ONE

MIXED PRESENTATIONS OF **WORLD WAR I** IN THE PRIME MINISTERS OF THE U.K.

	(PRESENT)	(MISSING)
WILLIAM PITT II	WRLDARI	OW
HENRY ADDINGTON	WORDWAI	LR
SPENCER PERCEVAL I	WRLDWARI	O
ROBERT BANKS JENKINSON	WORWARI	LD
GEORGE CANNING JNR	WORLWARI	D
ARTHUR WELLESLEY	WRLWAR	ODI
CHARLES GREY II	WRLWARI	OD
HENRY WILLIAM LAMB	WRLDWARI	O
ROBERT PEEL II	WORLWRI	DA
JOHN RUSSELL II	WORLWAI	DR
HENRY JOHN TEMPLE	WORLDWA	RI
BENJAMIN DISRAELI	WRLDWARI	O
ARCHIBALD PHILIP PRIMROSE	WORLDARI	W
ROBERT ARTHUR TALBOT GASCOYNE-CECIL	WORLWARI	D
ARTHUR JAMES BALFOUR	WORLDAR	WI
HENRY CAMPBELL BANNERMAN	WRLDWAR	OI

MIXED PRESENTATIONS OF **WORLD WAR I** IN THE PRIME MINISTERS OF THE U.K.

	(PRESENT)	(MISSING)
HERBERT HENRY ASQUITH	WRLWARI	OD
DAVID LLOYD GEORGE I	***WORLD WAR I***	
ANDREW BONAR LAW I	***WORLD WAR I***	
STANLEY BALDWIN	WLDWAI	ORR
JAMES RAMSAY MACDONALD	WORLDWA	RI
ARTHUR NEVILLE CHAMBERLAIN	WRLDWARI	O
WINSTON LEONARD CHURCHILL	***WORLD WAR I***	
CLEMENT RICHARD ATTLEE	WRLDWARI	O
ROBERT ANTHONY EDEN	WORDWAR	LI
MAURICE HAROLD MACMILLAN	***WORLD WAR I***	
JAMES HAROLD WILSON	WORLDWAI	R
LEONARD JAMES CALLAGHAN	WORLDWA	RI
MARGARET HILDA ROBERTS THATCHER	***WORLD WAR I***	64-YEAR PHEN
JOHN ROY MAJOR	WORDAR	LWI
ANTHONY CHARLES LYNTON BLAIR	WORLWARI	D
JAMES GORDON BROWN	WORDWAR	LI
THERESA MARY BRASIER MAY	WRDWARI	OL
ALEXANDER BORIS DE PFEFFEL JOHNSON (((WORLD WAR I)))		

With a Presentation of WORLD WAR I, we see the name WINSTON LEONARD CHURCHILL again. We also see that DAVID LLOYD GEORGE I, the Prime Minister during much of the war, and ANDREW BONAR LAW I, who played multiple roles during the war, have WORLD WAR I in their names. MAURICE HAROLD MACMILLAN also has the Presentation. Before his Premiership, he was a Captain in the British Army during WORLD WAR I. Finally, we see the name of the first female Prime Minister, MARGARET HILDA ROBERTS THATCHER. She represents the 64-Year Phenomenon for WORLD WAR I (and THE GREAT WAR).

We see one Incidental Display in the name ALEXANDER BORIS DE PFEFFEL JOHNSON.

HERBERT HENRY ASQUITH

HERBERT HENRY ASQUITH (1852 - 1928), 1st Earl of Oxford and Asquith, was Prime Minister of the United Kingdom from 1908 to 1916. He was Prime Minister when his country entered into what was originally called The Great War. In fact, he asked the Monarch of the United Kingdom to declare war and to enter into The Great War. He formed a Coalition government. Interestingly, he served as his own Secretary of State for War for the four months immediately preceding the entrance of the United Kingdom into the war. His wartime government instituted conscription to fill the needs of the military. Asquith served for the first two years and four months of The Great War. He was considered a poor wartime leader. He passed the leadership to David Lloyd George in December of 1916.

Two men served as Prime Minister of the United Kingdom during WORLD WAR I—HERBERT HENRY ASQUITH and DAVID LLOYD GEORGE, and another Prime Minister—ANDREW BONAR LAW—served in a number of important capacities during and immediately after the war. At Level Three, WORLD WAR I can be found in the names DAVID LLOYD GEORGE I and ANDREW BONAR LAW I. HERBERT HENRY ASQUITH doesn't have any of the four expressions of WORLD WAR I that are part of the statistical tests that were performed in this book. He does have THE GREAT WAR encoded in his name and, therefore, this Presentation provides evidence supporting both Claim 1 and Claim 3.

COVERT PRESENTATION OF **THE GREAT WAR** IN **HERBERT HENRY ASQUITH**

H—H	H		
E—E	E		
R—R		R	
B			
E—E		E	
R—R			R
T—T	T		
H			
E = W			W
N			
R			
Y = G		G	
A—A		A	
S = A			A
Q			
U			
I			
T—T		T	
H			
	THE	**GREAT**	**WAR**

Of course, the first world war that was fought was not given a number—as in WORLD WAR I—often abbreviated WWI—until there was a WORLD WAR II—often abbreviated WWII. So, it was commonly known as THE GREAT WAR or WORLD WAR.

In this table, we find THE GREAT WAR encoded in the name HERBERT HENRY ASQUITH. Tables of THE GREAT WAR in the names of the Prime Ministers of the United Kingdom can be found in Appendix D.

DAVID LLOYD GEORGE I

> DAVID LLOYD GEORGE (1863 - 1945), 1st Earl Lloyd George of Dwyfor, served as Prime Minister of the United Kingdom from December 1916 until 1922. It was David Lloyd George who, while serving as the Chancellor or the Exchequer, gained the approval of nearly all of the cabinet for the United Kingdom's intervention into World War I. He served as Chancellor of the Exchequer (second in command to Prime Minister Herbert Henry Asquith), as Minister of Munitions and then as Secretary of State for War immediately before assuming the premiership. He centralized authority with a group of advisors, a small cabinet and a new cabinet office. George saw his nation through victory and he played a major role in the Paris Peace Conference.

DAVID LLOYD GEORGE became the Prime Minister two years after the entrance of the United Kingdom into the war and saw his nation through the war. The name DAVID LLOYD GEORGE I contains WORLD WAR I.

MIXED PRESENTATION OF **WORLD WAR I** IN **DAVID LLOYD GEORGE I**

D—D	D		
A—A		A	
V			
I = R		R	
D			
L—L	L		
L			
O—O	O		
Y			
D			
G			
E = W	W		
O			
R—R	R		
G			
E = W		W	
I—I			I
	WORLD	**WAR**	**I**

Several pages ago, in the summary of my findings of three wars and the U.S. Presidents, I discussed the incredible predictive value of the Code. I mentioned that the past, present, and future can be found in the Code. There is no better or more amazing example of this phenomenon than in the case of DAVID LLOYD GEORGE I. When he served as Prime Minister during the first of the two world wars, his name contained WORLD WAR—one of the two terms Britons most commonly used for the war at that time. Three years after the war ended, GEORGE's son, Gwilym Lloyd George, begat a son—DAVID LLOYD GEORGE II—changing the ex-Prime Minister's name to DAVID LLOYD GEORGE I. With this change in his name, his name now contained WORLD WAR I. In 1939—with the beginning of WORLD WAR II—the first world war now became known as WORLD WAR I. This is absolutely amazing!

ANDREW BONAR LAW I

ANDREW BONAR LAW (1858 - 1923) was the Prime Minister of the United Kingdom from October 23, 1922, until May 20, 1923. His most important accomplishment during his short term in relation to the war was to negotiate with the United States over Britain's war loan. But his involvement during World War I was quite substantial. He was Leader of the House of Commons during much of the war. He was also the Leader of the Conservative Party, and in that role, Andrew Bonar Law helped forge a Coalition Government with David Lloyd George, a coalition that was considered of the utmost importance to the United Kingdom during a time of war. Law actually turned down the offer of the premiership in favor of George. He was Chancellor of the Exchequer from the end of 1916 until the beginning of 1919 during much of the term of wartime Prime Minister, David Lloyd George.

The role of ANDREW BONAR LAW in forming and maintaining the Coalition Government during the war was of great importance—putting aside political differences when their nation was at war. As we also see in his biography, he was Chancellor of the Exchequer for over two years of the war.

MIXED PRESENTATION OF **WORLD WAR I** IN **ANDREW BONAR LAW I**

A—A	A		
N			
D—D	D		
R—R	R		
E			
W—W	W		
B			
O—O	O		
N			
A			
R—R		R	
L—L	L		
A			
W—W		W	
I—I			I
	WORLD	**WAR**	**I**

Just as we witnessed in the case of DAVID LLOYD GEORGE I and WORLD WAR I, we now see the same remarkable phenomenon in the name of Prime Minister ANDREW BONAR LAW I and WORLD WAR I. He was originally assigned the name ANDREW BONAR LAW. At the time of the first of the two world wars, his name already contained WORLD WAR—which was at that time a correct Presentation of the Event. In 1933, ten years after his death, his son Richard Kidston Law begat ANDREW BONAR LAW II. This changed the late Prime Minister's name to ANDREW BONAR LAW I. His name now contained WORLD WAR I. This was just in time as WORLD WAR II began in 1939—and with this came a change to the name of the first of the world wars from simply WORLD WAR to WORLD WAR I. So, the Code remained current and up-to-date the entire time. This is astonishing.

MAURICE HAROLD MACMILLAN

MAURICE HAROLD MACMILLAN (1894 - 1986), the first Earl of Stockton, served as Prime Minister of the United Kingdom from 1957 to 1963. (1) He served as a Captain with the Grenadier Guards in the British Army during World War I. (2) He fought in the front lines in France and was wounded during major battles. In fact, he was in the hospital during the last two years of World War I. During one battle, he lay seriously wounded—pretending to be dead to avoid being captured or killed by enemy soldiers as they passed by his body. (3) He was in the hospital during the last two years of World War I. (4) His wounds forever affected his walk and his handwriting. (5) He very openly expressed contempt for other politicians who had not served in either world war.

As we see in his biography, MAURICE HAROLD MACMILLAN served as a Captain with the Grenadier Guards in the British Army during WORLD WAR I. He fought on the front lines in France where he risked death and he came very close to dying.

MIXED PRESENTATION OF **WORLD WAR I** IN **MAURICE HAROLD MACMILLAN**

M			
A—A		A	
U			
R—R	R		
I—I			I
C			
E = W	W		
H			
A			
R—R		R	
O—O	O		
L—L	L		
D—D	D		
M			
A			
C			
M			
I			
L			
L			
A			
N = W		W	
	WORLD	**WAR**	**I**

THE 64-YEAR PHENOMENON

MIXED PRESENTATION OF WORLD WAR I IN MARGARET HILDA ROBERTS THATCHER

M			
A—A		A	
R—R	R		
G			
A			
R—R		R	
E = W	W		
T			
H			
I—I			I
L—L	L		
D—D	D		
A			
R			
O—O	O		
B			
E = W		W	
R			
T			
S			
T			
H			
A			
T			
C			
H			
E			
R			
	WORLD	**WAR**	**I**

This table shows WORLD WAR I in the name MARGARET HILDA ROBERTS THATCHER, who represents the 64-Year Phenomenon for WORLD WAR I and THE GREAT WAR. She became the Prime Minister on May 4, 1979, and she served until November 28, 1990. Her term covers the 64-year anniversary of nearly the entirety of WORLD WAR I.

FIRST WORLD WAR

A COMMON EXPRESSION FOR WORLD WAR ONE

COVERT PRESENTATIONS OF **FIRST WORLD WAR** IN THE PRIME MINISTERS OF THE U.K.

	(PRESENT)	(MISSING)
WILLIAM PITT II	IRTWRLDA	FSOWR
HENRY ADDINGTON	IRTWODWA	FSRLR
SPENCER PERCEVAL I	IRSWRLDWA	FTOR
ROBERT BANKS JENKINSON	FIRSTWORWA	LDR
GEORGE CANNING JNR	IRSWORKWA	FTDR
ARTHUR WELLESLEY	RSTWRLWA	FIODR
CHARLES GREY II	IRSWRLWAR	FTOD
HENRY WILLIAM LAMB	IRSTWRLDWA	FOR
JOHN RUSSELL II	IRSWOLWA	FTRDR
HENRY JOHN TEMPLE	STWOLDW	FIRAR
BENJAMIN DISRAELI	IRSTWRLDWAR	FO
ARCHIBALD PHILIP PRIMROSE	FIRSTWORLDAR	W
ROBERT ARTHUR TALBOT GASCOYNE-CECIL	FIRSTWORLWAR	D
ARTHUR JAMES BALFOUR	FRSTWORLDAR	IW
HENRY CAMPBELL BANNERMAN	RSTWRLDWA	FIOR
HERBERT HENRY ASQUITH	IRSTWRLWAR	FOD
DAVID LLOYD GEORGE I	FIRWOLDWA	STRR

COVERT PRESENTATIONS OF **FIRST WORLD WAR** IN THE PRIME MINISTERS OF THE U.K.

	(PRESENT)	(MISSING)
ANDREW BONAR LAW I	IRSTWORLDWA	FR
STANLEY BALDWIN	ISTWLDWA	FRORR
JAMES RAMSAY MACDONALD	RSWOLDWA	FITRR
ARTHUR NEVILLE CHAMBERLAIN	IRSTWRLDWAR	FO
WINSTON LEONARD CHURCHILL	***FIRST WORLD WAR***	
CLEMENT RICHARD ATTLEE	IRSTWRLDWA	FOR
ROBERT ANTHONY EDEN	FRTWORDWA	ISLR
EDWARD RICHARD GEORGE HEATH	IRSTWORLDWAR	F
JAMES HAROLD WILSON	FIRSWOLDWA	TRR
LEONARD JAMES CALLAGHAN	RSWOLDWA	FITRR
MARGARET HILDA ROBERTS THATCHER	IRSTWORLDWAR	F
JOHN ROY MAJOR	FRSWORDA	ITLWR
ANTHONY CHARLES LYNTON BLAIR	FIRSTWORLWA	DR
JAMES GORDON BROWN	FRSTWORDWA	ILR
DAVID WILLIAM DONALD CAMERON	FIRSTWORLDWAR	T
THERESA MARY BRASIER MAY	IRSTWRDWAR	FOL
ALEXANDER BORIS DE PFEFFEL JOHNSON	FIRSTWORLDWA	R

We see WINSTON LEONARD CHURCHILL with another Presentation of the FIRST WORLD WAR in his name.

Summary of Evidence Supporting the Claims: WORLD WAR ONE, WORLD WAR I, WWI, FIRST WORLD WAR in the names of British Prime Ministers

Claim 1—
DAVID LLOYD GEORGE I, the Prime Minister most central to WORLD WAR ONE/WORLD WAR I/WWI/FIRST WORLD WAR does have WORLD WAR I in his name.*

Claim 2—
The 64-Year Phenomenon: MARGARET HILDA ROBERTS THATCHER, the Prime Minister who was in office during the 64-year anniversary of the end of WORLD WAR I, has WORLD WAR I in her name.**

Claim 3—
The British Prime Ministers with the strongest involvement in or association with the war contain one or more Presentations in their names. DAVID LLOYD GEORGE I, ANDREW BONAR LAW I, WINSTON LEONARD CHURCHILL and MAURICE HAROLD MACMILLAN all have Level Two Presentations of WORLD WAR I in their names; and WINSTON LEONARD CHURCHILL also has WORLD WAR ONE and FIRST WORLD WAR in his name.***

*HERBERT HENRY ASQUITH, the other wartime Prime Minister, has THE GREAT WAR in his name. THE GREAT WAR was a very common name for the war during WORLD WAR ONE. His Presentation is, therefore, supporting evidence for Claim 1.

**MARGARET HILDA ROBERTS THATCHER also has THE GREAT WAR in her name.

***HERBERT HENRY ASQUITH has THE GREAT WAR in his name. This is supporting evidence for Claim 3.

THE PROBABILITY OF GEORGE WASHINGTON, WILLIAM HARRISON AND GEORGE III WILLIAM FREDERICK HAVING EXCLUSIVE AND CORRECT DISPLAYS OF AWOI IN THEIR NAMES

AND

ABRAHAM LINCOLN, HIRAM ULYSSES GRANT, RUTHERFORD BIRCHARD HAYES, HERBERT CLARK HOOVER, WILLIAM JEFFERSON BLYTHE III, BARACK HUSSEIN OBAMA II AND WILLIAM HOWARD TAFT, AT LEVEL TWO, HAVING EXCLUSIVE AND CORRECT DISPLAYS OF THE CIVIL WAR IN THEIR NAMES

AND

WOODROW WILSON, THEODORE ROOSEVELT, WIILLIAM HOWARD TAFT, JOHN CALVIN COOLIDGE, HERBERT CLARK HOOVER, FRANKLIN ROOSEVELT AND RONALD WILSON REAGAN HAVING EXCLUSIVE AND CORRECT DISPLAYS OF WORLD WAR ONE/WWI/ WORLD WAR I /FIRST WORLD WAR IN THEIR NAMES

AND

FRANKLIN ROOSEVELT, HERBERT CLARK HOOVER, DWIGHT DAVID EISENHOWER, JOHN FITZGERALD KENNEDY, RICHARD MILHAUS NIXON AND BARACK HUSSEIN OBAMA II HAVING EXCLUSIVE AND CORRECT DISPLAYS OF WORLD WAR TWO/WWII/WORLD WAR II/SECOND WORLD WAR IN THEIR NAMES

AND

DAVID LLOYD GEORGE I, ANDREW BONAR LAW I, WINSTON LEONARD CHURCHILL, MAURICE HAROLD MACMILLAN AND MARGARET HILDA ROBERTS THATCHER HAVING EXCLUSIVE AND CORRECT DISPLAYS OF WORLD WAR ONE/WWI/WORLD WAR I/FIRST WORLD WAR IN THEIR NAMES IS

1

IN

9,680,000,000,000,000,000,000

(ONE IN 9 SEXTILLION, 680 QUINTILLION)

The series of investigations of WORLD WAR ONE/WORLD WAR I/WWI/FIRST WORLD WAR and the United Kingdom resulted in further support for the Three Claims. In fact, the investigations for evidence brought results with the British Prime Ministers that were very similar to those I had found with the U.S. Presidents. So, the search continued. Name by name I knew I could take nothing for granted.

It was now time to look at WORLD WAR TWO/WORLD WAR II/WWII/SECOND WORLD WAR. Should I keep expecting the same results? A part of me was certain that I would, but that did nothing to diminish my sense of anticipation. Setting aside my notebooks filled with all of the tests and tables of the expressions of WORLD WAR ONE, I picked up a handful of new notebooks, ready to examine WORLD WAR TWO. Once again, I was filled with suspense.

WORLD WAR TWO

WINSTON LEONARD SPENCER-CHURCHILL

SIR WINSTON LEONARD SPENCER-CHURCHILL (1874 - 1965), born of mixed British and American heritage, was a British politician who served as Prime Minister of the United Kingdom for two terms, and Lord of the Admiralty and Minister of Munitions during World War One. He was also a writer who won a Nobel Prize for Literature. In the years leading up to World War Two, he was a leader among those who called for British rearmament in the face of the growing menace of Nazi Germany. When Neville Chamberlain resigned, Churchill became Prime Minister. During his first term (1940 - 1945), he chose to go to war—leading to Great Britain's full-scale participation in war. He led Great Britain as one of the Allies with the United States and the Soviet Union to victory in World War Two. Several years later, he served another term as Prime Minister. He is held in mostly high esteem in history.

COVERT PRESENTATION OF **WORLD WAR TWO** IN **WINSTON LEONARD CHURCHILL**

W—W	W		
I			
N = W		W	
S			
T—T			T
O—O	O		
N = W			W
L—L	L		
E			
O—O			O
N			
A—A		A	
R—R	R		
D—D	D		
C			
H			
U			
R—R		R	
C			
H			
I			
L			
L			
	WORLD	**WAR**	**TWO**

As I searched the names of the Prime Ministers of the United Kingdom, my excitement could hardly be contained. As I found each of the letters and realized that most of the names failed to have such a Display, I was overcome with anticipation. The suspense peaked as I got to the name WINSTON LEONARD CHURCHILL. And there it was. We do not even need Churchill's hyphenated surname Spencer. In fact, his hyphenated name is not needed for any of his Presentations in this book.

COVERT PRESENTATIONS OF **WORLD WAR TWO** IN THE PRIME MINISTERS OF THE U.K.

	(PRESENT)	(MISSING)
WILLIAM PITT II	WRLDART	OWWO
HENRY ADDINGTON	WORDWARTW	LO
SPENCER PERCEVAL I	WRLDWARW	OTO
ROBERT BANKS JENKINSON	WORWARTWO	LD
GEORGE CANNING JNR	WORLWARW	DTO
ARTHUR WELLESLEY	WRLWARTW	ODO
CHARLES GREY II	WRLWAR	ODTWO
HENRY WILLIAM LAMB	WRLDWARTW	OO
ROBERT PEEL II	WORLWRTW	DAO
JOHN RUSSELL II	WORLWA	DRTWO
HENRY JOHN TEMPLE	WORLDWATW	RO
BENJAMIN DISRAELI	WRLDWARTW	OO
ARCHIBALD PHILIP PRIMROSE	WORLDART	WWO
ROBERT ARTHUR TALBOT CASCOYNE-CECIL	WORLWARTWO	D
ARTHUR JAMES BALFOUR	WORLDARTO	WW
HENRY CAMPBELL-BANNERMAN	WRLDWARTW	OO
HERBERT HENRY ASQUITH	WRLWARTW	ODO
DAVID LLOYD GEORGE I	WORLDWARO	TW

COVERT PRESENTATIONS OF **WORLD WAR TWO** IN THE PRIME MINISTERS OF THE U.K.

	(PRESENT)	(MISSING)
ANDREW BONAR LAW I	WORLDWARTW	O
STANLEY BALDWIN	WRLDWATW	ORO
JAMES RAMSAY MACDONALD	WORLDWA	RTWO
ARTHUR NEVILLE CHAMBERLAIN	WRLDWARTW	OO
WINSTON LEONARD CHURCHILL	***WORLD WAR TWO***	
CLEMENT RICHARD ATTLEE	WRLDWARTW	OO
ROBERT ANTHONY EDEN	WORDWARTWO	L
MAURICE HAROLD MACMILLAN	WORLDWAR	TWO
EDWARD RICHARD GEORGE HEATH	WORLDWARTW	O
JAMES HAROLD WILSON	WORLDWARWO	T
LEONARD JAMES CALLAGHAN	WORLDWAW	RTO
MARGARET HILDA ROBERTS THATCHER	WORLDWARTW	O
JOHN ROY MAJOR	WORDARO	LWTW
ANTHONY CHARLES LYNTON BLAIR	WORLWARTWO	D
JAMES GORDON BROWN	WORDWARTWO	L
THERESA MARY BRASIER MAY	WRDWARTW	OLO
ALEXANDER BORIS DE PFEFFEL JOHNSON	(((WORLD WAR TWO)))	

Here we see how rare it is to find WORLD WAR TWO in a name. This table demonstrates the other side of these tests. The "correct predictions of no involvement or association" can be just as valid as the "correct predictions of involvement or association."

In this test of Prime Ministers of the United Kingdom, we only find a Presentation of WINSTON LEONARD CHURCHILL and an Incidental Display of ALEXANDER BORIS DE PFEFFEL JOHNSON.

WWII

A COMMON EXPRESSION FOR WORLD WAR TWO

OVERT PRESENTATIONS OF **WWII** IN THE PRIME MINISTERS OF THE U.K.

	(PRESENT)	(MISSING)
WILLIAM PITT I	WII	W
HENRY ADDINGTON	I	WWI
SPENCER PERCEVAL I	I	WWI
ROBERT BANKS JENKINSON	I	WWI
GEORGE CANNING JNR	I	WWI
ARTHUR WELLESLEY	W	WII
CHARLES GREY II	II	WW
HENRY WILLIAM LAMB	WII	W
ROBERT PEEL II	II	WW
JOHN RUSSELL II	II	WW
GEORGE HAMILTON GORDON	I	WWI
HENRY JOHN TEMPLE		WWII
BENJAMIN DISRAELI	II	WW
ARCHIBALD PHILIP PRIMROSE	II	WW
ROBERT ARTHUR TALBOT GASCOYNE-CECIL	I	WWI
ARTHUR JAMES BALFOUR		WWII
HENRY CAMPBELL BANNERMAN		WWII
HERBERT HENRY ASQUITH	I	WWI

OVERT PRESENTATIONS OF **WWII** IN THE PRIME MINISTERS OF THE U.K.

	(PRESENT)	(MISSING)
DAVID LLOYD GEORGE I	I	WWI
ANDREW BONAR LAW I	WWI	I
STANLEY BALDWIN	WI	WI
JAMES RAMSAY MACDONALD		WWII
ARTHUR NEVILLE CHAMBERLAIN	II	WW
WINSTON LEONARD CHURCHILL	WII	W
CLEMENT RICHARD ATTLEE	I	WWI
ROBERT ANTHONY EDEN		WWII
MAURICE HAROLD MACMILLAN	II	WW
EDWARD RICHARD GEORGE HEATH	WI	WI
JAMES HAROLD WILSON	WI	WI
LEONARD JAMES CALLAGHAN		WWII
MARGARET HILDA ROBERTS THATCHER	I	WWI
JOHN ROY MAJOR		WWII
ANTHONY CHARLES LYNTON BLAIR	I	WWI
JAMES GORDON BROWN	W	WII
THERESA MARY BRASIER MAY	I	WWI
ALEXANDER BORIS DE PFEFFEL JOHNSON	I	WWI

We now look for Overt Presentations of WWII in the names of Prime Ministers of the United Kingdom and we do not find any.

WORLD WAR II

A COMMON EXPRESSION FOR WORLD WAR TWO

MIXED PRESENTATIONS OF **WORLD WAR II** IN THE PRIME MINISTERS OF THE U.K.

	(PRESENT)	(MISSING)
WILLIAM PITT II	WRLDARII	OW
HENRY ADDINGTON	WORDWAI	LRI
WILLIAM WYNDHAM GRENVILLE	WRLDWARII	O
SPENCER PERCEVAL I	WRLDWARI	OI
ROBERT BANKS JENKINSON	WORWARI	LDI
GEORGE CANNING JNR	WORLWARI	DI
ARTHUR WELLESLEY	WRLWAR	ODII
CHARLES GREY II	WRLWARII	OD
HENRY WILLIAM LAMB	WRLDWARII	O
JOHN RUSSELL II	WORLWAII	DR
GEORGE HAMILTON GORDON	WORLDWARI	I
HENRY JOHN TEMPLE	WORLDWA	RII
BENJAMIN DISRAELI	WRLDWARII	O
ARCHIBALD PHILIP PRIMROSE	WORLDARII	W
ROBERT ARTHUR TALBOT GASCOYNE-CECIL	WORLWARI	DI
ARTHUR JAMES BALFOUR	WORLDAR	WII
HENRY CAMPBELL BANNERMAN	WRLDWAR	OII
DAVID LLOYD GEORGE I	WORLDWARI	I

MIXED PRESENTATIONS OF **WORLD WAR II** IN THE PRIME MINISTERS OF THE U.K.

	(PRESENT)	(MISSING)
ANDREW BONAR LAW I	WORLDWARI	I
STANLEY BALDWIN	WLDWAI	ORRI
JAMES RAMSAY MACDONALD	WORLDWA	RII
ARTHUR NEVILLE CHAMBERLAIN	WRLDWARII	O
WINSTON LEONARD CHURCHILL	***WORLD WAR II***	
CLEMENT RICHARD ATTLEE	WRLDWARI	OI
ROBERT ANTHONY EDEN	WORDWAR	LII
EDWARD RICHARD GEORGE HEATH	WORLDWARI	I
JAMES HAROLD WILSON	WORLDWAI	RI
LEONARD JAMES CALLAGHAN	WORLDWA	RII
MARGARET HILDA ROBERTS THATCHER	WORLD WARI	I
JOHN ROY MAJOR	WORDAR	LWII
ANTHONY CHARLES LYNTON BLAIR	WORLWARI	DI
JAMES GORDON BROWN	WORDWAR	LII
DAVID WILLIAM DONALD CAMERON	***WORLD WAR II***	**64-YEAR PHEN**
THERESA MARY BRASIER MAY	WRDWARI	OLI
ALEXANDER BORIS DE PFEFFEL JOHNSON	WORLDWARI	I

In this test we see that both WINSTON LEONARD CHURCHILL and the United Kingdom's 64-Year Phenomenon, DAVID WILLIAM DONALD CAMERON, have WORLD WAR II in their names.

64-YEAR PHENOMENON

MIXED PRESENTATION OF WORLD WAR II IN DAVID WILLIAM DONALD CAMERON

D—D	D		
A—A		A	
V			
I—I			I
D			
W—W	W		
I—I			I
L—L	L		
L			
I = R		R	
A			
M			
D			
O—O	O		
N = W		W	
B			
A			
L			
D			
C			
A			
M			
E			
R—R	R		
O			
N			
	WORLD	**WAR**	**II**

Here we find WORLD WAR II in the name of DAVID WILLIAM DONALD CAMERON who is the 64-Year Phenomenon for the United Kingdom and WORLD WAR II. He became Prime Minister during the year between the 64-year anniversary and 65-year anniversary at the end of WORLD WAR II.

SECOND WORLD WAR

A COMMON EXPRESSION FOR WORLD WAR TWO

COVERT PRESENTATIONS OF **SECOND WORLD WAR** IN THE PRIME MINISTERS OF THE U.K.

	(PRESENT)	(MISSING)
WILLIAM PITT II	SDWRLAR	SEONODW
HENRY ADDINGTON	EONDWRDWAR	SCOL
SPENCER PERCEVAL I	SECNDWRLWAR	OOD
ROBERT BANKS JENKINSON	SEONWORWAR	CDLD
GEORGE CANNING JNR	SECONWRWAR	DOLD
ARTHUR WELLESLEY	SECNWRLWAR	ODOD
CHARLES GREY II	SECNRLAR	ODWODW
HENRY WILLIAM LAMB	SECNDWRLDAR	OOW
ROBERT PEEL II	EONWRLR	SCDODWA
JOHN RUSSELL II	SECONRLA	DWODWR
GEORGE HAMILTON-GORDON	EONDWORLDWAR	SC
HENRY JOHN TEMPLE	SEONDWRLW	CODAR
BENJAMIN DISRAELI	SENDWRLDWAR	COO
ARCHIBALD PHILIP PRIMROSE	SECODRLDAR	NWOW
ROBERT ARTHUR TALBOT GASCOYNE-CECIL	SECONWORLWAR	DD
ARTHUR JAMES BALFOUR	SECODORLAR	NWDW
HENRY CAMPBELL BANNERMAN	SECNDWLDWAR	OO
HERBERT HENRY ASQUITH	SECNWRWAR	ODOLD

COVERT PRESENTATIONS OF **SECOND WORLD WAR** IN THE PRIME MINISTERS OF THE U.K.		
	(PRESENT)	(MISSING)
DAVID LLOYD GEORGE I	ECONDORLDAR	SWW
ANDREW BONAR LAW I	SEONDWRLWAR	COD
STANLEY BALDWIN	SECNDWRLWA	OODR
JAMES RAMSAY MACDONALD	SECONDRLDA	WOWR
ARTHUR NEVILLE CHAMBERLAIN	SECNDWRLDWAR	OO
WINSTON LEONARD CHURCHILL	SECONDWORLWAR	D
CLEMENT RICHARD ATTLEE	SECNDWRLDWAR	OO
ROBERT ANTHONY EDEN	EONDWORWAR	SCLD
EDWARD RICHARD GEORGE HEATH	SECONDWRDWAR	OL
JAMES HAROLD WILSON	SECONDWORLDAR	W
LEONARD JAMES CALLAGHAN	SECONDWRLDWA	OR
MARGARET HILDA ROBERTS THATCHER	SECONDWRLDAR	OW
JOHN ROY MAJOR	SONDORAR	ECWLDW
ANTHONY CHARLES LYNTON BLAIR	SECONWORLWAR	DD
JAMES GORDON BROWN	SEONDWORDWAR	CL
DAVID WILLIAM DONALD CAMERON	***SECOND WORLD WAR***64-YEAR PH	
THERESA MARY BRASIER MAY	SENDWRDAR	COOLW
ALEXANDER BORIS DE PFEFFEL JOHNSON	(((SECOND WORLD WAR)))	

As we see, DAVID WILLIAM DONALD CAMERON, who is the United Kingdom's 64-Year Phenomenon for WORLD WAR II, has both WORLD WAR II and SECOND WORLD WAR in his name.

We, again, find an Incidental Display in the name of ALEXANDER BORIS DE PFEFFEL JOHNSON, perhaps because of the many letters in his full name.

Summary of Evidence Supporting the Claims: WORLD WAR TWO, WORLD WAR II, WWII, SECOND WORLD WAR in the names of British Prime Ministers

Claim 1–
WINSTON LEONARD CHURCHILL, the Prime Minister most central to WORLD WAR TWO/WORLD WAR II/WWII/SECOND WORLD WAR, has the only Presentation of WORLD WAR TWO and of WORLD WAR II among the Prime Ministers after exclusions, with the exception of the 64-Year Phenomenon.

Claim 2–
The 64-Year Phenomenon: DAVID WILLIAM DONALD CAMERON, the Prime Minister who served approximately 64 years after WORLD WAR II ended, has WORLD WAR II and SECOND WORLD WAR in his name.

Claim 3–
WINSTON LEONARD CHRUCHILL, who was the Prime Minister most directly involved in and associated with WORLD WAR TWO/WORLD WAR II/WWII/SECOND WORLD WAR, has WORLD WAR TWO and WORLD WAR II in his name.

THE PROBABILITY OF GEORGE WASHINGTON, WILLIAM HARRISON AND GEORGE III WILLIAM FREDERICK HAVING EXCLUSIVE AND CORRECT DISPLAYS OF AWOI IN THEIR NAMES

AND

ABRAHAM LINCOLN, HIRAM ULYSSES GRANT, RUTHERFORD BIRCHARD HAYES, HERBERT CLARK HOOVER, WILLIAM JEFFERSON BLYTHE III, BARACK HUSSEIN OBAMA II AND WILLIAM HOWARD TAFT, AT LEVEL TWO, HAVING EXCLUSIVE AND CORRECT DISPLAYS OF THE CIVIL WAR IN THEIR NAMES

AND

WOODROW WILSON, THEODORE ROOSEVELT, FRANKLIN ROOSEVELT, WILLIAM HOWARD TAFT, JOHN CALVIN COOLIDGE, HERBERT CLARK HOOVER AND RONALD WILSON REAGAN HAVING EXCLUSIVE AND CORRECT DISPLAYS OF WORLD WAR ONE/WWI IN THEIR NAMES

AND

FRANKLIN ROOSEVELT, HERBERT CLARK HOOVER, DWIGHT DAVID EISENHOWER, JOHN FITZGERALD KENNEDY, RICHARD MILHAUS NIXON AND BARACK HUSSEIN OBAMA II HAVING EXCLUSIVE AND CORRECT DISPLAYS OF WORLD WAR TWO/WWII IN THEIR NAMES

AND

DAVID LLOYD GEORGE I, ANDREW BONAR LAW I, WINSTON LEONARD CHURCHILL, MAURICE HAROLD MACMILLAN AND MARGARET HILDA ROBERTS THATCHER HAVING EXCLUSIVE AND CORRECT DISPLAYS OF WORLD WAR ONE/WWI/WORLD WAR I/FIRST WORLD WAR IN THEIR NAMES

AND

WINSTON LEONARD CHURCHILL AND DAVID WILLIAM DONALD CAMERON HAVING EXCLUSIVE AND CORRECT DISPLAYS OF WORLD WAR TWO IN THEIR NAMES IS:

1

IN

17,600,000,000,000,000,000,000

(ONE IN OVER 17 SEXTILLION, 600 QUINTILLION)

Thus far, the series of investigations of the U.S. Presidents and THE CIVIL WAR and WORLD WAR ONE/WORLD WAR I/WWI/FIRST WORLD WAR, and WORLD WAR TWO/WORLD WAR II/WWII/SECOND WORLD WAR had already been found to support the Three Claims.

Now, I had just completed this series of tests on WORLD WAR ONE/WORLD WAR I/WWI/FIRST WORLD WAR and WORLD WAR TWO/WORLD WAR II/WWII/SECOND WORLD WAR and the Prime Ministers of the United Kingdom. As I slowly completed each one, I was seeing the same results. Everything continued to support the Three Claims.

It is common for researchers to perform tests of the same phenomenon many times. They do this to find further support for earlier findings. As you can see, all my findings yielded similar results. The world leaders involved in or associated with certain wars contained one or more of the expressions of those wars in their names. In fact, the Three Claims were supported by the evidence in all of my investigations.

At this point, my shock and disbelief were turning into full recognition of the reality of the Code. I was now more certain than ever that the Code was not a random occurrence, but that it was deliberately created and placed in the English language. The Code was not an accident, a coincidence or something that happened by chance. It was intended, planned, and designed. And it tells the story of human events even before the story has played out. Whatever force or phenomenon I had been witnessing up until this moment, I knew the Code was now very real.

As convinced as I was by the results of the tests thus far, I had no intention of slowing down. I felt driven to continue by the simple fact that there was nothing within the range of human experience (or at least nothing with which I was familiar) that resembled this—nothing I had ever seen before.

So, I decided it was time to look at the British Monarchs.

THE WORLD WARS AND THE BRITISH MONARCHS

GEORGE V (GEORGE V FREDERICK ERNEST ALBERT) (1865 - 1936) served as King of the United Kingdom during World War One. It was actually King George V who chose to declare war and engage the United Kingdom in World War One. On August 4, 1914, King George V made an entry into his diary, "I held a council at 10:45 to declare war with Germany. It is a terrible catastrophe but it is not our fault . . . Please to God it may soon be over."

GEORGE VI (ALBERT FREDERICK ARTHUR GEORGE VI) (1895 - 1952) served as King during World War Two. While it was George VI who appointed Winston Leonard Churchill as Prime Minister of the United Kingdom, it was Churchill's decision to resist Hitler and enter the United Kingdom in World War Two. George VI would dine daily with Churchill and discuss the war as it progressed and as it was coming to an end.

COVERT PRESENTATION OF WORLD WAR ONE IN KING GEORGE V FREDERICK ERNEST ALBERT

G			
E = W	W		
O—O	O		
R—R	R		
G			
E = W		W	
V			
F = O			O
R—R		R	
E			
D—D	D		
E—E			E
R			
I			
C			
K			
E			
R			
N—N			N
E			
S			
T			
A—A		A	
L—L	L		
B			
E			
R			
T			
	WORLD	**WAR**	**ONE**

There was new excitement as I studied the names of the British Monarchs for WORLD WAR ONE and WORLD WAR TWO. I found WORLD WAR ONE in the name GEORGE V FREDERICK ERNEST ALBERT also known as King George V.

LEVEL TWO PRESENTATION OF **WORLD WAR TWO** IN **ALBERT FREDERICK ARTHUR GEORGE VI**

	WORLD	WAR	TWO
A—A	A		
L—L	L		
B			
E = W	W		
R—R	R		
T—T			T
F = O			O
R			
E = W		W	
D—D	D		
E			
R—R		R	
I			
C			
K			
A			
R			
T			
H			
U			
R			
G			
E = W		W	
O—O	O		
R			
G			
E			
V			
I			
	WORLD	**WAR**	**TWO**

I also found WORLD WAR TWO where it belonged—in the name ALBERT FREDERICK ARTHUR GEORGE VI also known as King George VI. Actually, because of the great similarity between the names of the wars, these two Monarchs each have both world wars in their names, even though they were each associated with only one.

LEVEL TWO PRESENTATION OF WORLD WAR ONE IN ELIZABETH ALEXANDRA MARY WINDSOR

E = W		W	
L—L	L		
I—I			
Z			
A—A	A		
B			
E---E			E
T—T			
H			
A—A		A	
L			
E = N			N
X = O			O
A			
N			
D--D	D		
R—R	R		
A			
M			
A			
R—R		R	
Y			
W—W	W		
I			
N			
D			
S			
O—O	O		
R			
	WORLD	**WAR**	**ONE**

Here we find WORLD WAR ONE in the name ELIZABETH ALEXANDRA MARY WINDSOR—better known as Queen Elizabeth II. She is the 64-Year Phenomenon for WORLD WAR ONE.

LEVEL TWO PRESENTATION OF WORLD WAR TWO IN ELIZABETH ALEXANDRA MARY WINDSOR

E = W		W	
L—L	L		
I—I			
Z			
A—A	A		
B			
E = W			W
T—T			T
H			
A—A		A	
L			
E			
X = O			O
A			
N			
D--D	D		
R—R	R		
A			
M			
A			
R—R		R	
Y			
W—W	W		
I			
N			
D			
S			
O—O	O		
R			
	WORLD	**WAR**	**TWO**

We also find WORLD WAR TWO in the name of ELIZABETH ALEXANDRA MARY WINDSOR as she is the 64-Year Phenomenon for WORLD WAR TWO, as well. It is not surprising as she has been the Queen of the United Kingdom for 70 years at the time of the writing of this book.

COVERT PRESENTATION OF **EXPRESSIONS OF WORLD WAR ONE** IN THE NAMES OF BRITISH MONARCHS	
WILLIAM III	NEITHER WAR
GEORGE LOUIS	NEITHER WAR
GEORGE II AUGUSTUS	NEITHER WAR
WILLIAM IV HENRY	NEITHER WAR
ALEXANDRINA VICTORIA	(((WORLD WAR ONE/WORLD WAR I)))
ALBERT EDWARD VII	NEITHER WAR
GEORGE V FREDERICK ERNEST ALBERT	***WORLD WAR ONE*** ***WORLD WAR I*** ***FIRST WORLD WAR***
ELIZABETH II ALEXANDRA MARY WINDSOR	***WORLD WAR ONE*** 64-YEAR PH ***WORLD WAR I*** ***FIRST WORLD WAR*** 64-YEAR PH

ELIZABETH II ALEXANDRA MARY WINDSOR, known as QUEEN ELIZABETH, is the 64-Year Phenomenon for two wars—WORLD WAR I and for WORLD WAR II. She shares WORLD WAR I with Prime Minister MARGARET HILDA ROBERTS THATCHER.

Two Kings were near namesakes. They both have GEORGE, ALBERT, and FREDERICK in their names, so they are each excluded from one of the exhibits.

COVERT PRESENTATION OF **EXPRESSIONS OF WORLD WAR TWO** IN THE NAMES OF BRITISH MONARCHS

WILLIAM III	NEITHER WAR
GEORGE LOUIS	NEITHER WAR
GEORGE II AUGUSTUS	NEITHER WAR
WILLIAM IV HENRY	NEITHER WAR
ALEXANDRINA VICTORIA	(((WORLD WAR TWO/WORLD WAR II)))
ALBERT EDWARD VII	NEITHER WAR
ALBERT FREDERICK ARTHUR GEORGE VI	***WORLD WAR TWO*** ***WORLD WAR II***
ELIZABETH II ALEXANDRA MARY WINDSOR	***WORLD WAR TWO*** 64-YEAR PH ***WORLD WAR II*** ***SECOND WORLD WAR***64-YEAR PH

ALBERT FREDERICK ARTHUR GEORGE VI was King of the United Kingdom during WORLD WAR TWO. ELIZABETH II ALEXANDRA MARY WINDSOR, known as QUEEN ELIZABETH, is the 64-Year Phenomenon for WORLD WAR I and for WORLD WAR II, as mentioned. She shares the 64-Year Phenomenon for WORLD WAR II with DAVID WILLIAM DONALD CAMERON.

Two Kings were near namesakes. As mentioned on the previous page, they share GEORGE, ALBERT and FREDERICK in their names.

Summary of Evidence Supporting the Claims: WORLD WAR ONE, WORLD WAR I, WWI, FIRST WORLD WAR in the names of British Monarchs

Claim 1—
GEORGE V FREDERICK ERNEST ALBERT, the Monarch of the United Kingdom most central to WORLD WAR ONE/WORLD WAR I/WWI/FIRST WORLD WAR, has WORLD WAR ONE, WORLD WAR I and FIRST WORLD WAR in his name.

Claim 2—
The 64-Year Phenomenon: ELIZABETH II ALEXANDRA MARY WINDSOR, the Monarch who served 64 years after the war, has WORLD WAR ONE, WORLD WAR I and FIRST WORLD WAR in her name.

Claim 3—
GEORGE V FREDERICK ERNEST ALBERT, who was the Monarch most directly involved in and associated with the war, has WORLD WAR ONE, WORLD WAR I and FIRST WORLD WAR in his name.

THE PROBABILITY OF GEORGE WASHINGTON, WILLIAM HARRISON AND GEORGE III WILLIAM FREDERICK HAVING EXCLUSIVE AND CORRECT DISPLAYS OF AWOI IN THEIR NAMES

AND

ABRAHAM LINCOLN, HIRAM ULYSSES GRANT, RUTHERFORD BIRCHARD HAYES, HERBERT CLARK HOOVER, WILLIAM JEFFERSON BLYTHE III, BARACK HUSSEIN OBAMA II AND WILLIAM HOWARD TAFT, AT LEVEL TWO, HAVING EXCLUSIVE AND CORRECT DISPLAYS OF THE CIVIL WAR IN THEIR NAMES

AND

THOMAS WOODROW WILSON, THEODORE ROOSEVELT, FRANKLIN ROOSEVELT, WILLIAM HOWARD TAFT, JOHN CALVIN COOLIDGE AND RONALD WILSON REAGAN HAVING EXCLUSIVE AND CORRECT DISPLAYS OF WORLD WAR ONE/WWI IN THEIR NAMES

AND

FRANKLIN ROOSEVELT, HERBERT CLARK HOOVER, DWIGHT DAVID EISENHOWER, JOHN FITZGERALD KENNEDY, RICHARD MILHAUS NIXON AND BARACK HUSSEIN OBAMA II HAVING EXCLUSIVE AND CORRECT DISPLAYS OF WORLD WAR TWO/WWII IN THEIR NAMES

AND

DAVID LLOYD GEORGE I, ANDREW BONAR LAW I, WINSTON LEONARD CHURCHILL, MAURICE HAROLD MACMILLAN AND MARGARET HILDA ROBERTS THATCHER HAVING EXCLUSIVE AND CORRECT DISPLAYS OF WORLD WAR ONE/WWI/WORLD WAR I/FIRST WORLD WAR IN THEIR NAMES

AND

WINSTON LEONARD CHURCHILL AND DAVID WILLIAM DONALD CAMERON HAVING EXCLUSIVE AND CORRECT DISPLAYS OF WORLD WAR TWO/WWII/WORLD WAR II/SECOND WORLD WAR IN THEIR NAMES

AND

GEORGE V FREDERICK ERNEST ALBERT AND ELIZABETH II ALEXANDRA MARY WINDSOR HAVING EXCLUSIVE AND CORRECT DISPLAYS OF WORLD WAR I IN THEIR NAMES IS:

1
IN

44,230,000,000,000,000,000,000

(ONE IN 44 SEXTILLION, 320 QUINTILLION)

Summary of Evidence Supporting the Claims: WORLD WAR TWO, WORLD WAR II, WWII, SECOND WORLD WAR in the names of British Monarchs

Claim 1—
ALBERT FREDERICK ARTHUR GEORGE VI, the Monarch of the United Kingdom most central to WORLD WAR TWO/WORLD WAR II/WWII/SECOND WORLD WAR has WORLD WAR TWO, WORLD WAR II and SECOND WORLD WAR in his name.

Claim 2—
The 64-Year Phenomenon: ELIZABETH II ALEXANDRA MARY WINDSOR, the Monarch who served 64 years after the war, has WORLD WAR TWO, WORLD WAR II and SECOND WORLD WAR in her name.

Claim 3—
ALBERT FREDERICK ARTHUR GEORGE VI, who was the Monarch most directly involved in and associated with the war, has WORLD WAR TWO, WORLD WAR II and SECOND WORLD WAR in his name.

THE PROBABILITY OF GEORGE WASHINGTON, WILLIAM HARRISON AND GEORGE III WILLIAM FREDERICK BEING THE ONLY PRESIDENT AND MONARCH DURING THE AMERICAN WAR OF INDEPENDENCE AND HAVING EXCLUSIVE AND CORRECT DISPLAYS OF AWOI IN THEIR NAMES

AND

ABRAHAM LINCOLN, HIRAM ULYSSES GRANT, RUTHERFORD BIRCHARD HAYES, HERBERT CLARK HOOVER, WILLIAM JEFFERSON BLYTHE III, BARACK HUSSEIN OBAMA II AND WILLIAM HOWARD TAFT, AT LEVEL TWO, HAVING EXCLUSIVE AND CORRECT DISPLAYS OF THE CIVIL WAR IN THEIR NAMES

AND

WOODROW WILSON, THEODORE ROOSEVELT, FRANKLIN ROOSEVELT, WILLIAM HOWARD TAFT AND RONALD WILSON REAGAN HAVING EXCLUSIVE AND CORRECT DISPLAYS OF WORLD WAR ONE/WWI IN THEIR NAMES

AND

FRANKLIN ROOSEVELT, HERBERT HOOVER, DWIGHT DAVID EISENHOWER, JOHN FITZGERALD KENNEDY, RICHARD MILHAUS NIXON AND BARACK HUSSEIN OBAMA II HAVING EXCLUSIVE AND CORRECT DISPLAYS OF WORLD WAR TWO/WWII IN THEIR NAMES

AND

DAVID LLOYD GEORGE, ANDREW BONAR LAW, WINSTON LEONARD CHURCHILL, MAURICE HAROLD MACMILLAN AND MARGARET HILDA ROBERTS THATCHER HAVING EXCLUSIVE AND CORRECT DISPLAYS OF WORLD WAR ONE/WWI/WORLD WAR I/FIRST WORLD WAR IN THEIR NAMES

AND

WINSTON LEONARD CHURCHILL AND DONALD DAVID WILLIAM CAMERON HAVING EXCLUSIVE AND CORRECT DISPLAYS OF WORLD WAR TWO/WWII/WORLD WAR II/SECOND WORLD WAR IN THEIR NAMES

AND

KING GEORGE V FREDERICK ERNEST ALBERT AND QUEEN ELIZABETH II ALEXANDRA MARY WINDSOR HAVING EXCLUSIVE AND CORRECT DISPLAYS OF WORLD WAR I IN THEIR NAMES

AND

KING ALBERT FREDERICK ARTHUR GEORGE VI AND QUEEN ELIZABETH II ALEXANDRA MARY WINDSOR HAVING EXCLUSIVE AND CORRECT DISPLAYS OF WORLD WAR TWO IN THEIR NAMES IS:

1
IN

79,930,000,000,000,000,000,000

(ONE IN 79 SEXTILLION, 930 QUINTILLION)

It had appeared to me that the names of the British Monarchs should also be examined. If it had been found that a search of their names failed to support my claims, there would be challenges and questions as to why. But this was clearly not the case. The results again supported my claims.

Rigorous investigations had been performed on wars involving the United States—the American War of Independence (AWOI), THE CIVIL WAR, and both world wars. Prime Ministers and Monarchs were also tested for the AWOI and both world wars. The Three Claims have been confirmed by exhaustive searches of the names of Heads of State of both countries. Each series of investigations has provided the same results and the probability of this phenomenon occurring by chance is approaching impossible.

By this time, I had gone from three notebooks to ten to twenty, and now, all the way to having over fifty notebooks filled with the names of the leaders involved in all of these wars. And I had gone from initially wondering if the book would amount to even eighty pages to now wondering where the book would end. Or if it ever would.

As I reflected on all of the amazing discoveries I had made thus far, I wondered if there was anything else I could explore.

DER HOLOCAUST

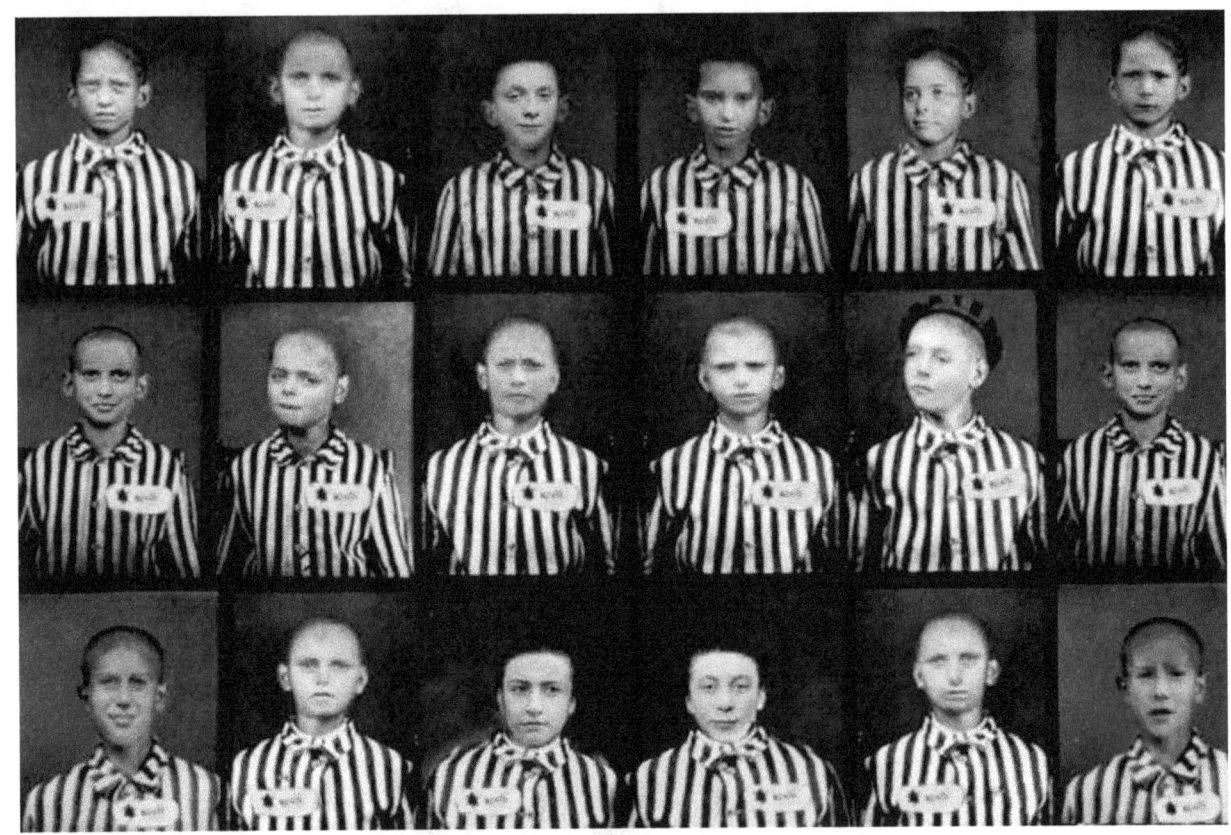

The HOLOCAUST was a genocide committed during World War II, in which Nazi Germany and its co-conspirators systematically murdered between five million and seven million European Jews, approximately two-thirds of the Jewish population of Europe at that time. While the mass killings were perpetrated between 1941 and 1945, it can be said that the Holocaust really began with the rise of Hitler and the Nazis in 1933. Although the Jews were the original target of what the Nazis called "the Final Solution," the Nazis persecuted and murdered many other groups—including homosexual men, the Roma, Soviet prisoners and citizens, Jehovah's Witnesses, Poles and political opponents. They may have murdered as many as seventeen million people or more. It was the intention of the Nazi leaders to expand the Holocaust to include the murder of all Jews—even those in the neutral nations such as Spain, Portugal and Sweden. Eventually, no Jew on Earth would have been spared.

"The great masses of the people will more easily fall victims to a big lie than to a small one."

"Success is the sole earthly judge of right and wrong."

"The victor will never be asked to tell the truth."

"What good fortune for governments that people do not think."

"Humanitarianism is the expression of cowardice and stupidity."

"If you tell a big enough lie and you tell it frequently enough, it will be believed."

"I do not see why men should not be just as cruel as nature."

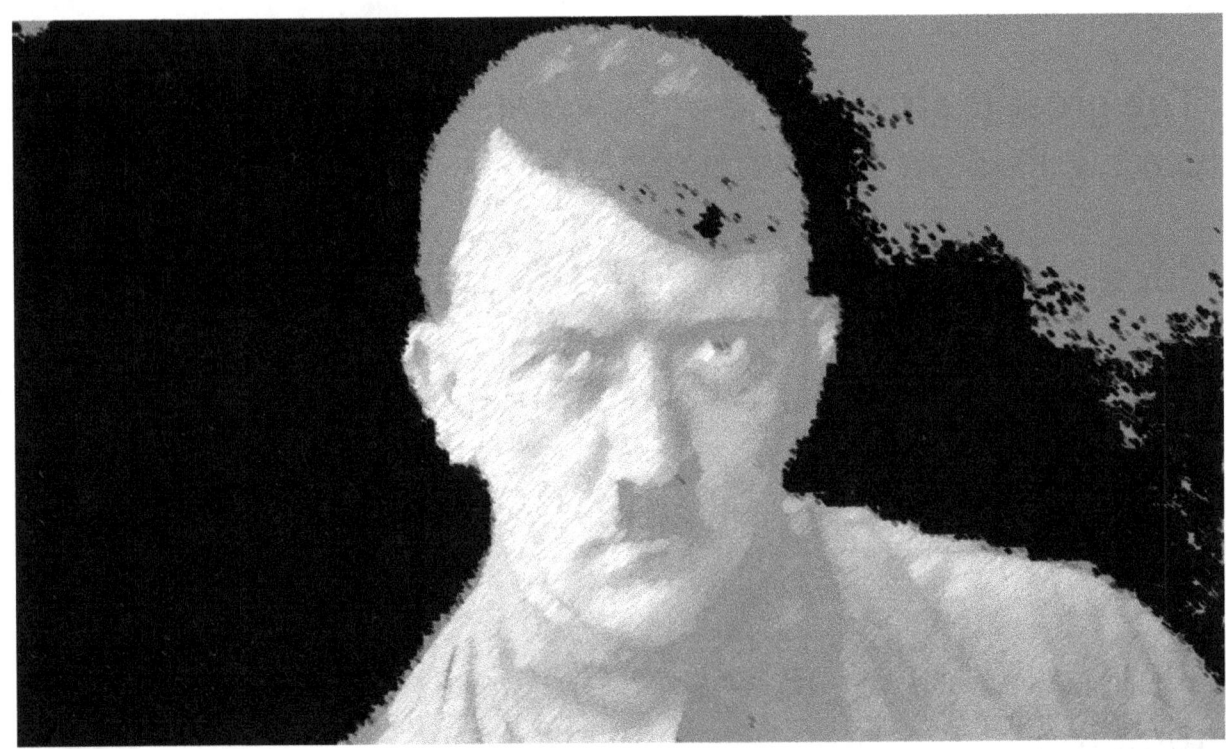

ADOLFUS JACOB HITLER

ADOLFUS JACOB HITLER (1889 - 1945*) was born April 20, 1889, in Braunau am Inn, Austria, and was raised by a dictatorial father and an indulgent mother. In his younger years, he wanted to be an artist, but his father discouraged him, and later, his applications to art schools were rejected. Hitler moved to Munich in 1913 and served in the Bavarian army in World War One. In 1919, he joined the German Workers' Party, the precursor to the Nazi Party, was appointed leader of the Party in 1921, and tried to seize power in 1923 in a failed coup for which he was arrested. While in jail, he wrote *Mein Kampf*. The Nazi Party rose in 1933, and by the end of the year, Hitler had become Chancellor of Germany. In 1934, he appointed himself Dictator. The Weimar Republic soon became Nazi Germany. His aims were to remove the Jews from Germany and to remove restrictions and what he perceived as injustices placed on Germany by France and Britain after World War I. Under his dictatorship, Germany began World War II and orchestrated the Holocaust. *Despite the many inconsistencies in reports and evidence of his death, most historians believe he committed suicide in his bunker on April 30, 1945.

OVERT PRESENTATION OF DER HOLOCAUST IN ADOLFUS JACOB HITLER

A—A		A
D—D	D	
O—O		O
L—L		L
F		
U—U		U
S—S		S
J		
A		
C—C		C
O—O		O
B		
H—H		H
I		
T—T		T
L		
E—E	E	
R—R	R	
	DER	**HOLOCAUST**

One day, as I was driving, it suddenly occurred to me that DER HOLOCAUST, the German term for the HOLOCAUST, might be found in the name of ADOLFUS JACOB HITLER. Letter by letter, I performed the work in my head, all the while in a state of absolute suspense. When I found it was true, I checked and doublechecked and I was soon overwhelmed with the absolute horror of this discovery. I couldn't wait to get home. I told Blythe I had found something really shocking, but that I didn't want to share it with her until I had studied it further. She waited anxiously. I examined the names of all the German Chancellors.

OVERT PRESENTATIONS OF **DER HOLOCAUST** IN THE NAMES OF GERMAN CHANCELLORS

	(PRESENT)	(MISSING)
OTTO EDUARD LEOPOLD	DEROLOAUT	HCS
GEORG LEO CAPRIVI	EROLOCA	DHUST
CHLODWIG CARL VIKTOR	DRHOLOCAT	EUS
BERNHARD HEINRICH KARL MARTIN VON BULOW	DERHOLOCAUT	S
THEOBALD THEODOR FRIEDRICH ALFRED VON BETHMANN-HOLLWEG	DERHOLOCAT	US
GEORG MICHAELIS	ERHOLCAS	DOUT
GEORG FRIEDRICH HERTLING	DERHOLCT	OAUS
MAXIMILIAN ALEXANDER FRIEDRICH WILHELM	DERHLCA	OOUST
FRIEDRICH EBERT	DERHCT	OLOAUS
PHILIPP HENRICH SCHEIDEMANN	DERHLCAS	OOUT
GUSTAV ADOLF BAUER	DEROLAUST	HOC
HERMANN MULLER	ERHLAU	DOOCST
CONSTANTIN FEHRENBACH	ERHOCAST	DLOU
KARL JOSEPH WIRTH	ERHOLAST	DOCU
WILHELM CARL JOSEF CUNO	ERHOLOCAUS	DT
GUSTAV STRESEMANN	ERAUST	DHOLOC
HANS LUTHER	ERHLAUST	DOOC
WILHELM MARX	ERHLA	DOOCUST
HEINRICH ALOYSIUS MARIA ELISABETH BRUNING	ERHOLCAUST	DO
FRANZ JOSEPH HERMANN MARIA VON PAPEN	ERHOOAS	DLCUT
KURT FERDINAND FRIEDRICH HERMANN VON SCHLEICHER	DERHOLCAUST	O
ADOLFUS JACOB HITLER	***DER HOLOCAUST***	
PAUL JOSEPH GOEBBELS	EHOLOAUS	DRCT
JOHANN LUDWIG VON KROSIGK	DRHOLOAUS	ECT
KONRAD HERMANN JOSEPH ADENAUER	DERHOOAUS	LCT
LUDWIG WILHELM ERHARD	DERHLAU	OOCST
KURT GEORG KIESINGER	EROUST	DHLOCA
GEBHARD MULLER	DERHLAU	OOCST
REINHOLD MAIER	DERHOLA	OCUST
HERBERT ERNST KARL FRAHM	ERHLAST	DOOCU
WALTER SCHEEL	ERHLCAST	DOOU
HELMUT HENRICH WALDEMAR SCHMIDT	DERHLCAUST	OO
HELMUT JOSEF MICHAEL KOHL	EHOLOCAUST	DR
GERHARD FRITZ KURT SCHRODER	DERHOCAUST	LO
ANGELA DOROTHEA KASNER MERKEL	DERHOLOAST	CU

HITLER was alone with this monstrous Presentation. It was time to tell Blythe. As I did, I stressed each word, including HITLER's full name. I told her that the actual letters of the German term for Holocaust—DER HOLOCAUST—was in the name of only one German Chancellor—ADOLFUS JACOB HITLER. At first, she looked at me in disbelief. Then disbelief turned to chilling realization. Then tears. She did not look away from me the whole time. Then she said, "Oh, my God . . . Oh, my God! Could it be that all the evil that men do is in their name!"

LEVEL TWO: OVERT PRESENTATION OF HOLOCAUST IN ADOLFUS JACOB HITLER

A—A	A
D	
O—O	O
L—L	L
F	
U—U	U
S—S	S
J	
A	
C—C	C
O—O	O
B	
H—H	H
I	
T—T	T
L	
E	
R	
HOLOCAUST	

It took some time for us to comprehend the full magnitude of this discovery. As we pondered this secret that had just been unearthed, we experienced the most powerful emotions we had felt thus far.

We also acknowledged that the Code not only exists in the English language—but also in the German language. Not that I ever thought for a minute that it could only be found in English—but I had only been investigating the presence of the Code in the English language, thus far, and now I was performing a test in German.

I decided to test the simpler term—HOLOCAUST. Obviously, if ADOLFUS JACOB HITLER has an Overt Presentation of DER HOLOCAUST in his name—he also has a simple Overt Presentation of HOLOCAUST in his name. So, I did a table for HOLOCAUST and ADOLFUS JACOB HITLER.

OVERT PRESENTATIONS OF HOLOCAUST IN THE NAMES OF GERMAN CHANCELLORS

	(PRESENT)	(MISSING)
OTTO EDUARD LEOPOLD	OLOAUT	HCS
GEORG LEO CAPRIVI	OLOCA	HUST
CHLODWIG CARL VIKTOR	HOLOCAT	US
BERNHARD HEINRICH KARL MARTIN VON BULOW	HOLOCAUT	S
THEOBALD THEODOR FRIEDRICH ALFRED VON BETHMANN-HOLLWEG	HOLOCAT	US
GEORG MICHAELIS	HOLCAS	OUT
GEORG FRIEDRICH HERTLING	HOLCT	OAUS
MAXIMILIAN ALEXANDER FRIEDRICH WILHELM	HLCA	OOUST
FRIEDRICH EBERT	HCT	OLOAUS
PHILIPP HENRICH SCHEIDEMANN	HLCAS	OOUT
GUSTAV ADOLF BAUER	OLAUST	HOC
HERMANN MULLER	HLAU	OOCST
CONSTANTIN FEHRENBACH	HOCAST	LOU
KARL JOSEPH WIRTH	HOLAST	OCU
WILHELM CARL JOSEF CUNO	HOLOCAUS	T
GUSTAV STRESEMANN	AUST	HOLOC
HANS LUTHER	HLAUST	OOC
WILHELM MARX	HLA	OOCUST
HEINRICH ALOYSIUS MARIA ELISABETH BRUNING	HOLCAUST	O
FRANZ JOSEPH HERMANN MARIA VON PAPEN	HOOAS	LCUT
KURT FERDINAND FRIEDRICH HERMANN VON SCHLEICHER	HOLCAUST	O
ADOLFUS JACOB HITLER	*****HOLOCAUST*****	
PAUL JOSEPH GOEBBELS	HOLOAUS	CT
JOHANN LUDWIG VON KROSIGK	HOLOAUS	CT
KONRAD HERMANN JOSEPH ADENAUER	HOOAUS	LCT
LUDWIG WILHELM ERHARD	HLAU	OOCST
KURT GEORG KIESINGER	OUST	HLOCA
GEBHARD MULLER	HLAU	OOCST
REINHOLD MAIER	HOLA	OCUST
HERBERT ERNST KARL FRAHM	HLAST	OOCU
WALTER SCHEEL	HLCAST	OOU
HELMUT HENRICH WALDEMAR SCHMIDT	HLCAUST	OO
HELMUT JOSEF MICHAEL KOHL	*****HOLOCAUST*****	**64-YEAR PHEN**
GERHARD FRITZ KURT SCHRODER	HOCAUST	LO
ANGELA DOROTHEA KASNER MERKEL	HOLOAST	CU

Here we see a thorough search of the Chancellors of Germany for an Overt Presentation of HOLOCAUST. It is only found in two names—the name of the evil orchestrator of the HOLOCAUST, ADOLFUS JACOB HITLER, and the 64-Year Phenomenon—HELMUT JOSEF MICHAEL KOHL.

64-YEAR PHENOMENON

LEVEL TWO: OVERT PRESENTATION OF HOLOCAUST IN HELMUT JOSEF MICHAEL KOHL

H—H	H
E	
L—L	L
M	
U—U	U
T—T	T
J	
O—O	O
S—S	S
E	
F	
M	
I	
C—C	C
H	
A—A	A
E	
L	
K	
O—O	O
H	
L	
	HOLOCAUST

HITLER is only joined by HELMUT JOSEF MICHAEL KOHL who is the 64-Year Phenomenon for Germany and the HOLOCAUST. He was still serving as Chancellor during the 64-year anniversary and through the 65-year anniversary of the day ADOLFUS HITLER became the Chancellor of Germany. That day—January 30, 1933—burns in history as the turning point—the defining moment that led to the HOLOCAUST.

LEVEL TWO: COVERT PRESENTATIONS OF **DER HOLOCAUST** IN THE NAMES OF GERMAN CHANCELLORS

	(PRESENT)	(MISSING)
OTTO EDUARD LEOPOLD	DEROLOCAUT	HS
GEORG LEO CAPRIVI	EROLOCA	HUST
CHLODWIG CARL VIKTOR	DERHOLOCAUT	S
GEORGE MICHAELIS	DERHOLCAS	OUT
GEORG FRIEDRICH HERTLING	DERHOLOCT	AUS
FRIEDRICH EBERT	DERHOCT	LOAUS
PHILIPP HENRICH SCHEIDEMANN	DERHLCAUS	OOT
GUSTAV ADOLF BAUER	DEROLOCAUST	H
HERMANN MULLER	DERHLCAU	OOST
CONSTANTINE FEHRENBACH	ERHOLOCAST	DU
KARL JOSEPH WIRTH	ERHOLAST	DOCU
WILHELM CARL JOSEF CANO	DERHOLOCAUS	T
GUSTAV STRESEMANN	DERAUST	HOLOC
HANS LUTHER	ERHLAUST	DOOC
WILHELM MARX	DERHOLCA	OUST
FRANZ JOSEPH HERMANN MARIA VON PAPEN	DERHOOAS	LCUT
ADOLFUS HITLER	***DER HOLOCAUST***	
PAUL JOSEPH GOEBBELS	EHOLOCAUST	DR
JOHANN LUDWIG VON KROSIGK	DERHOLOAUST	C
KONRAD HERMAN JOSEPH ADENAUER	DERHOOAUST	LC
LUDWIG WILHELM ERHARD	DERHLCAU	OOST
KURT GEORGE KIESINGER	EROUST	DHLOCA
GEBHARD MULLER	DERHLCAUT	OOS
REINHOLD MAIER	DERHOLA	OCUST
HERBERT ERNST KARL FRAHM	DERHOLAST	OCU
WALTER SCHEEL	ERHLCAUST	DOO
HELMUT HENRICH WALDEMAR SCHMIDT	DERHLCAUST	OO
HELMUT JOSEF MICHAEL KOHL	***DER HOLOCAUST***	**64-YEAR PHEN**
GERHARD FRITZ KURT SCHRODER	DERHOOCAUST	L
ANGELA DOROTHEA KASNER MERKEL	DERHOLOCAST	U

A search for Level Two Covert Displays of DER HOLOCAUST is equally shocking. Instead of being joined by several other German Chancellors, HITLER is still only joined by HELMUT JOSEF MICHAEL KOHL. But Hitler does not even need his middle name. While KOHL joins him at Level Two, at Level One—ADOLFUS HITLER stands alone.

LEVEL ONE: COVERT PRESENTATION OF **DER HOLOCAUST** IN **ADOLFUS HITLER**		
A—A		A
D—D	D	
O—O		O
L—L		L
F = O		O
U—U		U
S—S		S
H—H		H
I		
T—T		T
L = C		C
E—E	E	
R—R	R	
	DER	**HOLOCAUST**

I now made the move to look at Covert Presentations at Level One. This would mean using only the surname and the most used given name. I examined the name of ADOLFUS HITLER. I was amazed yet again. A Covert Presentation of DER HOLOCAUST uses all but one of the letters of HITLER's name—even without using his middle name. Similar to the two Displays of an "A" left in Abraham Lincoln and the two Displays of "O" left in the name Woodrow Wilson, I was shocked—even after all I had seen—to find that DER HOLOCAUST uses all the letters of ADOLFUS HITLER but one—a single "I." Of course, HITLER was at the very center of DER HOLOCAUST and becoming the Chancellor of Germany was the one defining moment that led to all the occurrences that fall under the umbrella of DER HOLOCAUST. Again, I told Blythe and she gave me an unforgettable look of utter astonishment and horror.

LEVEL TWO: COVERT PRESENTATION OF DER HOLOCAUST IN HELMUT JOSEF MICHAEL KOHL

H—H		H
E—E	E	
L—L		L
M = D	D	
U—U		U
T—T		T
J		
O—O		O
S—S		S
E		
F		
M		
I = R	R	
C—C		C
H—H		
A—A		A
E—E		
L		
K		
O—O		O
H		
L		
	DER	**HOLOCAUST**

HELMUT JOSEF MICHAEL KOHL, who plays the role of the 64-Year Phenomenon for DER HOLOCAUST/HOLOCAUST, not only has a Level Two Covert Presentation of DER HOLOCUAST in his name, but he also has an Overt Presentation of HOLOCAUST in his name.

LEVEL TWO: COVERT PRESENTATIONS OF **HOLOCAUST** IN THE NAMES OF GERMAN CHANCELLORS		
	(PRESENT)	(MISSING)
OTTO EDUARD LEOPOLD	OLOCAUT	HS
GEORG LEO CAPRIVI	OLOCA	HUST
CHLODWIG CARL VIKTOR	HOLOCAUT	S
GEORGE MICHAELIS	HOLCAS	OUT
GEORG FRIEDRICH HERTLING	HOLOCT	AUS
FRIEDRICH EBERT	HOCT	LOAUS
PHILIPP HENRICH SCHEIDEMANN	HLCAS	OOUT
GUSTAV ADOLF BAUER	OLOCAUST	H
HERMANN MULLER	HLCAU	OOST
CONSTANTINE FEHRENBACH	HOLOCAST	U
KARL JOSEPH WIRTH	HOLAST	OCU
WILHELM CARL JOSEF CANO	HOLOCAUS	T
GUSTAV STRESEMANN	AUST	HOLOC
HANS LUTHER	HLAUST	OOC
WILHELM MARX	HOLCA	OUST
FRANZ JOSEPH HERMANN MARIA VON PAPEN	HOOAS	LCUT
ADOLFUS HITLER	***HOLOCAUST***	
PAUL JOSEPH GOEBBELS	***HOLOCAUST***	
JOHANN LUDWIG VON KROSIGK	HOLOAUST	C
KONRAD HERMAN JOSEPH ADENAUER	HOOAUST	LC
LUDWIG WILHELM ERHARD	HLCAU	OOST
KURT GEORGE KIESINGER	OUST	HLOCA
GEBHARD MULLER	HLCAUT	OOS
REINHOLD MAIER	HOLA	OCUST
HERBERT ERNST KARL FRAHM	HOLAST	OCU
WALTER SCHEEL	HLCAUST	OO
HELMUT JOSEF MICHAEL KOHL	***HOLOCAUST***	**64-YEAR PHEN**
HELMUT HENRICH WALDEMAR SCHMIDT	HLCAUST	OO
GERHARD FRITZ KURT SCHRODER	HOOCAUST	L
ANGELA DOROTHEA KASNER MERKEL	HOLOCAST	U

This test examines Level Two Covert Displays of HOLOCAUST for all the other German Chancellors. HITLER's name is listed without his middle name to show that, covertly, HOLOCAUST is found in just his first and last name. Look who joins him in having a Covert Presentation of HOLOCAUST.

Special Note: Five names have been excluded for length of name. Exclusions are explained in Appendix B.

PAUL JOSEPH GOEBBELS

> PAUL JOSEPH GOEBBELS (1897 - 1945) was the Minister of Propaganda in Nazi Germany from 1933 to 1945 and Chancellor of Germany for one day—from April 30, 1945, to May 1, 1945. Early in his life he considered becoming a priest and later he aspired to be an author. He attended the University of Heidelberg in pursuit of a doctoral degree in philology. He asked a retiring Jewish professor to supervise his doctoral thesis, but that professor recommended another Jewish professor who supervised his thesis. So, he earned his PhD in philology in 1921 under the supervision of a Jew. In 1922, he began a five-year romance with a half-Jewish schoolteacher. Goebbels joined the Nazi Party in 1924 and he quickly rose in the Party. In 1933, he was given the role of Propaganda Minister because of his strong anti-Semitism and his abilities at public speaking. As of 1933, his Propaganda Ministry dominated the news media. Goebbels is known as one of the first to advocate for the Holocaust. He became Hitler's closest and most trusted confidant. As the war came to an end, Hitler wrote a last will and testament that made Goebbels the Chancellor if he should die. So, at the time of Hitler's alleged suicide, Goebbels took his position as Chancellor, which he held for just one day. His biographies report that the next day Goebbels and his wife murdered their six children with cyanide and committed suicide. Biographies also state that the exact details of the Goebbels' deaths are in serious dispute.

PAUL JOSEPH GOEBBELS was the Minister of Propaganda from 1933 until 1945 and one of the first to recommend the HOLOCAUST. His propaganda promoted HITLER and anti-Semitism. He was Chancellor of Germany for just one day.

COVERT PRESENTATION OF HOLOCAUST IN PAUL JOSEPH GOEBBELS

P	
A—A	A
U—U	U
L—L	L
J	
O—O	O
S—S	S
E	
P	
H—H	H
G	
O—O	O
E	
B = T	T
B	
E	
L = C	C
S	
	HOLOCAUST

As I conducted the search of the names of the German Chancellors for Covert Presentations of HOLOCAUST, I had no idea what to expect. Would HITLER remain almost exclusive, only joined by KOHL because of the 64-Year Phenomenon? As I went through the names, eliminating those with twenty-nine letters or more, I was not finding anyone as I approached the name of HITLER. I wondered if I would find any new names after him. The very next name after HITLER's really jumped out at me. I saw the name PAUL JOSEPH GOEBBELS and there it was—the word HOLOCAUST. I still consider it one of the most chilling revelations I experienced during my journey.

Summary of Evidence Supporting the Claims: HOLOCAUST and DER HOLOCAUST in the names of German Chancellors

Claim 1—
ADOLFUS JACOB HITLER, the Fuhrer of the Third Reich, who played the most central role in the HOLOCAUST/DER HOLOCAUST, has the only Overt Presentation of HOLOCAUST and, in fact, of DER HOLOCAUST. He also has the only Level One Covert Presentation of DER HOLOCAUST. In all, he has four Superior Presentations.

Claim 2—
The 64-Year Phenomenon: HELMUT JOSEF MICHAEL KOHL, who began to serve as German Chancellor approximately 64 years after a major turning point in the HOLOCAUST, has an Overt Presentation of HOLOCAUST and a Covert Presentation of DER HOLOCAUST in his name.

Claim 3—
Both German Chancellors with a strong involvement in or association with the HOLOCAUST have a Presentation of HOLOCAUST and/or DER HOLOCAUST in their names. These are ADOLFUS JACOB HITLER and PAUL JOSEPH GOEBBELS.

THE PROBABILITY OF GEORGE WASHINGTON AND GEORGE III WILLIAM FREDERICK BEING THE ONLY PRESIDENT AND MONARCH DURING THE AMERICAN WAR OF INDEPENDENCE AND HAVING EXCLUSIVE AND CORRECT DISPLAYS OF AWOI IN THEIR NAMES

AND

ABRAHAM LINCOLN, HIRAM ULYSSES GRANT, RUTHERFORD BIRCHARD HAYES, HERBERT CLARK HOOVER, WILLIAM JEFFERSON BLYTHE III, BARACK HUSSEIN OBAMA II AND WILLIAM HOWARD TAFT, AT LEVEL TWO, HAVING EXCLUSIVE AND CORRECT DISPLAYS OF THE CIVIL WAR IN THEIR NAMES

AND

WOODROW WILSON, THEODORE ROOSEVELT, FRANKLIN ROOSEVELT, WILLIAM HOWARD TAFT, JOHN CALVIN COOLIDGE, HERBERT CLARK HOOVER AND RONALD WILSON REAGAN HAVING EXCLUSIVE AND CORRECT DISPLAYS OF WORLD WAR ONE/WWI IN THEIR NAMES

AND

FRANKLIN ROOSEVELT, HERBERT HOOVER, DWIGHT DAVID EISENHOWER, JOHN FITZGERALD KENNEDY, RICHARD MILHAUS NIXON AND BARACK HUSSEIN OBAMA II HAVING EXCLUSIVE AND CORRECT DISPLAYS OF WORLD WAR TWO/WWII IN THEIR NAMES

AND

DAVID LLOYD GEORGE I, ANDREW BONAR LAW I, WINSTON LEONARD CHURCHILL, MAURICE HAROLD MACMILLAN AND MARGARET HILDA ROBERTS THATCHER HAVING EXCLUSIVE AND CORRECT DISPLAYS OF WORLD WAR ONE/WWI/WORLD WAR I/FIRST WORLD WAR IN THEIR NAMES

AND

WINSTON LEONARD CHURCHILL AND DONALD WILLIAM DAVID CAMERON HAVING EXCLUSIVE AND CORRECT DISPLAYS OF WORLD WAR TWO/WWII/WORLD WAR II/SECOND WORLD WAR IN THEIR NAMES

AND

KING GEORGE V FREDERICK ERNEST ALBERT AND QUEEN ELIZABETH II ALEXANDRA MARY WINDSOR HAVING EXCLUSIVE AND CORRECT DISPLAYS OF WORLD WAR I IN THEIR NAMES

AND

KING ALBERT FREDERICK ARTHUR GEORGE VI AND QUEEN ELIZABETH II ALEXANDRA MARY WINDSOR HAVING EXCLUSIVE AND CORRECT DISPLAYS OF WORLD WAR TWO IN THEIR NAMES

AND

ADOLFUS JACOB HITLER, PAUL JOSEPH GOEBBELS AND HELMUT JOSEF MICHAEL KOHL HAVING EXCLUSIVE AND CORRECT DISPLAYS OF HOLOCAUST AND/OR DER HOLOCAUST IN THEIR NAMES IS:

1
IN
4,335,000,000,000,000,000,000,000,000

(ONE IN 4 OCTILLION, 335 SEXTILLION)

I had already experienced seeing perfect or near perfect results throughout all the investigations I had conducted. So, it was not that I was expecting anything less when I examined the German Chancellors and the Holocaust. Yet, when the names appeared, I was aghast and struck with shock and horror that the name of such an atrocity should appear in the most evil of names ever spoken. I had real shivers and goose bumps as I found the actual letters of DER HOLOCAUST in the name of ADOLFUS JACOB HITLER.

I experienced the same feeling again when I found that HITLER was alone with the Overt Presentation, and again, when I found he was alone with a Covert Presentation at Level One, and again, when I found HOLOCUAST in the name PAUL JOSEPH GOEBBELS. And the goose bumps came back when I discovered that when the Covert Presentation is removed from HITLER's name, there is only one letter—an "I" that is left in his name. There is no way to communicate what a dark and yet compelling moment this was for me.

Reflecting on the finding that the name ADOLFUS HITLER is permeated with the words DER HOLOCAUST made me once again think about the discovery that the Code is also in the German language. So, now I pondered, "What if there is a secret code in most or, even, all languages?" The whole idea was startling. And the implications were unfathomable.

I was not prepared for my next discovery.

DER HOLOCAUST AND THE PRIME MINISTERS OF THE UNITED KINGDOM

"I have nothing to offer but blood, toil, tears and sweat."

"History will be kind to me for I intend to write it."

Winston Churchill

WINSTON LEONARD SPENCER-CHURCHILL

SIR WINSTON LEONARD SPENCER-CHURCHILL (1874 - 1965) was a supporter of the Balfour Declaration, written by his friend and colleague, Arthur Balfour, which promised support for the Zionist movement. Before the Second World War, to defend the Jews, he called for boycotts against Nazi Germany for their persecution of Jews. During his first term as Prime Minister of the United Kingdom (1940 - 1945), he chose to resist Hitler. In doing so, he may have been the world leader who did the most to stop Hitler, to save the Jews from complete annihilation, and to save the world from Nazi Germany. In his book *Churchill and the Jews: A Lifelong Friendship*, Martin Gilbert, the great Churchill biographer, describes Churchill as a defender of Zionism, a strong opponent of anti-Semitism, an advocate of boycotts against Nazi Germany, the leader to first resist Hitler and one of the leaders of the Allies who did stop Hitler and the Holocaust. Winston Leonard Churchill was truly, as Gilbert's subtitle suggests, a lifelong friend of the Jews.

OVERT PRESENTATION OF DER HOLOCAUST IN WINSTON LEONARD CHURCHILL

Letter	DER	HOLOCAUST
W		
I		
N		
S—S		S
T—T		T
O—O		O
N		
L—L		L
E—E	E	
O—O		O
N		
A—A		A
R—R	R	
D—D	D	
C		
H—H		H
U—U		U
R		
C—C		C
H		
I		
L		
L		
	DER	**HOLOCAUST**

One day soon after I had performed the tests with HITLER's name, I thought of the role that WINSTON CHURCHILL played in stopping HITLER and—some say—in saving the world. I was walking toward a bookstore at a large shopping mall. It suddenly occurred to me to look for the actual letters of DER HOLOCAUST in the name WINSTON LEONARD CHURCHILL. As previously mentioned, DER is German, and so DER HOLOCAUST is the common German term for the HOLOCAUST. So, I thought, what if the German term was found in the name of their biggest enemy? I solved it in my head—by now I was quite adept at the process—and there it was!

OVERT PRESENTATIONS OF **DER HOLOCAUST** IN THE PRIME MINISTERS OF THE U.K.

	(PRESENT)	(MISSING)
WILLIAM PITT II	LAT	DERHOOCUS
HENRY ADDINGTON	DERHOAT	LOCUS
WILLIAM WYNDHAM GRENVILLE	DERHLA	OOCUST
WILLIAM HENRY CAVENDISH CAVENDISH-BENTINCK	DERHLCAST	OOU
SPENCER PERCEVAL I	ERLCAS	DHOOUT
ROBERT BANKS JENKINSON	EROOAST	DHLCU
GEORGE CANNING JNR	EROCA	DHLOUST
FREDERICK JOHN ROBINSON	DERHOOCS	LAUT
ARTHUR WELLESLEY	ERHLAUST	DOOC
CHARLES GREY II	ERHLCAS	DOOUT
HENRY WILLIAM LAMB	ERHLA	DOOCUST
ROBERT PEEL II	EROLT	DHOCAUS
JOHN RUSSELL II	ERHOLUS	DOCAT
EDWARD GEORGE GEOFFREY SMITH-STANLEY	DERHOLOAST	CU
GEORGE HAMILTON-GORDON	DERHOLOAT	CUS
HENRY JOHN TEMPLE	ERHOLT	DOCAUS
BENJAMIN DISRAELI	DERLAS	HOOCUT
WILLIAM EWART GLADSTONE	DEROLAST	HOCU
ARCHIBALD PHILIP PRIMROSE	DERHOLCAS	OUT
ROBERT ARTHUR TALBOT GASCOYNE-CECIL	ERHOLOCAUST	D
ARTHUR JAMES BALFOUR	ERHOLAUST	DOC
HENRY CAMPBELL	ERHLCA	DOOUST
HERBERT HENRY ASQUITH	ERHAUST	DOLOC
DAVID LLOYD GEORGE I	DEROLOA	HCUST
ANDREW BONAR LAW I	DEROLA	HOCUST

OVERT PRESENTATIONS OF **DER HOLOCAUST** IN THE PRIME MINISTERS OF THE U.K.

	(PRESENT)	(MISSING)
STANLEY BALDWIN	DELAST	RHOOCU
JAMES RAMSAY MACDONALD	DEROLCAS	HOUT
ARTHUR NEVILLE CHAMBERLAIN	ERHLCAUT	DOOS
WINSTON LEONARD CHURCHILL	***DER HOLOCAUST***	
CLEMENT RICHARD ATTLEE	DERHLCAT	OOUS
ROBERT ANTHONY EDEN	DERHOOAT	LCUS
MAURICE HAROLD MACMILLAN	DERHOLCAU	OST
ALEXANDER FREDERICK DOUGLAS-HOME	DERHOLOCAUS	T
JAMES HAROLD WILSON	DERHOLOAS	CUT
EDWARD RICHARD GEORGE HEATH	DERHOCAT	LOUS
LEONARD JAMES CALLAGHAN	DERHOLCAS	OUT
MARGARET HILDA ROBERTS THATCHER	DERHOLCAST	OU
JOHN ROY MAJOR	RHOOA	DELCUST
ANTHONY CHARLES LYNTON BLAIR	ERHOLOCAST	DU
JAMES GORDON BROWN	DEROOAS	HLCUT
DAVID WILLIAM DONALD CAMERON	DEROLOCA	HUST
THERESA MARY BRASIER MAY	ERHAST	DOLOCU
ALEXANDER BORIS DE PFEFFEL JOHNSON	HOLOAS	CUT

I turned around, went back to my car and rushed home, naturally while obeying the speed limit and all other relevant traffic laws. I went immediately to my notebooks and started scribbling names. He alone among all the British Prime Ministers had the actual letters of DER HOLOCAUST in his name. I rushed to tell Blythe. I asked her, "Do you know what world leader did the most to stop Hitler?" "Roosevelt?" "No." "Churchill?" "Yes." She gasped and said, "Don't tell me! "HOLOCAUST?" "Yes. DER HOLOCAUST." Then she asked, "Is he alone with the words?" "Yes."

COVERT PRESENTATIONS OF **DER HOLOCAUST** IN THE PRIME MINISTERS OF THE U.K.

	(PRESENT)	(MISSING)
WILLIAM PITT II	DERLCAT	HOOUS
HENRY ADDINGTON	DERHOAT	LOCUS
WILLIAM HENRY CAVENDISH CAVENDISH-BENTINCK	DERHLCAUST	OO
WILLIAM WYNDHAM GRENVILLE	DERHLHAUS	OOT
SPENCER PERCEVAL I	DERLCAUS	HOOT
ROBERT BANKS JENKINSON	EROOAST	DHLCU
GEORGE CANNING JNR	EROCAS	DHLOUT
FREDERICK JOHN ROBINSON	DERHOOCAST	LU
ARTHUR WELLESLEY	ERHLCAUST	DOO
CHARLES GREY II	ERHLCAS	DOOUT
HENRY WILLIAM LAMB	DERHLCAUST	OO
ROBERT PEEL II	EROLT	DHOCAUS
JOHN RUSSELL II	ERHOLCAUS	DOT
EDWARD GEORGE GEOFFREY SMITH-STANLEY	DERHOLOAST	CU
GEORGE HAMILTON-GORDON	DERHOLOAT	CUS
HENRY JOHN TEMPLE	DERHOLAT	OCUS
BENJAMIN DISRAELI	DERLAST	HOOCU
WILLIAM EWART GLADSTONE	DEROLCAUST	HO
ARCHIBALD PHILIP PRIMROSE	DERHOLCAUST	O
ROBERT ARTHUR TALBOT GASCOYNE-CECIL	ERHOLOCAUST	D

COVERT PRESENTATIONS OF **DER HOLOCAUST** IN THE PRIME MINISTERS OF THE U.K.

	(PRESENT)	(MISSING)
ARTHUR JAMES BALFOUR	***DER HOLOCAUST***	
HENRY CAMPBELL	DERHLCAUT	OOS
HERBERT HENRY ASQUITH	ERHAUST	DOLOC
DAVID LLOYD GEORGE I	DEROLOCA	HUST
ANDREW BONAR LAW I	DEROLAST	HOCU
STANLEY BALDWIN	DERLCAST	HOOU
JAMES RAMSAY MACDONALD	DEROLCAS	HOUT
ARTHUR NEVILLE CHAMBERLAIN	DERHLCAUST	OO
WINSTON LEONARD CHURCHILL	***DER HOLOCAUST***	
CLEMENT RICHARD ATTLEE	DERHLAUST	OO
ROBERT ANTHONY EDEN	DERHOOAT	LCUS
MAURICE HAROLD MACMILLAN	DERHOLCAUS	OT
ALEXANDER FREDERICK DOUGLAS-HOME	(((DER HOLOCAUST)))	
JAMES HAROLD WILSON	DERHOLOCAS	UT
EDWARD RICHARD GEORGE HEATH	DERHOCAST	LOU
LEONARD JAMES CALLAGHAN	DERHOLCAS	OT
MARGARET HILDA ROBERTS THATCHER	DERHOLCAST	OU
JOHN ROY MAJOR	DRHOOAS	ELCUT
ANTHONY CHARLES LYNTON BLAIR	ERHOLOCAUST	D
JAMES GORDON BROWN	DEROOAST	HLCU
DAVID WILLIAM DONALD CAMERON	DEROLOCAUS	HT
THERESA MARY BRASIER MAY	DERHAST	OLOCU
ALEXANDER BORIS DE PFEFFEL JOHNSON	DERHOLOCAST	U

WINSTON LEONARD CHURCHILL was the one who could be said to have done the most to stop HITLER. After finding an Overt Presentation of DER HOLOCAUST in his name, I extended the search and looked for Covert Presentations in the names of British Prime Ministers. Of course, we have letter restrictions.

We find a Covert Presentation of DER HOLOCAUST in the name WINSTON LEONARD CHURCHILL. He is joined by ARTHUR JAMES BALFOUR, the author of the Balfour Declaration that declared British support for the Jewish Zionist Movement.

ARTHUR JAMES BALFOUR

ARTHUR JAMES BALFOUR (1848 - 1930) was a British statesman who held many positions in the United Kingdom, including Prime Minister. Perhaps the most important impact Balfour had on the world came from a public announcement he made in the form of a letter to Baron Rothschild and the Zionist Federation of Great Britain and Ireland—known as the Balfour Declaration. In the document, Balfour expresses support for the Zionists and the Jewish people in the establishment of a home for the Jewish people in Palestine. The document would become of great importance in the world, in the history of the Jewish people and in the creation of the State of Israel.

> Foreign Office,
> November 2nd, 1917.
>
> Dear Lord Rothschild,
>
> I have much pleasure in conveying to you, on behalf of His Majesty's Government, the following declaration of sympathy with Jewish Zionist aspirations which has been submitted to, and approved by, the Cabinet
>
> "His Majesty's Government view with favour the establishment in Palestine of a national home for the Jewish people, and will use their best endeavours to facilitate the achievement of this object, it being clearly understood that nothing shall be done which may prejudice the civil and religious rights of existing non-Jewish communities in Palestine, or the rights and political status enjoyed by Jews in any other country"
>
> I should be grateful if you would bring this declaration to the knowledge of the Zionist Federation.
>
> *[signature: Arthur James Balfour]*

This document became a strong inspiration and motivating factor to the Jewish diaspora. It was core to the British Mandate for Palestine and the founding document of Mandatory Palestine, which would become Israel and the Palestinian territories. It also became one of the causes of Israeli-Palestinian conflict. Chaim Weizmann called it the "'unique act of the world moral conscience,'" and Sir Isaiah Berlin called it the "'greatest event in Jewish history since the destruction of Judaea.'" Some historians believe that the Holocaust played a major role in prompting world condemnation of anti-Semitism and that the Balfour Declaration played an important part in nurturing growing support for a Jewish homeland. Both were significant organizing factors in the establishment of the State of Israel.

OVERT PRESENTATIONS OF **HOLOCAUST** IN THE PRIME MINISTERS OF THE U.K.

	(PRESENT)	(MISSING)
WILLIAM PITT II	LAT	HOOCUS
HENRY ADDINGTON	HOAT	LOCUS
WILLIAM WYNDHAM GRENVILLE	HLA	OOCUST
SPENCER PERCEVAL I	LCAS	HOOUT
ROBERT BANKS JENKINSON	OOAST	HLCU
GEORGE CANNING JNR	OCA	HLOUST
FREDERICK JOHN ROBINSON	HOOCS	LAUT
ARTHUR WELLESLEY	HLAUST	OOC
CHARLES GREY II	HLCAS	OOUT
HENRY WILLIAM LAMB	HLA	OOCUST
ROBERT PEEL II	OLT	HOCAUS
JOHN RUSSELL II	HOLUS	OCAT
GEORGE HAMILTON-GORDON	HOLOAT	CUS
HENRY JOHN TEMPLE	HOLT	OCAUS
BENJAMIN DISRAELI	LAS	HOOCUT
WILLIAM EWART GLADSTONE	OLAST	HOCU
ARCHIBALD PHILIP PRIMROSE	HOLCAS	OUT
ARTHUR JAMES BALFOUR	HOLAUST	OC
HENRY CAMPBELL	HLCA	OOUST
HERBERT HENRY ASQUITH	HAUST	OLOC

OVERT PRESENTATIONS OF **HOLOCAUST** IN THE PRIME MINISTERS OF THE U.K.

	(PRESENT)	(MISSING)
DAVID LLOYD GEORGE I	OLOA	HCUST
ANDREW BONAR LAW I	OLA	HOCUST
STANLEY BALDWIN	LAST	HOOCU
JAMES RAMSAY MACDONALD	OLCAS	HOUT
ARTHUR NEVILLE CHAMBERLAIN	HLCAUT	OOS
WINSTON LEONARD CHURCHILL	***HOLOCAUST***	
CLEMENT RICHARD ATLEE	HLCAT	OOUS
ROBERT ANTHONY EDEN	HOOAT	LCUS
MAURICE HAROLD MACMILLAN	HOLCAU	OST
ALEXANDER FREDERICK DOUGLAS-HOME	HOLOCAUS	T
JAMES HAROLD WILSON	HOLOAS	CUT
EDWARD RICHARD GEORGE HEATH	HOCAT	LOUS
LEONARD JAMES CALLAGHAN	HOLCAS	OUT
MARGARET HILDA ROBERTS THATCHER	HOLAST	OCU
JOHN ROY MAJOR	HOOA	LUST
ANTHONY CHARLES LYNTON BLAIR	JOLOCAST	U
JAMES GORDON BROWN	OOAS	HLCUT
DAVID WILLIAM DONALD CAMERON	OLOCA	HUST
THERESA MARY BRASIER MAY	HAST	OLOCU
ALEXANDER BORIS DE PFEFFEL JOHNSON	HOLOAS	CUT

I knew that WINSTON LEONARD CHURCHILL would have an Overt Presentation of HOLOCAUST in his name, as he had DER HOLOCAUST. But I was surprised to see that he remained alone with an Overt Presentation of HOLOCAUST.

COVERT PRESENTATIONS OF **HOLOCAUST** IN THE PRIME MINISTERS OF THE U.K.

	(PRESENT)	(MISSING)
WILLIAM PITT II	LCAT	HOOUS
HENRY ADDINGTON	HOAT	LOCUS
WILLIAM WYNDHAM GRENVILLE	HLCAUS	OOT
SPENCER PERCEVAL I	LCAUS	HOOT
ROBERT BANKS JENKINSON	OOAST	HLCU
GEORGE CANNING JNR	OCA	HLOUST
FREDERICK JOHN ROBINSON	HOOCAST	LU
ARTHUR WELLESLEY	HLCAUST	OO
CHARLES GREY	HLCAS	OOUT
HENRY WILLIAM LAMB	DERHLCAUST	OO
ROBERT PEEL II	OLT	HOCAUS
JOHN RUSSELL II	HOLCAUS	OT
GEORGE HAMILTON-GORDON	HOLOAT	CUS
HENRY JOHN TEMPLE	HOLAT	OCUS
BENJAMIN DISRAELI	LAST	HOOCU
WILLIAM EWART GLADSTONE	OLCAUST	HO
ARCHIBALD PHILIP PRIMROSE	HOLCAUST	O

COVERT PRESENTATIONS OF **HOLOCAUST** IN THE PRIME MINISTERS OF THE U.K.

	(PRESENT)	(MISSING)
ARTHUR JAMES BALFOUR	***HOLOCAUST***	
HENRY CAMPBELL	HLCAUT	OOS
HERBERT HENRY ASQUITH	HAUST	OLOC
DAVID LLOYD GEORGE I	OLOCA	HUST
ANDREW BONAR LAW I	OLAST	HOCU
STANLEY BALDWIN	LCAST	HOOU
JAMES RAMSAY MACDONALD	OLCAS	HOUT
ARTHUR NEVILLE CHAMBERLAIN	HLCAUST	OO
WINSTON LEONARD CHURCHILL	***HOLOCAUST***	
CLEMENT RICHARD ATTLEE	HLCAUST	OO
ROBERT ANTHONY EDEN	HOOAT	LCUS
MAURICE HAROLD MACMILLAN	HOLCAUS	OT
ALEXANDER FREDERICK DOUGLAS-HOME	(((HOLOCAUST)))	
JAMES HAROLD WILSON	HOLOCAS	UT
EDWARD RICHARD GEORGE HEATH	HOCAST	LOU
LEONARD JAMES CALLAGHAN	HOLCAUS	OT
MARGARET HILDA ROBERTS THATCHER	HOLAST	OCU
JOHN ROY MAJOR	HOOAS	LCUT
ANTHONY CHARLES LYNTON BLAIR	***HOLOCAUST***	64-YEAR PHEN
JAMES GORDON BROWN	OOAST	HLCU
DAVID WILLIAM DONALD CAMERON	OLOCAUS	HT
THERESA MARY BRASIER MAY	HAST	OLOCU
ALEXANDER BORIS DE PFEFFEL JOHNSON	HOLOCAST	U

WINSTON LEONARD CHURCHILL and ARTHUR JAMES BALFOUR have Covert Presentations of HOLOCAUST in their names. They are joined by ANTHONY CHARLES LYNTON BLAIR—the 64-Year Phenomenon.

64-YEAR PHENOMENON

COVERT PRESENTATION OF **HOLOCAUST** IN **ANTHONY CHARLES LYNTON BLAIR**

A—A	A
N	
T	
H—H	H
O—O	O
N	
Y	
C—C	C
H	
A	
R	
L = U	U
E	
S—S	S
L—L	L
Y	
N	
T—T	T
O—O	O
N	
B	
L	
A	
I	
R	
	HOLOCAUST

ANTHONY CHARLES LYNTON BLAIR is the 64-Year Phenomenon for the HOLOCAUST and the UNITED KINGDOM. Here we see that he has HOLOCAUST in his name.

Summary of Evidence Supporting the Claims: HOLOCAUST and DER HOLOCAUST in the names of British Prime Ministers

Claim 1_
WINSTON LEONARD CHURCHILL, the British Prime Minister who played the most central role in putting an end to HITLER and the HOLOCAUST, or DER HOLOCAUST, has the only Overt Presentation of DER HOLOCAUST in a complete list of all the Prime Ministers of the United Kingdom. He has, without a doubt, the Superior Presentation.

Claim 2_
The 64-Year Phenomenon: ANTHONY CHARLES LYNTON BLAIR has a Covert Presentation of HOLOCAUST in his name.

Claim 3_
The British Prime Ministers with the strongest involvement in or association with the HOLOCAUST have a Presentation of HOLOCAUST and/or DER HOLOCAUST in their names. WINSTON LEONARD CHURCHILL has an Overt Presentation of HOLOCAUST and an Overt Presentation of DER HOLOCAUST in his name. ARTHUR JAMES BALFOUR, who wrote the Balfour Declaration, has Covert Presentations of HOLOCAUST and DER HOLOCAUST in his name.

THE PROBABILITY OF GEORGE WASHINGTON AND GEORGE III WILLIAM FREDERICK HAVING EXCLUSIVE AND CORRECT DISPLAYS OF AWOI IN THEIR NAMES

AND

ABRAHAM LINCOLN, HIRAM ULYSSES GRANT, RUTHERFORD BIRCHARD HAYES, HERBERT CLARK HOOVER, WILLIAM JEFFERSON BLYTHE III, BARACK HUSSEIN OBAMA II AND WILLIAM HOWARD TAFT, AT LEVEL TWO, HAVING EXCLUSIVE AND CORRECT DISPLAYS OF THE CIVIL WAR IN THEIR NAMES

AND

THOMAS WOODROW WILSON, THEODORE ROOSEVELT, FRANKLIN ROOSEVELT, WILLIAM HOWARD TAFT, JOHN CALVIN COOLIDGE, HERBERT CLARK HOOVER AND RONALD WILSON REAGAN HAVING EXCLUSIVE AND CORRECT DISPLAYS OF WORLD WAR ONE/WWI/FIRST WORLD WAR IN THEIR NAMES

AND

FRANKLIN ROOSEVELT, HERBERT HOOVER, DWIGHT DAVID EISENHOWER, JOHN FITZGERALD KENNEDY, RICHARD MILHAUS NIXON AND BARACK HUSSEIN OBAMA II HAVING EXCLUSIVE AND CORRECT DISPLAYS OF WORLD WAR TWO/WWII/WORLD WAR II/SECOND WORLD WAR IN THEIR NAMES

AND

DAVID LLOYD GEORGE I, ANDREW BONAR LAW I, WINSTON LEONARD CHURCHILL, MAURICE HAROLD MACMILLAN AND MARGARET HILDA ROBERTS THATCHER HAVING EXCLUSIVE AND CORRECT DISPLAYS OF WORLD WAR ONE/WWI/WORLD WAR I/FIRST WORLD WAR IN THEIR NAMES

AND

WINSTON LEONARD CHURCHILL AND DONALD DAVID WILLIAM CAMERON HAVING EXCLUSIVE AND CORRECT DISPLAYS OF WORLD WAR ONE/WWI/WORLD WAR I/FIRST WORLD WAR IN THEIR NAMES

AND

KING GEORGE V FREDERICK ERNEST ALBERT AND QUEEN ELIZABETH II ALEXANDRA MARY WINDSOR HAVING EXCLUSIVE AND CORRECT DISPLAYS OF WORLD WAR I IN THEIR NAMES

AND

KING ALBERT FREDERICK ARTHUR GEORGE VI AND QUEEN ELIZABETH II ALEXANDRA MARY WINDSOR HAVING EXCLUSIVE AND CORRECT DISPLAYS OF WORLD WAR TWO IN THEIR NAMES

AND

ADOLFUS JACOB HITLER, PAUL JOSEPH GOEBBELS AND HEMUT JOSEF MICHAEL KOHL HAVING EXCLUSIVE AND CORRECT DISPLAYS OF HOLOCAUST/DER HOLOCAUST IN THEIR NAMES

AND

WINSTON LEONARD CHURCHILL, ARTHUR JAMES BALFOUR AND ANTHONY CHARLES LYNTON BLAIR HAVING EXCLUSIVE AND CORRECT DISPLAYS OF HOLOCAUST/DER HOLOCAUST IN THEIR NAMES IS:

1
IN
8,803,000,000,000,000,000,000,000,000

(ONE IN OVER 8 OCTILLION, 803 SEPTILLION)

Just as the Code had predicted ADOLFUS HITLER to be the central evil perpetrator of the HOLOCAUST, the Code had also predicted that WINSTON CHURCHILL would be the individual who would most resist him and stop him. Although I knew it to be true, the Code was too perfect for me to believe.

At this point the rigorous investigations for the book were coming to an end, but I had one more test to complete. This next test was unnecessary, due to the fact that WINSTON CHURCHILL satisfies the rules for DER HOLOCAUST and the Three Claims have been supported by what I have consistently found throughout my investigations. Nonetheless, I still wanted to see if I would find DER HOLOCAUST in the name of the one Monarch who dined with Churchill throughout the war and, who served as King throughout the time of the HOLOCAUST. So, I decided to look.

This was it—the final inquiry! And I just had to see it.

DER HOLOCAUST AND THE BRITISH MONARCHS

COVERT PRESENTATION OF DER HOLOCAUST IN ALBERT FREDERICK ARTHUR GEORGE VI

A—A		A
L—L		L
B		
E—E	E	
R—R	R	
T—T		T
F = O		O
R		
E		
D—D	D	
E		
R		
I		
C—C		C
K		
A = S		S
R		
T		
H—H		H
U—U		U
R		
G		
E		
O--O		O
R		
G		
E		
	DER	**HOLOCAUST**

ALBERT FREDERICK ARTHUR GEORGE VI served as the Monarch of the United Kingdom during the HOLOCAUST and his name does contain a Covert Presentation of DER HOLOCAUST.

COVERT PRESENTATIONS OF **DER HOLOCAUST** IN THE NAMES OF BRITISH MONARCHS		
	(PRESENT)	(MISSING)
WILLIAM III	DELCA	RHOOUST
GEORGE LOUIS	EROLOAUS	DHCT
GEORGE II AUGUSTUS	EROLCAUST	DHO
GEORGE III WILLIAM FREDERICK	DEROLOCAUT	HS
GEORGE IV AUGUSTUS FREDERICK	DEROLOCAUST	H
WILLIAM IV HENRY	DERHLCA	OOUST
ALEXANDRINA VICTORIA	DEROLOCAST	HU
ALBERT EDWARD VII	DERLAST	HOOCU
GEORGE V FREDERICK ERNEST ALBERT	DEROLOCAST	HU
EDWARD VIII ALBERT CHRISTIAN GEORGE ANDREW PATRICK DAVID	DEROLCAST	HOU
ALBERT FREDERICK ARTHUR GEORGE VI	***DER HOLOCAUST***	
ELIZABETH II ALEXANDRA MARY WINDSOR	DERHOLOCAST	U

Among the British Monarchs, we find that the final results support the Three Claims. King ALBERT FREDERICK ARTHUR GEORGE VI, who appointed CHURCHILL Prime Minister and who was King during WORLD WAR TWO and during the HOLOCAUST, does, in fact, share a Covert Presentation of DER HOLOCAUST with WINSTON CHURCHILL. He is alone among all of the British Monarchs; ALBERT FREDERICK ARTHUR GEORGE VI has an exclusive Presentation of DER HOLOCAUST. A 64-Year Phenomenon for the British has already been satisfied by Prime Minister ANTHONY CHARLES LYNTON BLAIR.

On the other hand, just as I did not test for THE GREAT WAR, I did not test for SHOAH—the other term for the HOLOCAUST. If I had, we would have found an Overt Presentation of SHOAH in both WINSTON LEONARD CHURCHILL and ANTHONY CHARLES LYNTON BLAIR, and we would have found further support for Claim 2 with the finding of an exclusive Covert Presentation among the British Monarchs in the name ELIZABETH II ALEXANDRIA MARY WINDSOR.

Summary of Evidence Supporting the Claims: HOLOCAUST and DER HOLOCAUST in the names of the British Monarchs

Claim 1_
ALBERT FREDERICK ARTHUR GEORGE VI, the King of the United Kingdom during the HOLOCAUST/DER HOLOCAUST and the King who appointed WINSTON LEONARD CHURCHILL Prime Minister, is the only British Monarch to contain the Covert Presentations of HOLOCAUST and DER HOLOCAUST in his name.

Claim 2_
The 64-Year Phenomenon:* ANTHONY CHARLES LYNTON BLAIR, who was Prime Minister approximately 64 years after a major turning point in the HOLOCAUST, already suffices for the 64-Year Phenomenon of DER HOLOCAUST for the British.

Claim 3_
ALBERT FREDERICK ARTHUR GEORGE VI, the only British Monarch involved in and associated with the HOLOCAUST/DER HOLOCAUST, has Covert Presentations of HOLOCAUST and DER HOLOCAUST in his name.

*ELIZABETH II ALEXANDRIA MARY WINDSOR has an exclusive Covert Presentation of SHOAH—the alternative term for the HOLOCAUST—in her name. As she does qualify as the 64-Year Phenomenon among the British Monarchs, she does give further support for Claim 1.

THE PROBABILITY OF GEORGE WASHINGTON AND GEORGE III WILLIAM FREDERICK HAVING EXCLUSIVE AND CORRECT DISPLAYS OF AWOI IN THEIR NAMES

AND

ABRAHAM LINCOLN, HIRAM ULYSSES GRANT, RUTHERFORD BIRCHARD HAYES, HERBERT CLARK HOOVER, WILLIAM JEFFERSON BLYTHE III, BARACK HUSSEIN OBAMA II AND WILLIAM HOWARD TAFT, AT LEVEL TWO, HAVING EXCLUSIVE AND CORRECT DISPLAYS OF THE CIVIL WAR IN THEIR NAMES

AND

WOODROW WILSON, THEODORE ROOSEVELT, FRANKLIN ROOSEVELT, WILLIAM HOWARD TAFT, JOHN CALVIN COOLIDGE, HERBERT CLARK HOOVER AND RONALD WILSON REAGAN HAVING EXCLUSIVE AND CORRECT DISPLAYS OF WORLD WAR ONE/WWI IN THEIR NAMES

AND

FRANKLIN ROOSEVELT, HERBERT CLARK HOOVER, DWIGHT DAVID EISENHOWER, JOHN FITZGERALD KENNEDY, RICHARD MILHAUS NIXON AND BARACK HUSSEIN OBAMA II HAVING EXCLUSIVE AND CORRECT DISPLAYS OF WORLD WAR TWO/WWII IN THEIR NAMES

AND

DAVID LLOYD GEORGE I, ANDREW BONAR LAW I, WINSTON LEONARD CHURCHILL, MAURICE HAROLD MACMILLAN AND MARGARET HILDA ROBERTS THATCHER HAVING EXCLUSIVE AND CORRECT DISPLAYS OF WORLD WAR ONE/WWI/WORLD WAR I/FIRST WORLD WAR IN THEIR NAMES

AND

WINSTON LEONARD CHURCHILL, ARTHUR JAMES BALFOUR AND DONALD DAVID WILLIAM CAMERON HAVING EXCLUSIVE AND CORRECT DISPLAYS OF WORLD WAR ONE/WWI/WORLD WAR I/FIRST WORLD WAR IN THEIR NAMES

AND

KING GEORGE V FREDERICK ERNEST ALBERT AND QUEEN ELIZABETH II ALEXANDRA MARY WINDSOR HAVING EXCLUSIVE AND CORRECT DISPLAYS OF WORLD WAR I IN THEIR NAMES

AND

KING ALBERT FREDERICK ARTHUR GEORGE VI AND QUEEN ELIZABETH II ALEXANDRA MARY WINDSOR HAVING EXCLUSIVE AND CORRECT DISPLAYS OF WORLD WAR TWO/WWII/WORLD WAR II/FIRST WORLD WAR IN THEIR NAMES

AND

ADOLFUS JACOB HITLER, PAUL JOSEPH GOEBBELS AND HEMUT JOSEF MICHAEL KOHL HAVING EXCLUSIVE AND CORRECT DISPLAYS OF HOLOCAUST IN THEIR NAMES

AND

WINSTON LEONARD CHURCHILL AND DAVID WILLIAM DONALD CAMERON HAVING EXCLUSIVE AND CORRECT DISPLAYS OF HOLOCAUST IN THEIR NAMES

AND

ALBERT FREDERICK ARTHUR GEORGE VI, THE KING OF THE UNITED KINGDOM, HAVING EXCLUSIVE AND CORRECT DISPLAYS OF DER HOLOCAUST IN HIS NAME IS:

1

IN

5,830,000,000,000,000,000,000,000,000,000

(ONE IN 5 NONILLION, 830 OCTILLION)

The many series of searches for evidence were over. It seemed so long ago that I began this journey. But after studying a revolution, a civil war, two world wars, a holocaust, three nations, and many leaders—there was no doubt in my mind.

With these findings came a huge sense of relief. I could, at long last, breathe. During my journey, I would often ponder if my discovery was, indeed, a discovery or a fluke? Now there was an answer. This was no fluke; the Code was—is—real.
I sat back and relaxed. But at the same time, I stared in wonderment. I felt a rush at the awesomeness of it all.

I shuffled through the pages of work I had done, looking at the tables and the results and the names and everything. And I knew I had found something that was more than amazing, greater than astonishing, and way beyond baffling, and whatever other words I have used to convey the slow unveiling of it all.

Which is to say: There are no words.

Perhaps, you have your own words. Or, like many, you are speechless.

SECTION III

SUPPLEMENTAL EVIDENCE OF THE CODE

PRESENTATIONS IN THE NAMES OF WORLD LEADERS STANDING ALONE AND IN CLUSTERS

THE PRESENTATIONS STANDING ALONE AND IN CLUSTERS

What you are about to see is a demonstration of the phenomenon in this book in visual patterns. When we exclude the Exceptions and the 64-Year Phenomena, and just view the Presentations of Heads of State with a strong and direct relationship with a Historical Event, we always find stand-alone Presentations or Clusters of Presentations.

The appearance of all the stand-alone Presentations and Clusters of Presentations make for quite a striking display. The long strings of names of those without a Presentation, association or involvement listed before and after the stand-alone Presentations and Clusters isolate the Presentations. In this way, we are provided strong visual patterns that demonstrate the exclusivity of the phenomenon covered in this book.

LEVEL ZERO: THE SEARCH FOR **AWOI** IN THE NAMES OF U.S. PRESIDENTS
(WITH SURNAME ONLY)

WASHINGTON	***AWOI***
ADAMS	
JEFFERSON	
MADISON	
MONROE	
ADAMS	
JACKSON	
VAN BUREN	
TYLER	
POLK	
TAYLOR	
FILLMORE	
PIERCE	
BUCHANAN	
LINCOLN	
JOHNSON	
GRANT	
HAYES	
GARFIELD	
ARTHUR	
CLEVELAND	
HARRISON	
MCKINLEY	
ROOSEVELT	
TAFT	
WILSON	
HARDING	
COOLIDGE	
HOOVER	
ROOSEVELT	
TRUMAN	
EISENHOWER	
KENNEDY	
JOHNSON	
NIXON	
KING	
CARTER	
REAGAN	
BUSH	
BLYTHE	
BUSH	
OBAMA	
TRUMP	
BIDEN	

Level Zero tests were not performed in the series of tests in this book. But the test is revealed here so that we can see that WASHINGTON is totally alone in having AWOI at Level Zero—surname only.

LEVEL ONE: THE SEARCH FOR **AWOI** IN THE NAMES OF U.S. PRESIDENTS
(WITHOUT THE 64-YEAR PHENOMENON)

GEORGE WASHINGTON   *****AWOI*****
JOHN ADAMS
THOMAS JEFFERSON
JAMES MADISON
JAMES MONROE
JOHN ADAMS
ANDREW JACKSON
MARTIN VAN BUREN
JOHN TYLER
JAMES POLK
ZACHARY TAYLOR
MILLARD FILLMORE
FRANKLIN PIERCE
JAMES BUCHANAN
ABRAHAM LINCOLN
ANDREW JOHNSON
ULYSSES GRANT
RUTHERFORD HAYES
JAMES GARFIELD
CHESTER ARTHUR
GROVER CLEVELAND
BENJAMIN HARRISON
WILLIAM MCKINLEY
THEODORE ROOSEVELT
WILLIAM TAFT
WOODROW WILSON
WARREN HARDING
CALVIN COOLIDGE
HERBERT HOOVER
FRANKLIN ROOSEVELT
HARRY TRUMAN
DWIGHT EISENHOWER
JOHN KENNEDY
LYNDON JOHNSON
RICHARD NIXON
LESLIE KING
JAMES CARTER
RONALD REAGAN
GEORGE BUSH
WILLIAM BLYTHE
GEORGE BUSH
BARACK OBAMA
DONALD TRUMP
JOSEPH BIDEN

As we can see, WASHINGTON is not only totally alone in having AWOI at Level Zero, he is also alone at Level One when we remove the 64-Year Phenomenon.

LEVEL THREE: COVERT PRESENTATIONS OF **THE CIVIL WAR** IN THE NAMES OF U.S. PRESIDENTS
(EXCLUDING 64-YEAR PHENOMENONA AND TWO PRESIDENTS WITH STRONG HISTORIC ASSOCIATIONS)

GEORGE WASHINGTON
JOHN ADAMS JR
THOMAS JEFFERSON II
JAMES MADISON JR
JAMES MONROE
ANDREW JACKSON JR
MARTIN VAN BUREN SR
WILLIAM HENRY HARRISON I
JOHN TYLER JR
JAMES KNOX POLK
ZACHARY TAYLOR II
MILLARD FILLMORE
FRANKLIN PIERCE SR
JAMES BUCHANAN JR
ABRAHAM LINCOLN II   ***THE CIVIL WAR***
ANDREW JOHNSON SR
HIRAM ULYSSES GRANT   ***THE CIVIL WAR***
RUTHERFORD BIRCHARD HAYES I ***THE CIVIL WAR***
JAMES ABRAM GARFIELD I
CHESTER ALAN ARTHUR I
STEPHEN GROVER CLEVELAND
BENJAMIN HARRISON
WILLIAM MCKINLEY JR
THEODORE ROOSEVELT JR
WILLIAM HOWARD TAFT I   ***THE CIVIL WAR***
THOMAS WOODROW WILSON
WARREN GAMALIEL HARDING
JOHN CALVIN COOLIDGE JR
FRANKLIN DELANO ROOSVELT SR
HARRY S. TRUMAN
DWIGHT DAVID EISENHOWER I
JOHN FITZGERALD KENNEDY SR
LYNDON BAINES JOHNSON
RICHARD MILHAUS NIXON
LESLIE LYNCH KING JR
JAMES EARL CARTER JR
RONALD WILSON REAGAN
GEORGE HERBERT WALKER BUSH
GEORGE WALKER BUSH
BARRACK HUSSEIN OBAMA II   ***THE CIVIL WAR***
DONALD JOHN TRUMP SR
JOSEPH ROBINETTE BIDEN JR

When we exclude the two 64-Year Phenomena and the two Presidents who have THE CIVIL WAR in their names because of strong associations, we see an interesting Cluster around the middle of the list.

LEVEL THREE: COVERT PRESENTATIONS OF **WORLD WAR I** IN THE NAMES OF U.S. PRESIDENTS
(EXCLUDING THE 64-YEAR PHENOMENON AND OTHER EXCEPTIONS)

GEORGE WASHINGTON
JOHN ADAMS JR
THOMAS JEFFERSON II
JAMES MADISON JR
JAMES MONROE
JOHN QUINCY ADAMS
ANDREW JACKSON JR
MARTIN VAN BUREN SR
JOHN TYLER JR
JAMES KNOX POLK
ZACHARY TAYLOR II
MILLARD FILLMORE
FRANKLIN PIERCE SR
JAMES BUCHANAN JR
ANDREW JOHNSON SR
HIRAM ULYSSES GRANT
CHESTER ALAN ARTHUR I
STEPHEN GROVER CLEVELAND
BENJAMIN HARRISON
WILLIAM MCKINLEY JR
THEODORE ROOSEVELT JR   ***WORLD WAR ONE***
WILLIAM HOWARD TAFT I   ***WORLD WAR I/WWI***
THOMAS WOODROW WILSON   ***WORLD WAR ONE/WWI***
WARREN GAMALIEL HARDING
JOHN CALVIN COOLIDGE JR   ***WORLD WAR I***
HERBERT CLARK HOOVER SR   ***FIRST WORLD WAR***
FRANKLIN DELANO ROOSEVELT SR   ***WORLD WAR ONE/FIRST WORLD WAR***
HARRY S. TRUMAN
LYNDON BAINES JOHNSON
LESLIE LYNCH KING JR
JAMES EARL CARTER JR
GEORGE HERBERT WALKER BUSH
GEORGE WALKER BUSH
DONALD JOHN TRUMP SR
JOSEPH ROBINETTE BIDEN JR

Here we find with the exclusion of the 64-Year Phenomenon and those excluded for other reasons, that we have a very strong and exclusive Cluster.

LEVEL THREE: COVERT PRESENTATIONS OF **WORLD WAR II** IN THE NAMES OF U.S. PRESIDENTS
(EXCLUDING THE 64-YEAR PHENOMENON AND OTHER EXCEPTIONS)

GEORGE WASHINGTON
JOHN ADAMS JR
THOMAS JEFFERSON II
JAMES MADISON JR
JAMES MONROE
JOHN QUINCY ADAMS
ANDREW JACKSON JR
MARTIN VAN BUREN SR
JOHN TYLER JR
JAMES KNOX POLK
ZACHARY TAYLOR II
MILLARD FILLMORE
FRANKLIN PIERCE SR
JAMES BUCHANAN JR
ANDREW JOHNSON SR
HIRAM ULYSSES GRANT
CHESTER ALAN ARTHUR I
STEPHEN GROVER CLEVELAND
BENJAMIN HARRISON
WILLIAM MCKINLEY JR
THEODORE ROOSEVELT JR
WILLIAM HOWARD TAFT I
THOMAS WOODROW WILSON
WARREN GAMALIEL HARDING
JOHN CALVIN COOLIDGE JR
HERBERT CLARK HOOVER SR   ***WORLD WAR TWO***
FRANKLIN DELANO ROOSEVELT SR   ***WORLD WAR TWO/SECOND WORLD WAR***
HARRY S. TRUMAN
DWIGHT DAVID EISENHOWER I   ***WWII***
JOHN FITZGERALD KENNEDY JR   ***WORLD WAR TWO***
LYNDON BAINES JOHNSON
RICHARD MILHAUS NIXON   ***WORLD WAR II***
LESLIE LYNCH KING JR
JAMES EARL CARTER JR
GEORGE HERBERT WALKER BUSH
GEORGE WALKER BUSH
DONALD JOHN TRUMP SR
JOSEPH ROBINETTE BIDEN JR

Observing Presentations of WORLD WAR TWO and the other expressions, we find a Cluster of five Presentations among seven. Again, we have excluded the Exceptions.

LEVEL THREE: COVERT PRESENTATIONS OF **WORLD WAR ONE** IN THE PRIME MINISTERS OF THE U.K.
(EXCLUDING THE 64-YEAR PHENOMENON, THE FAILURE—BORIS JOHNSON—AND EXCEPTIONS)

WILLIAM PITT II
HENRY ADDINGTON
WILLIAM HENRY CAVENDISH CAVENDISH-BENTINCK
SPENCER PERCEVAL I
ROBERT BANKS JENKINSON
GEORGE CANNING JNR
ARTHUR WELLESLEY
CHARLES GREY II
ROBERT PEEL II
HENRY WILLIAM LAMB
JOHN RUSSELL II
HENRY JOHN TEMPLE
BENJAMIN DISRAELI
ARCHIBALD PHILIP PRIMROSE
ROBERT ARTHUR TALBOT GASCOYNE-CECIL
ARTHUR JAMES BALFOUR
HENRY CAMPBELL-BANNERMAN
HERBERT HENRY ASQUITH   ***THE GREAT WAR***
DAVID LLOYD GEORGE I   ***WORLD WAR I***
ANDREW BONAR LAW I   ***WORLD WAR I***
STANLEY BALDWIN
JAMES RAMSAY MACDONALD
ARTHUR NEVILLE CHAMBERLAIN
WINSTON LEONARD CHURCHILL   ***WORLD WAR ONE***
CLEMENT RICHARD ATTLEE
ROBERT ANTHONY EDEN
MAURICE HAROLD MACMILLAN   ***WORLD WAR I***
JAMES HAROLD WILSON
LEONARD JAMES CALLAGHAN
JOHN ROY MAJOR
ANTHONY CHARLES LYNTON BLAIR
JAMES GORDON BROWN
THERESA MARY BRASIER (MAY)

Excluding the exceptions and the 64-Year Phenomenon, we find a Cluster of Presentations of WORLD WAR ONE and other expressions among the British Prime Ministers.

LEVEL THREE: COVERT PRESENTATIONS OF **WORLD WAR TWO** IN THE PRIME MINISTERS OF THE U.K.
(EXCLUDING THE 64-YEAR PHENOMENON, THE FAILURE—BORIS JOHNSON—AND EXCEPTIONS)

WILLIAM PITT II
HENRY ADDINGTON
WILLIAM HENRY CAVENDISH CAVENDISH-BENTINCK
SPENCER PERCEVAL I
ROBERT BANKS JENKINSON
GEORGE CANNING JNR
ARTHUR WELLESLEY
CHARLES GREY II
WILLIAM LAMB
ROBERT PEEL II
HENRY JOHN RUSSELL II
HENRY JOHN TEMPLE
BENJAMIN DISRAELI
WILLIAM EWART GLADSTONE
ARCHIBALD PHILIP PRIMROSE
ROBERT ARTHUR TALBOT CASCOYNE-CECIL
ARTHUR JAMES BALFOUR
HENRY CAMPBELL-BANNERMAN
HERBERT HENRY ASQUITH
DAVID LLOYD GEORGE I
ANDREW BONAR LAW I
STANLEY BALDWIN
JAMES RAMSAY MACDONALD
ARTHUR NEVILLE CHAMBERLAIN
WINSTON LEONARD CHURCHILL   ***WORLD WAR TWO/WORLD WAR II***
CLEMENT RICHARD ATTLEE
ROBERT ANTHONY EDEN
MAURICE HAROLD MACMILLAN
JAMES HAROLD WILSON
LEONARD JAMES CALLAGHAN
MARGARET HILDA ROBERTS (THATCHER)
JOHN ROY MAJOR
ANTHONY CHARLES LYNTON BLAIR
JAMES GORDON BROWN
THERESA MARY BRASIER (MAY)

Here we find **WINSTON LEONARD CHURCHILL** alone with both WORLD WAR TWO and WORLD WAR II.

OVERT PRESENTATIONS OF **DER HOLOCAUST** IN THE NAMES OF GERMAN CHANCELLORS

OTTO EDUARD LEOPOLD
GEORG LEO CAPRIVI
CHLODWIG CARL VIKTOR
BERNHARD HEINRICH KARL MARTIN VON BULOW
THEOBALD THEODOR FRIEDRICH ALFRED VON BETHMANN-HOLLWEG
GEORG MICHAELIS
GEORG FRIEDRICH HERTLING
MAXIMILIAN ALEXANDER FRIEDRICH WILHELM
FRIEDRICH EBERT
PHILIPP HENRICH SCHEIDEMANN
GUSTAV ADOLF BAUER
HERMANN MULLER
CONSTANTIN FEHRENBACH
KARL JOSEPH WIRTH
WILHELM CARL JOSEF CUNO
GUSTAV STRESEMANN
HANS LUTHER
WILHELM MARX
HEINRICH ALOYSIUS MARIA ELISABETH BRUNING
FRANZ JOSEPH HERMANN MARIA VON PAPEN
KURT FERDINAND FRIEDRICH HERMANN VON SCHLEICHER
ADOLFUS JACOB HITLER   *****DER HOLOCAUST*****
PAUL JOSEPH GOEBBELS
JOHANN LUDWIG VON KROSIGK
KONRAD HERMANN JOSEPH ADENAUER
LUDWIG WILHELM ERHARD
KURT GEORG KIESINGER
GEBHARD MULLER
REINHOLD MAIER
HERBERT ERNST KARL FRAHM
WALTER SCHEEL
HELMUT HENRICH WALDEMAR SCHMIDT
HELMUT JOSEF MICHAEL KOHL
GERHARD FRITZ KURT SCHRODER
ANGELA DOROTHEA KASNER MERKEL

Here we see how the name ADOLFUS JACOB HITLER stands out in the list of names of the German Chancellors with an Overt Presentation of DER HOLOCAUST.

OVERT PRESENTATIONS OF **HOLOCAUST** IN THE NAMES OF GERMAN CHANCELLORS
EXCLUDING THE 64-YEAR PHENOMENON

OTTO EDUARD LEOPOLD
GEORG LEO CAPRIVI
CHLODWIG CARL VIKTOR
BERNHARD HEINRICH KARL MARTIN VON BULOW
THEOBALD THEODOR FRIEDRICH ALFRED VON BETHMANN-HOLLWEG
GEORG MICHAELIS
GEORG FRIEDRICH HERTLING
MAXIMILIAN ALEXANDER FRIEDRICH WILHELM
FRIEDRICH EBERT
PHILIPP HENRICH SCHEIDEMANN
GUSTAV ADOLF BAUER
HERMANN MULLER
CONSTANTIN FEHRENBACH
KARL JOSEPH WIRTH
WILHELM CARL JOSEF CUNO
GUSTAV STRESEMANN
HANS LUTHER
WILHELM MARX
HEINRICH ALOYSIUS MARIA ELISABETH BRUNING
FRANZ JOSEPH HERMANN MARIA VON PAPEN
KURT FERDINAND FRIEDRICH HERMANN VON SCHLEICHER
ADOLFUS JACOB HITLER   ***HOLOCAUST***
PAUL JOSEPH GOEBBELS
JOHANN LUDWIG VON KROSIGK
KONRAD HERMANN JOSEPH ADENAUER
LUDWIG WILHELM ERHARD
KURT GEORG KIESINGER
GEBHARD MULLER
REINHOLD MAIER
HERBERT ERNST KARL FRAHM
WALTER SCHEEL
HELMUT HENRICH WALDEMAR SCHMIDT
HELMUT JOSEF MICHAEL KOHL
GERHARD FRITZ KURT SCHRODER
ANGELA DOROTHEA KASNER MERKEL

Even when we remove DER from DER HOLOCAUST, leaving only HOLOCAUST and we eliminate the 64-Year Phenomenon, we find that HITLER still stands alone with an Overt Presentation.

COVERT PRESENTATIONS OF **HOLOCAUST** IN THE NAMES OF GERMAN CHANCELLORS
EXCLUDING THE 64-YEAR PHENOMENON

OTTO EDUARD LEOPOLD
GEORG LEO CAPRIVI
CHLODWIG CARL VIKTOR
BERNHARD HEINRICH KARL MARTIN VON BULOW
THEOBALD THEODOR FRIEDRICH ALFRED VON BETHMANN-HOLLWEG
GEORG MICHAELIS
GEORG FRIEDRICH HERTLING
MAXIMILIAN ALEXANDER FRIEDRICH WILHELM
FRIEDRICH EBERT
PHILIPP HENRICH SCHEIDEMANN
GUSTAV ADOLF BAUER
HERMANN MULLER
CONSTANTIN FEHRENBACH
KARL JOSEPH WIRTH
WILHELM CARL JOSEF CUNO
GUSTAV STRESEMANN
HANS LUTHER
WILHELM MARX
HEINRICH ALOYSIUS MARIA ELISABETH BRUNING
FRANZ JOSEPH HERMANN MARIA VON PAPEN
KURT FERDINAND FRIEDRICH HERMANN VON SCHLEICHER
ADOLFUS JACOB HITLER   ***HOLOCAUST***
PAUL JOSEPH GOEBBELS   ***HOLOCAUST***
JOHANN LUDWIG VON KROSIGK
KONRAD HERMANN JOSEPH ADENAUER
LUDWIG WILHELM ERHARD
KURT GEORG KIESINGER
GEBHARD MULLER
REINHOLD MAIER
HERBERT ERNST KARL FRAHM
WALTER SCHEEL
HELMUT HENRICH WALDEMAR SCHMIDT
HELMUT JOSEF MICHAEL KOHL
GERHARD FRITZ KURT SCHRODER
ANGELA DOROTHEA KASNER MERKEL

Excluding the 64-Year Phenomenon, we see another Cluster, which shocked us when we first observed it earlier in the book.

OVERT PRESENTATIONS OF **DER HOLOCAUST** IN THE PRIME MINISTERS OF THE U.K.
(NO EXCLUSIONS)

WILLIAM PITT II
HENRY ADDINGTON
WILLIAM WYNDHAM GRENVILLE
WILLIAM HENRY CAVENDISH CAVENDISH-BENTINCK
SPENCER PERCEVAL I
ROBERT BANKS JENKINSON
GEORGE CANNING JNR
FREDERICK JOHN ROBINSON
ARTHUR WELLESLEY
CHARLES GREY II
ROBERT PEEL II
HENRY WILLIAM LAMB
JOHN RUSSELL II
EDWARD GEORGE GEOFFREY SMITH-STANLEY
GEORGE HAMILTON-GORDON
HENRY JOHN TEMPLE
BENJAMIN DISRAELI
WILLIAM EWART GLADSTONE
ARCHIBALD PHILIP PRIMROSE
ROBERT ARTHUR TALBOT GASCOYNE-CECIL
ARTHUR JAMES BALFOUR
HENRY CAMPBELL
HERBERT HENRY ASQUITH
DAVID LLOYD GEORGE I
ANDREW BONAR LAW I
STANLEY BALDWIN
JAMES RAMSAY MACDONALD
ARTHUR NEVILLE CHAMBERLAIN
WINSTON LEONARD CHURCHILL   *****DER HOLOCAUST*****
CLEMENT RICHARD ATTLEE
ROBERT ANTHONY EDEN
MAURICE HAROLD MACMILLAN
ALEXANDER FREDERICK DOUGLAS-HOME
JAMES HAROLD WILSON
EDWARD RICHARD GEORGE HEATH
LEONARD JAMES CALLAGHAN
MARGARET HILDA ROBERTS (THATCHER)
JOHN ROY MAJOR
ANTHONY CHARLES LYNTON BLAIR
JAMES GORDON BROWN
DAVID WILLIAM DONALD CAMERON
THERESA MARY BRASIER (MAY)
ALEXANDER BORIS DE PFEFFEL JOHNSON

In this final list, we see again that WINSTON LEONARD CHURCHILL is alone with DER HOLOCAUST.

COMPARISON OF NAME LENGTH IN THE NAMES OF WORLD LEADERS WITH PRESENTATIONS OR INCIDENTAL DISPLAYS

As we examine the results of this series of tests, we are looking to see if the Head of State who played the central role in the Historical Event has the name of the Event with the use of the fewest number of letters in that leader's name.

As we see here, WASHINGTON is the only U.S. President with AWOI (the initialism of the American War of Independence) in his name at Level Zero. Level Zero only uses one of the names—often the surname of a leader.

At Level One, GEORGE WASHINGTON (Level One is the first given name or most used given name plus the surname) contains AWOI with fewer letters than the excluded U.S. Presidents. WILLIAM HARRISON has AWOI because he is the 64-Year Phenomenon.

Heads of State excluded from the tests because of having Incidental Displays for the Events in their names are included in these lists to show that they require more letters in their name to have the Display.

AWOI

LEVEL ZERO

(SURNAME ONLY)

1. WASHINGTON (10 LETTERS)*

LEVEL ONE

1. GEORGE WASHINGTON (16)
2. WILLIAM HARRISON (15)

LEVEL TWO

(ALL EXCLUDED FROM THE TEST)

1. WILLIAM HOWARD TAFT (17)**
2. RONALD WILSON REAGAN (18)***
3. THOMAS WOODROW WILSON (19)****
4. DWIGHT DAVID EISENHOWER (21)*****
5. WILLIAM JEFFERSON BLYTHE (22)******

*WASHINGTON is the only name at Level Zero—surname only—that contains AWOI.

**Name excluded from the test because having both 'WWI' and 'WORLD WAR I' in his name gives him over a 90% chance of having 'AWOI' in his name.

***Name excluded because having both 'WORLD WAR ONE' and 'WORLD WAR I' in his name gives him over a 90% chance of having 'AWOI' in his name.

****Name excluded because having both 'WWI' and 'WORLD WAR ONE' in his name gives him over a 90% chance of having 'AWOI' in his name.

*****Name excluded because having 'WWII' in his name gives him over a 70% chance of having 'AWOI' in his name.

******Name excluded because having 'WORLD WAR ONE,' 'WORLD WAR TWO,' 'WORLD WAR I,' and 'WORLD WAR II' in his name gives him over a 90% chance of having 'AWOI' in his name.

Looking at the names of the Presidents strongly involved in or associated with THE CIVIL WAR, we see that the least number of sounds in a name that has THE CIVIL WAR is 13 and this is the name of ABRAHAM LINCOLN.

Including U.S. Presidents at all levels, the name with the least letters that has THE CIVIL WAR is ABRAHAM LINCOLN II. His name is 16 letters. The next is 17. The names with only 17 letters are HIRAM ULYSSES GRANT, who was second in importance in THE CIVIL WAR, and WILLIAM HOWARD TAFT, who has a strong association with the war.

THE CIVIL WAR

LEVEL ONE

(WITH SUBSTITUTION)

(SOUNDS)

1. A-B-R-A-H-A-M L-I-N-C-OL-N (13 SOUNDS)*
   (Only two sounds of an "A" are left in his name)

(NO ONE ELSE ADDED AT LEVEL ONE)

LEVELS TWO AND THREE

1. ABRAHAM LINCOLN II (16 LETTERS) (LEVEL THREE)**
2. HIRAM ULYSSES GRANT (17) (LEVEL TWO)
3. WILLIAM HOWARD TAFT (17) (LEVEL TWO)
4. HERBERT CLARK HOOVER (18) (LEVEL TWO)
5. BARACK HUSSEIN OBAMA II (20) (LEVEL THREE)
6. WILLIAM JEFFERSON BLYTHE (22) (LEVEL TWO)
7. RUTHERFORD BIRCHARD HAYES (23) (LEVEL TWO)

*Substitution is used in this Level One presentation and makes 'ABRAHAM LINC (OL) N' alone at Level One. He has the presentation with the fewest sounds—13. In the Introduction of the book, I explain this phenomenon. When a digraph (two letters) or a trigraph (three letters) makes the same identical sound as a single letter, the single letter can substitute for the digraph or trigraph.

**At Level Three, 'ABRAHAM LINCOLN II' does not use substitution and is the name with the fewest letters—16.

The U.S. President with WORLD WAR ONE with the fewest number of letters required in the name is WOODROW WILSON. He has it at Level One with only 13 letters.

As we see, the name of WOODROW WILSON has WWI with the fewest letters, as well, and that is also with just 13 letters.

WORLD WAR ONE/WORLD WAR I/WWI/FIRST WORLD WAR PRESIDENTS OF THE UNITED STATES

WORLD WAR ONE

LEVEL ONE
1. WOODROW WILSON (13 LETTERS)*
2. FRANKLIN ROOSEVELT (17)
3. THEODORE ROOSEVELT (17)

LEVEL TWO
1. RONALD WILSON REAGAN (18)
2. JOHN FITZGERALD KENNEDY (21)

WORLD WAR I

1. FRANKLIN ROOSEVELT (17)
2. WILLIAM HOWARD TAFT (17)
3. RONALD WILSON REAGAN (18)

WWI

LEVEL ONE
1. WOODROW WILSON (13)**

LEVEL TWO
1. WILLIAM HOWARD TAFT (17)

FIRST WORLD WAR

LEVEL THREE

1. HERBERT CLARK HOOVER SR (20)
2. FRANKLIN DELANO ROOSEVELT SR (25)

*At Level One, WOODROW WILSON has WORLD WAR ONE in his name with the fewest letters—13.

**At Level One, WOODROW WILSON has WWI in his name with the fewest letters—13.
So, WOODROW WILSON has two presentations in his name with the fewest letters.

FRANKLIN ROOSEVELT has WORLD WAR TWO in his name with 17 letters available. He is joined by his fifth cousin, Theodore Roosevelt, in having only 17, but Theodore is excluded from the test because his son and grandson, THEODORE II and THEODORE III, were high ranking Veterans of that war, and THEODORE III died in the war.

DWIGHT EISENHOWER, whose involvement in WWII was just as important, has WWII in his name with only 16 letters available.

FRANKLIN D ROOSEVELT is the only U.S. President with SECOND WORLD WAR in his name. He has it with only 18 letters available.

WORLD WAR TWO/WORLD WAR II/WWII/SECOND WORLD WAR PRESIDENTS OF THE UNITED STATES

WORLD WAR TWO

LEVEL ONE
1. FRANKLIN ROOSEVELT (17 LETTERS)*
2. THEODORE ROOSEVELT (17)**

LEVEL TWO
3. HERBERT CLARK HOOVER (18)
4. JOHN FITZGERALD KENNEDY (21)

WORLD WAR II

LEVEL TWO
1. RICHARD MILHAUS NIXON (19)

LEVEL THREE
1. BARACK HUSSEIN OBAMA II (20)

WWII

LEVEL ONE
1. DWIGHT EISENHOWER (16)***

LEVEL TWO
1. WILLIAM HOWARD TAFT (17)****

SECOND WORLD WAR

ALL LEVELS
1. FRANKLIN D ROOSEVELT (18)*****

*At Level One, FRANKLIN ROOSEVELT has WORLD WAR TWO with 17 letters available, as does his fifth cousin, THEODORE ROOSEVELT.

**His cousin, is excluded, as his namesake son and grandson served in the war.

***DWIGHT EISENHOWER has WWII in his name using only 16 letters.

****WILLIAM HOWARD TAFT is excluded from the test at Level Two because he has more than an 80% chance of having WWII in his name by the fact that he has a Presentation of WWI in his name.

*****FRANKLIN D ROOSEVELT is the only U.S. President with 'SECOND WORLD WAR' in his name. He has it using only 18 levels.

Examining the names of the Prime Ministers of the United Kingdom in WORLD WAR ONE/WORLD WAR I/WWI/FIRST WORLD WAR, also known as THE GREAT WAR, especially early in the war and especially in the United Kingdom, we find three Prime Ministers involved to a great degree. ANDREW BONAR LAW I, has both WORLD WAR I and WWI with only 15 letters available. He played a central role as leader of the Conservative Party in forming a Coalition Government early in the war. He was also Chancellor of the Exchequer during the last two years of the war, and he was Prime Minister during the immediate aftermath of the war. DAVID L GEORGE I has WORLD WAR I with only 13 letters available. HERBERT HENRY ASQUITH has THE GREAT WAR with only 19 letters available—the fewest of any of the Prime Ministers. Considering all the tests in the book, the only Historical Event with two leaders serving for a significant amount of time during the Event is this one.

WORLD WAR ONE/WORLD WAR I/WWI/FIRST WORLD WAR PRIME MINISTERS OF THE UNITED KINGDOM

WORLD WAR ONE

LEVEL TWO
1. WINSTON LEONARD CHURCHILL (23 LETTERS)
2. ALEXANDER BORIS DE PFEFFEL JOHNSON (30)

WORLD WAR I

ALL LEVELS
1. DAVID L GEORGE I (13)*
2. ANDREW BONAR LAW I (15)**
3. MAURICE HAROLD MACMILLAN (22)
4. WINSTON LEONARD CHURCHILL (23)
5. MARGARET HILDA ROBERTS THATCHER (28)
6. ALEXANDER BORIS DE PFEFFEL JOHNSON (30)****

WWI

LEVEL THREE
1. ANDREW BONAR LAW I (15)***

FIRST WORLD WAR

LEVEL TWO
1. WINSTON LEONARD CHURCHILL (23)

*At all levels, DAVID L GEORGE I has WORLD WAR I in his name with the fewest letters—13.

**ANDREW BONAR LAW I has the second fewest letters with 15.

***At Level Three, ANDREW BONAR LAW I has WWI in his name with the fewest letters—15.

****ALEXANDER BORIS DE PFEFFEL JOHNSON has been excluded from the test, and he has the expressions in the most letters in both cases.

Examining the names of the Prime Ministers of the United Kingdom in WORLD WAR TWO/WORLD WAR II/WWII/SECOND WORLD WAR, we find that the only Prime Minister with a Presentation of WORLD WAR TWO is WINSTON LEONARD CHURCHILL. One Incidental Display of ALEXANDER BORIS DE PFEFFEL JOHNSON requires his full name of 30 letters to have the Display.

WINSTON LEONARD CHURCHILL also has WORLD WAR II with the fewest letters required—only 23.

In all cases, the Incidental Display has the name requiring the most letters to get the Display. Prime Ministers with more letters are not listed.

WORLD WAR TWO/WORLD WAR II/WWI/SECOND WORLD WAR PRIME MINISTERS OF THE UNITED KINGDOM

WORLD WAR TWO
LEVEL TWO
1. WINSTON LEONARD CHURCHILL (23 LETTERS)*
2. ALEXANDER BORIS DE PFEFFEL JOHNSON (30)

WORLD WAR II
LEVEL TWO
1. WINSTON LEONARD CHURCHILL (23)**
2. DAVID WILLIAM DONALD CAMERON (25)

SECOND WORLD WAR
LEVEL TWO
1. DAVID WILLIAM DONALD CAMERON (25)**
2. ALEXANDER BORIS DE PFEFFEL JOHNSON (30)

*At Level One, WINSTON LEONARD CHURCHILL does not require the hyphenated name SPENCER and only requires 23 letters to present with WORLD WAR TWO. Note that JOHNSON requires 30 letters.

**WINSTON LEONARD CHURCHILL has 'WORLD WAR II' with the fewest number of letters—23. DAVID WILLIAM DONALD CAMERON (the 64-Year Phenomenon) has it in 25.

As we see, CHURCHILL is the only Prime Minister with two Presentations or Displays, and he contains them both with the fewest number of letters.

As we have seen up until now, aside from the three British Prime Ministers of the United Kingdom who played a role in WORLD WAR ONE, all the central leaders have had more than one Presentation of a Historical Event with the fewest number of letters in their name. GEORGE WASHINGTON, ABRAHAM LINCOLN, WOODROW WILSON, FRANKLIN ROOSEVELT, and WINSTON CHURCHILL all have the fewest number of letters in their names among those with the Presentation or the Display.

With ADOLFUS HITLER (Level One) and ADOLFUS JACOB HITLER (Level Two), the modern embodiment of evil contains exclusive rights to an Overt Presentation of DER HOLOCAUST—which he has with a mere 18 letters, and to a Level One Covert Presentation of the same expression with only 13 letters—leaving only one letter unused.

DER HOLOCAUST (GERMANY)

OVERT PRESENTATION

1. ADOLFUS JACOB HITLER (18 LETTERS)*

COVERT PRESENTATION

1. ADOLFUS HITLER (13)**
2. HELMUT JOSEF MICHAEL KOHL (22)***
3. BERNHARD HEINRICH KARL MARTIN VON BULOW (34)****
4. KURT FERDINAND FRIEDRICH HERMANN VON SCHLEICHER (42)*****
5. THEOBALD THEODORE FRIEDRICH ALFRED VON BETHMANN-HOLLWEG (48)******

*ADOLFUS JACOB HITLER is the only German Chancellor who has an Overt Presentation of 'DER HOLOCAUST' in his name.

**ADOLFUS HITLER has the Covert Presentation in the fewest letters.

***HELMUT JOSEF MICHAEL KOHL is the 64-Year Phenomenon.

****BULOW is excluded from the test for length of name.

*****VON SCHLEICHER is excluded for length of name.

******BETHMANN-HOLLWEG is excluded for length of name.

ADOLFUS HITLER also has the only Overt Presentation or Display of HOLOCAUST and he has a Covert Presentation of HOLOCAUST with the fewest number of letters.

HELMUT JOSEF MICHAEL KOHL has an Overt Presentation of HOLOCAUST in 22 letters.

PAUL JOSEPH GOEBBELS has a Covert Presentation of HOLOCAUST in only 16 letters.

These leaders all have their Presentations in fewer letters than the German Chancellors who have an Incidental Display because of having so many letters in their name.

HOLOCAUST (GERMANY)

OVERT PRESENTATION

1. ADOLFUS JACOB HITLER (18 LETTERS)*
2. HELMUT JOSEF MICHAEL KOHL (22)***

COVERT PRESENTATION

1. ADOLFUS HITLER (13)**
2. PAUL JOSEPH GOEBBELS (18)****
3. HELMUT JOSEF MICHAEL KOHL (22)***
4. BERNHARD HEINRICH KARL MARTIN VON BULOW (34)*****
5. KURT FERDINAND FRIEDRICH HERMANN VON SCHLEICHER (42)******
6. THEOBALD THEODORE FRIEDRICH ALFRED VON BETHMANN-HOLLWEG (48)*******

*The only Overt Presentation of 'HOLOCAUST' in the name of a German Chancellor is in the name ADOLFUS JACOB HITLER.

**ADOLFUS is the only German Chancellor with 'HOLOCAUST' in his name at Level One and with the fewest letters—13.

***HELMUT JOSEF KOHL is the 64-Year Phenomenon.

****PAUL JOSEPH GOEBBELS, HITLER's colleague, has 'HOLOCAUST' in 18 letters.

*****BULOW is excluded from the test for length of name.

******VON SCHLEICHER is excluded for length of name.

*******BETHMANN-HOLLWEG is excluded for length of name.

In the final analysis of this phenomenon, it is true one more time. WINSTON LEONARD CHURCHILL—without his hyphenated name from his mother—Spencer, has the only Overt Presentation of DER HOLOCAUST and HOLOCAUST, and he has a Covert Presentation of HOLOCAUST with the fewest letters required than any of the other British Prime Ministers.

DER HOLOCAUST (UNITED KINGDOM)

OVERT PRESENTATION

1. WINSTON LEONARD CHURCHILL (23 LETTERS)*

COVERT PRESENTATION

1. WINSTON LEONARD CHURCHILL (23)*
2. ALEXANDER FREDERICK DOUGLAS-HOME (29)

HOLOCAUST (UNITED KINGDOM)

OVERT PRESENTATION

1. WINSTON LEONARD CHURCHILL (23)*

COVERT PRESENTATION

1. ARTHUR JAMES BALFOUR (18)
2. WINSTON LEONARD CHURCHILL (23)*
3. ANTHONY CHARLES LYNTON BLAIR (25)
4. ALEXANDER FREDERICK DOUGLAS-HOME (29)

*The only Overt Presentation of 'DER HOLOCAUST' in the name of a British Prime Minister is in the name WINSTON LEONARD CHURCHILL (without the hyphenated name—SPENCER).

What is amazing—even beyond the findings we have already seen—and the Clusters we have just now seen—is that upon further examination we find that the names of each of the central leaders have the Presentation of the Historical Event they are associated with by themselves or with the fewest letters in their name.

WOODROW WILSON, who has 13 letters in his name, has WORLD WAR ONE, which is 11 letters, encoded in his name, leaving two copies of the letter "O."

ABRAHAM LINCOLN—with Substitution—has THE CIVIL WAR in a name of only 13 sounds or 13 letters. After taking THE CIVIL WAR from his name, his name is left with two copies of and two sounds of the letter "A."

DER HOLOCAUST is 12 letters. ADOLFUS HITLER is 13 letters. And yet, ADOLFUS HITLER has this 12-letter expression in his 13-letter name as a Covert Level One Presentation—leaving only one copy of the letter "I."

So, in addition to the astonishing findings you have already seen, the Clusters and the Comparison of Name Length in the names of Heads of State with Presentations and Displays, provide further evidence of the existence of the phenomena we are witnessing in this book.

SECTION IV

SUMMARY

SUMMARY OF THE EVIDENCE OF THE CLAIMS IN THIS BOOK

Claim 1:

The Head of State or Military Leader most central to a war or other Historical Event has a Superior Presentation of the Event in his or her name.

1. AWOI—GEORGE WASHINGTON, who was President of the United States, only shares the acronym AWOI (American War of Independence) at Level One with WILLIAM HARRISON. At Level Zero, he is alone.

2. AWOI—GEORGE III WILLIAM FREDERICK, who was the King of Great Britain and Ireland at the time of the AWOI, shares AWOI with no other British Monarch (after exclusions).

3. THE CIVIL WAR—ABRAHAM LINCOLN, who was president of the United States during THE CIVIL WAR, shares the term with no one at Level One.

4. WWI—WOODROW WILSON, who was President of the United States during WWI, has the only initialism at Level One.

5. WORLD WAR ONE—WOODROW WILSON shares WORLD WAR ONE with only two others at Level One.

6. WWII—DWIGHT EISENHOWER, who was Supreme Commander of the Allied Forces in Europe, has the sole Superior Presentation of WWII after an exclusion.

7. WORLD WAR TWO—FRANKLIN ROOSEVELT, who was President of the United States, shares WORLD WAR TWO with no other President at Level One after exclusions.

8. SECOND WORLD WAR—FRANKLIN DELANO ROOSEVELT also has SECOND WORLD WAR at Level Two and shares this with no other United States President.

9. WORLD WAR I is in the names of the two Prime Ministers, DAVID LLOYD GEORGE I, who was Prime Minister for the last 23 months of WORLD WAR I, and ANDREW BONAR LAW I, who served as Chancellor of the Exchequer during WORLD WAR I. THE GREAT WAR is in the name of HERBERT HENRY ASQUITH.

10. WORLD WAR ONE and WORLD WAR TWO are in the names of the two Kings of the United Kingdom who served, respectively, during WORLD WAR ONE and WORLD WAR TWO. They are GEORGE V FREDERICK ERNEST ALBERT and ALBERT FREDERICK ARTHUR GEORGE VI.

11. WORLD WAR TWO—WINSTON LEONARD CHURCHILL, who was the Head of State who declared war on Germany, has a Presentation.

12. DER HOLOCAUST—ADOLFUS JACOB HITLER, who was at the very center of DER HOLOCAUST, is the only German Chancellor to have DER HOLOCAUST as an Overt Presentation in his name.

13. DER HOLOCAUST—ADOLFUS HITLER has the only Covert Presentation of DER HOLOCAUST at Level One.

14. DER HOLOCAUST—WINSTON LEONARD CHURCHILL, who chose to resist HITLER, and was—above all other world leaders—the most responsible for stopping HITLER and ending the HOLOCAUST, is the only Prime Minister with an Overt Presentation of DER HOLOCAUST in his name.

15. DER HOLOCAUST—ALBERT FREDERICK ARTHUR GEORGE VI appointed CHURCHILL Prime Minister and they would dine together every evening throughout the war and during the worst years of DER HOLOCAUST. He is the only Monarch of the United Kingdom to have DER HOLOCAUST in his name.

THE CORRELATION BETWEEN CENTRAL INVOLVEMENT IN AN HISTORICAL EVENT AND SUPERIOR PRESENTATION IS +1. In other words, it occurs in all cases.

Claim 2:

The leader who serves from the 64th anniversary to the 65th anniversary of the turning point of a Historical Event has the Event in his or her name. If, however, a new leader takes office during that one-year period of time, that new leader becomes the 64-Year Phenomenon and is the one who contains the Event in their name. If more than one leader takes office during that one-year period of time, it is the first of those who becomes the 64-Year Phenomenon and is the one who contains the Event in his or her name.

1. WILLIAM HARRISON served his brief term from March 4, 1841, until April 4, 1841. He was the first to become President after the 64th anniversary of the Declaration of Independence—a defining moment in the AMERICAN WAR OF INDEPENDENCE. He has a Presentation of AWOI in his name.

2. HERBERT CLARK HOOVER began his one term as President on March 4, 1929, and he served until March 4, 1933. So, during the entire year from the 64th anniversary of the end of the war (May 26, 1929) until the 65th anniversary (May 26, 1930), HERBERT CLARK HOOVER was President. He is the 64-Year Phenomenon of THE CIVIL WAR and he contains THE CIVIL WAR in his name.

3. WILLIAM JEFFERSON BLYTHE III (the birth name of Bill Clinton) began his term on January 20, 1993, and he served until January 20, 2001. The 128th anniversary (64 X 2) of the end of THE CIVIL WAR was May 26, 1993, and the 129th was May 26, 1994. He is the second 64-Year Phenomenon for THE CIVIL WAR.

4. RONALD WILSON REAGAN began his term on January 20, 1981, and he served until January 20, 1989. He served during the years of the 64th and 65th anniversaries of WORLD WAR I, November 11, 1945, and November 11, 1946. He has WORLD WAS ONE and WORLD WAR I in his name.

5. BARACK HUSSEIN OBAMA II served as President from January 20, 2009, until January 20, 2017, covering the year between the 64th and 65th anniversaries of WORLD WAR II, and he has WORLD WAR II in his full name.

6. ELIZABETH II ALEXANDRA MARY WINDSOR has served as Queen of the United Kingdom since 1952. If we add 64 years to 1914 (the beginning of WORLD WAR ONE) or 1918 (the end of WORLD WAR ONE) or any year in the aftermath, we get a year that Queen Elizabeth was the Monarch of the United Kingdom. She contains WORLD WAR I, WORLD WAR ONE, and FIRST WORLD WAR in her name.

7. ELIZABETH II ALEXANDRA MARY WINDSOR has remained Queen of the United Kingdom even during WORLD WAR TWO and during the 64 years after and remains Queen at the time of this writing. She also contains WORLD WAR II, WORLD WAR TWO, and SECOND WORLD WAR in her name.

8. MARGARET HILDA ROBERTS THATCHER served as Prime Minister of the United Kingdom from 1979 until 1990, covering 64 years after 1915 through 1926. She has WORLD WAR I in her name.

9. DONALD WILLIAM DAVID CAMERON served as Prime Minister of the United Kingdom from May 11, 2010, until November 23, 2016. He has WORLD WAR II and SECOND WORLD WAR in his name.

10. The turning point in the HOLOCAUST considered the most defining moment is when ADOLFUS JACOB HITLER became Chancellor of Germany and the Nazi party began to rule Germany. This was January 30, 1933.

HELMUT JOSEPH MICHAEL KOHL served as Chancellor of Germany from October 1, 1982, until October 27, 1998. HITLER became Chancellor on January 30, 1933, a turning point that set the HOLOCAUST in motion. Add 64 years and we get January 30, 1997. Kohl was already Chancellor on that date and remained Chancellor on the date of the 65-year anniversary—making him the 64-Year Phenomenon for the HOLOCAUST for Germany.

11. ANTHONY CHARLES LYNTON BLAIR served as the Prime Minister of the United Kingdom from May 2, 1997, to June 27, 2007. He became Prime Minister during the year that began with the 64-year anniversary of the turning point of the HOLOCAUST, and he continued beyond the 65-year anniversary. This makes him the 64-Year Phenomenon for the HOLOCAUST for the United Kingdom.

THE CORRELATION IS +1. It occurs in all cases.

Claim 3:

Heads of State and Military Leaders who were most strongly involved in or associated with the Historical Event have a Presentation of the Event in their name. We see this in all the Events in this book.

THE CORRELATION IS +1. It occurs in all cases.

INTERPRETING THE EVIDENCE

What you have just read is a revelation and a demonstration that the English alphabet is a secret code hidden in the English language. I did not invent the code—I discovered it. It is not a code that requires computer software. Anyone can review the tables and tests in this book by hand and get the same results.

You have already read the story. To say that the findings are amazing is an understatement, and to say it is an understatement is itself an understatement. You can clearly see that it is true, and I can only assume you are as astounded as I was when I discovered it and as I still am.

It is still hard for me to believe; I have tried to convince myself that it cannot be. But if you skim through this book, no matter where you stop, there is another piece of evidence. What if I had found that the only Display of the American Revolutionary War was in the name of Andrew Johnson and the only expression for The Civil War was in the name of James Knox Polk? If that had been the case, I would have looked no further. But as you see, all the tests reveal the same thing. They all confirm there is a code.

The Presidents of the United States, Prime Ministers of the United Kingdom, British Monarchs, and Chancellors of Germany contain correct "predictions" of their involvement in or association with Historical Events or they show their noninvolvement or lack of association over 98% of the time. The probability of all of these being accurate, the occurrence of these correlations even with the astronomical odds against it, is unheard of in a test. If tests for a new drug presented statistics like just the first test in this book, the drug would be approved immediately.

One of the most fascinating discoveries in the book is that the central Head of State in each Historical Event has a Superior Presentation of the Event in their name. There are no exceptions. Washington has it, Lincoln has it. Wilson has two, FDR has two, Hitler has two, Churchill has Superior Presentations of two Events and the British Monarchs during the American War of Independence, the world wars, and the Holocaust have theirs.

Yes, there are some challenges and questions. The challenges are important to address, and they are addressed in the appendices. The questions are important to answer, as well, and they are also answered and explained fully. Nothing can shake the reality of these discoveries.

THE DISCOVERY

If you have read the book up to this point, you know by now that the Code is a given fact. It is indisputable. The Three Claims are supported by evidence beyond evidence. The statistical tests show that the findings are statistically significant. Still more statistics show there is an incredibly low probability for all the tests having such results. There is a 1 in 5.8 nonillion (5.8×10^{30}) chance of all this happening randomly.

But not only is the Code a fact—the Code foretells history and the people who are destined to become central figures in this history. Presidents, Prime Ministers, Monarchs, and Chancellors have Historical Events spelled out in their names at birth. And, by the appearance of these Events in their name, these Events have been predicted. Thus, the Code foretells the American War of Independence, The Civil War, World War One, World War Two, and the Holocaust.

We are told, for example, that there will be The Civil War and that it will involve Abraham Lincoln and Ulysses Grant. Herbert Hoover will serve approximately 64 years after the declared end of The Civil War. Each Event is foretold with the same accuracy and precision as this one.

As I realized the foretelling of these Historical Events was deliberate, I felt my perception of the world being challenged. Certainly, this kind of order to things called into question my whole worldview. I was experiencing an inner revolution. The most radical of revolutions!

I don't think I am alone when I say such a thing. Everyone's experience is going to be unique, certainly, but it would be hard to imagine anyone reading this book and walking away unaffected. And so now you know, the English alphabet is a secret code that has been deliberately etched into the English language. And we write, speak, and share a language that foretells the future!

THE SCHEMA

According to Swiss psychologist Jean Piaget, as children and continuing as adults, we develop a "schema," a framework through which we understand the world around us. When confronted with something new, we find a way to assimilate it into our schema. When it does not fit into our pre-existing schema, we are forced to change our schema to accommodate the new information. On very rare occasions, we must overthrow the old schema. It can be likened to a revolution of the mind. None of the new information we are presented with in this book appears to fit into most schemas. The idea that the names of wars and other Historical Events are encoded in the names of world leaders associated with these Events does not make sense in most people's world. For this reason, the Code is certain to challenge our schemas.

I don't consider it appropriate for me to try to speak for you. I can only speak for myself. I have always been a reasonable man—a logical man—a man who claims nothing until after seeing the facts. So, this whole book has entailed quite a leap for me. And I don't mean a leap of faith. The leap of faith required *before* researching this book was quite a leap. But my next leap of faith is barely a hop because something is right in front of me, waving its arms. My leap, then? My leap is a leap from the reality we see and hear and smell and taste and touch every day to an experience of something that is uncanny—unheard-of—and so unusual and out of the ordinary that I must rethink everything I have ever believed to be true.

There is most definitely a force at work here. It is up to you how you perceive who or what this force is. It's my guess that more people will perceive a "who" than a "what." An inanimate object cannot predict the future.

THE WATCHMAKER ANALOGY

The Watchmaker Analogy is a teleological argument for the existence of God. The argument is "a design implies a designer." If someone is walking and they come across a rock, they might pick up the rock. They might look at it, and they might assume that it is a product of nature. But if someone is walking and comes across a watch, they will perceive it differently. They will say that the watch is a design and that it is not just a product of nature—but that it was designed by a designer.

The Watchmaker Argument, as a whole, is controversial. David Hume argued that we have no knowledge of world-making, so we can't compare world-making to watch-making. He also argued that one can't make such an argument based on an analogy. Comparing a watch to the universe in one respect does not prove that they are alike in any other respect. Believers, skeptics, critics, and nonbelievers have kept the argument alive. I bring up to the Watchmaker Argument because a new discovery has been made that absolutely implies it is a design.

The Code is a design. There is no question. The evidence of the design is overwhelming. And the design of the Code implies a designer.

Let us present this as a categorical syllogism:

> Major Premise: A Design implies a Designer
> Minor premise: The Code is a Design
> Conclusion: The Code has a Designer

With this syllogism, we are presented with a truth in a way that is nice and tidy and to the point. Each step is clear. Each proposition is clear. But the Code goes further than this and into a new realm. The Code is not just a design; the Code predicts the future. So let us observe the logic of another syllogism:

> Major Premise: Only God knows the future
> Minor premise: The Code can foretell the future
> Conclusion: The Code is the work of God

Forgive me for the change in the syllogism; I would rather state it as "the Code is from God" than say "the Code is the work of God."

The two syllogisms we just read bring logic to our assertion that the Code is the work of God. As we see, then, the Watchmaker Analogy applies to the Code. You can argue that some designs that have been applied to the Watchmaker Analogy do not stand up for everyone. For example, some people see the Perfection of the Universe as a Design, and there are others who do not see the Perfection of the Universe as a Design. In fact, there are those who do not see the Perfection of the Universe. There are arguments; there is debate.

But I assert to you that the findings in this book cannot be denied. The Design is evident. As much as some might want to deny it or argue it at some point, there is no point at which it can be dismissed. The Code is no rock—it is a watch.

So, I will remind you of the conversation I had with my wife so long ago, before my discovery.

Blythe asked, "Do you think you can find a code hidden in the English language?"

I replied, "Yes. If there is a code, I will find it."

After reflecting a moment, Blythe said, "If you can, you will do much more than find a code. You will prove there is a God!"

IMPLICATIONS

The implications of the discovery of the Code are vast and far-reaching. Never before in the history of the world has there been such a discovery. For some, the Code will be experienced merely as mind-boggling or as an interesting curiosity. For others, it will be life-changing and transformative. Some will find the Code as evidence of God—of fate—or of a meaning and purpose to the Universe.

In addition to the personal meaning the Code may bring into each person's life, many fields of study will never be the same.

Linguistics, especially etymology, will acquire a new dimension. The numerical value of words will be introduced as a new world for exploration. Gematria will be considered to have been confirmed as real and this will bring many more people to its study. Many of those who have studied Gematria for years will find joy in exploring new directions.

The study of History will acquire multiple new dimensions. As we see the names of Historical Events in the names of leaders destined to be involved in those Events, we will see predictions, decisions, choice, and destiny unfold right before our eyes in a never-ending story.

Philosophy will be forever changed. For every unanswered question that has been proposed by philosophers, there will be a new one that is similar. The question, "Why is there something instead of nothing?" will be joined by "Why is this 'something' predetermined?" The question, "How do we conceive of the relationship between free will and fate?" will be expounded upon by thinkers. Completely new philosophical questions will also be asked in light of the discovery such as, "How should I live my life?"—"How will I live my life?

Religion and spirituality will undergo a transformation. How evidence of the existence of God will be received, perceived, questioned and pondered will be at the discretion of each person. And, if there is fate and if consciousness pervades the Universe, will this diminish our fear of death and our fear of ceasing to be?

That which I have mentioned here will only be a small part of what is to come of this discovery and will only be the beginning. The implications will be as far reaching as our imaginations, and each and every one of us will have a chance to experience our world in an exciting new light.

There will be a rebirth of wonder.

SECTION V

APPENDICES

APPENDIX A

LEGAL AND HISTORICAL DOCUMENTS

This is the Certificate of Birth for Barack Hussein Obama II. Note that the suffix to his name is the Roman numeral II rather than Jr. Eleven Presidents have the suffix "'Jr.'" (one of them in both his birth name and in his adopted name) and eight have the suffix "'Sr.'" Obama is one of 10 Presidents with a Roman numeral suffix to his name.

This is the Certificate of Birth for Adolfus Hitler. The middle name Jacob is not listed in this certificate. It is not known what the protocol was for this birth certificate template at that time or if middle names were added shortly after. It is not known if the space below the name Adolfus was intended as space for other given names.

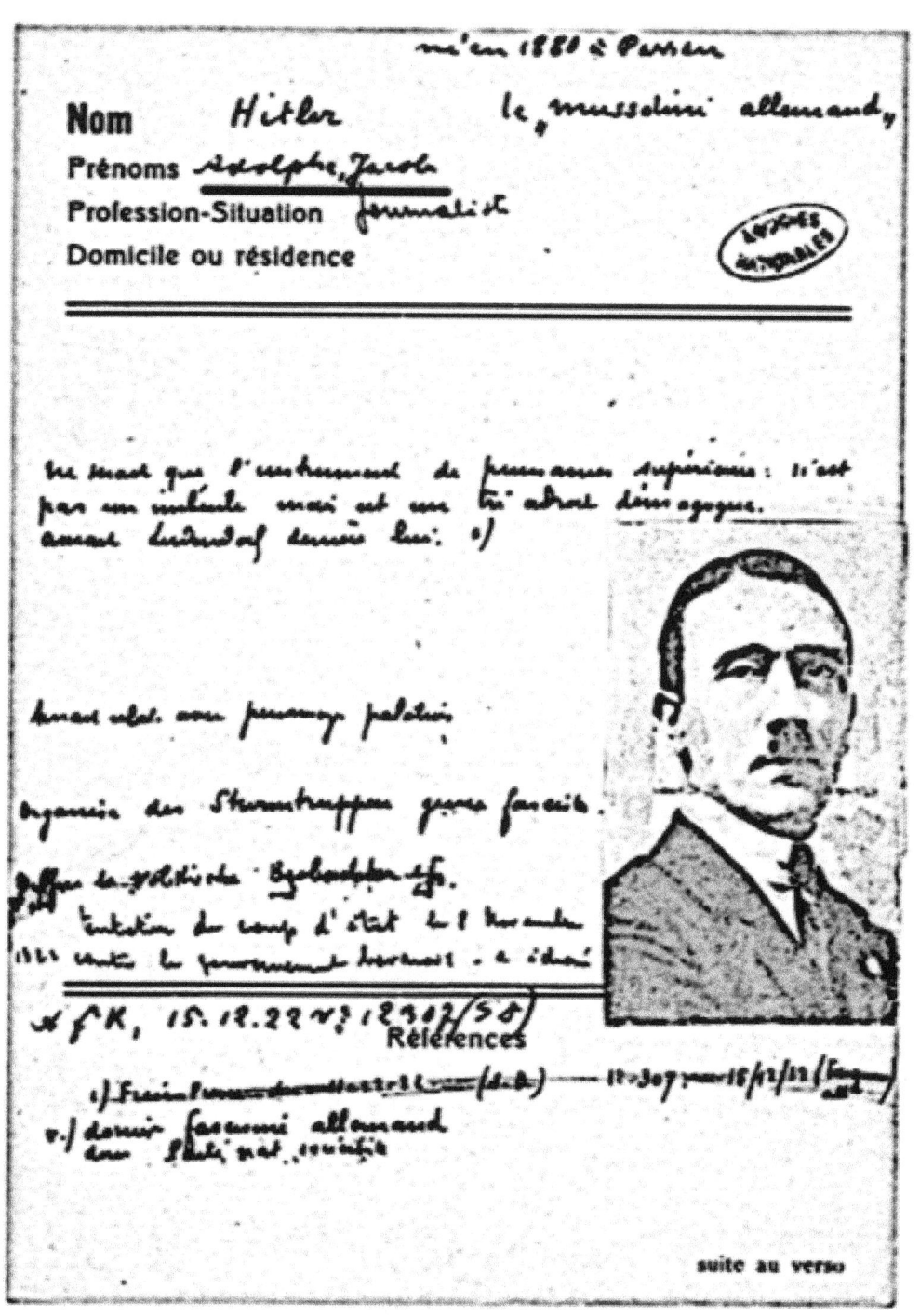

Prénoms is the French term for forenames and refers to the given names that precede the surname. As we see on this 1924 French Police File Card, according to the police and to Hitler himself, Hitler's middle name is, unquestionably, Jacob.

APPENDIX B

EXCLUSIONS FROM TESTS

EXCLUSIONS

In some of the statistical tests you see performed in this book, I have excluded what we must consider to be exceptions. These exclusions are made to make the statistical tests valid and reliable.

NAMESAKE OF A VETERAN EXCEPTION

When performing any type of research, one must be vigilant to rule out alternative explanations for any finding. The Namesake of a Veteran Exception is important to this study for that very reason. If two people have the same name, they will have the same letters, numbers, and words in their names. If one of their given names and their surnames is the same, their middle names can differ so long as the words, acronyms or abbreviations are found in the shared names. If someone has a meaningful Presentation of an Event in their name, their namesakes for whom there is no meaning must be excluded from the statistical tests.

This study looks for the names of Historical Events in the names of Heads of State and Military Leaders. Leaders have the Event in their name if they played a central role in it or if they had a strong involvement in or a strong association with the Event. It is interesting to note that people from the rest of the population can also have an Historical Event, such as a war, in their name for other meaningful reasons. For example, a person died in the Event, played an important role in the Event, and/or the Event had a strong impact on the person's life.

All of the world leaders discussed here have Veteran Namesakes who likely have more of an involvement in a war than merely serving in that war. Being a namesake requires that a world leader be excluded from the tests.

President WILLIAM HENRY HARRISON SR has WORLD WAR I and WORLD WAR II in his name. His great-great-grandson and namesake, WILLIAM HENRY HARRISON III, served in WORLD WAR I in the Aviation Section (Signal Corps), and he went on to serve five terms as a U.S. Representative. Lieutenant General WILLIAM HENRY HARRISON MORRIS, JR served in both world wars—he was promoted to Captain in 1917 and Major in 1918, and to Brigadier General for a time in WORLD WAR II and, finally to Lieutenant General. He was known for an act of extraordinary bravery in WORLD WAR I. As a result of being a namesake of numerous Veterans of both world wars, WILLIAM HENRY HARRISON SR has been excluded from the tests.

Multiple men who are likely named after President RUTHERFORD BIRCHARD HAYES served in WORLD WAR I and/or II, and, therefore, he has been excluded.

Of the many men who served in one or both of the world wars with the same name as President JAMES ABRAM GARFIELD, one was his own grandson JAMES ABRAM GARFIELD II, who served as Captain and Major during WORLD WAR I. As a result, he has been excluded.

THEODORE ROOSEVELT JR
THEODORE ROOSEVELT III
THEODORE ROOSEVELT IV

THEODORE ROOSEVELT JR was President of the United States. He played a leading role in the Preparedness Movement to arm the U.S. in case of an emergency entrance into the war that would one day be known as WORLD WAR ONE. His association with WORLD WAR ONE, and the fact that his five children participated in the war, gives THEODORE ROOSEVELT a reason for a Presentation of WORLD WAR ONE in his name. With a son, THEODORE ROOSEVELT III, who fought in both world wars, and a grandson, THEODORE ROOSEVELT IV, who fought in WORLD WAR TWO, we see that THEODORE ROOSEVELT JR also qualifies for the Namesake Exception. His son and grandson have the words, so he must also. Therefore, his name is excluded from WORLD WAR TWO.

WILLIAM JEFFERSON BLYTHE SR
WILLIAM JEFFERSON BLYTHE JR
WILLIAM JEFFERSON BLYTHE III

The President we know as Bill Clinton was born WILLIAM JEFFERSON BLYTHE III. His father, WILLIAM JEFFERSON BLYTHE JR served in WORLD WAR II. Historically, it is important in terms of him being the father of a U.S. President, and it was one of the most important events in his short life—he only lived to be 28 years of age.

British Prime Minister WILLIAM WYNDHAM GRENVILLE contains WWI and WWII in his name. WYNDHAM is his mother's maiden name and GRENVILLE is his father's surname. It is WILLIAM WYNDHAM that contains WWI and WWII. There is a long list of soldiers and sailors who fought in one or both the world wars named WILLIAM WYNDHAM. One such WILLIAM WYNDHAM was a Major in 1916. Others with the name show up on muster rolls, hospital records, and service records during WWI and WWII.

FREDERICK JOHN ROBINSON, Prime Minister of the United Kingdom, is excluded from the test of WORLD WAR ONE and WORLD WAR TWO, as there are a great number of men named FREDERICK ROBINSON who served in one of the world wars, and who held high positions.

British Prime Minister GEORGE HAMILTON GORDON contains WORLD WAR ONE in his name. A great number of males were named after him and some of them served in WORLD WAR ONE. If a name contains WORLD WAR ONE—this greatly increases the chance that the name will also contain WORLD WAR TWO. This is the case for GEORGE HAMILTON GORDON.

The name of Prime Minister WILLIAM EWART GLADSTONE is certainly distinct with its middle name EWART. He also had a number of men named after him, including many who served in WORLD WAR I or WORLD WAR II.

Prime Minister EDWARD RICHARD GEORGE HEATH does have WORLD WAR I in his name without the need of his first name, EDWARD. There were quite a few men who served in WORLD WAR I for the United Kingdom and for the United States named either RICHARD GEORGE HEATH or GEORGE RICHARD HEATH.

In addition, ALEXANDER FREDERICK DOUGLAS-HOME, Prime Minister of the United Kingdom, had several namesakes in both world wars. Captain ALEXANDER FREDERICK DOUGLAS, born September 2, 1871, served in WORLD WAR ONE and has Presentations of WORLD WAR ONE/ WORLD WAR I/ FIRST WORLD WAR in his name. Major ALEXANDER FREDERICK DOUGLAS-SMITH, who died October 8, 1944, during WORLD WAR TWO, has Presentations of WORLD WAR TWO/SECOND WORLD WAR in his name. There is no need for the hyphenated surname HOME in order to display the world war expressions in their names.

It is highly probable that in each case of a world leader with the name of a Veteran, one or more of the Veterans had a personal and meaningful reason for having the war in his name. The leader who shares a name with someone with a Presentation of the Historical Event in his name cannot help but have the Event, as well. For this reason, the leader who shares his name with a Veteran of the Event must be excluded from the test.

NAMESAKES OF OTHER HEADS OF STATE AND LEADERS

GEORGE III WILLIAM FREDERICK
GEORGE IV AUGUSTUS FREDERICK
GEORGE V FREDERICK ERNEST ALBERT
ALBERT FREDERICK ARTHUR GEORGE VI

These four British Monarchs share two of their names—GEORGE and FREDERICK. Two also share ALBERT. The last two also share a "V," and three share an "I." So, some of them must be excluded from certain tests as they automatically have many of the same or nearly same Displays. When you see any of their names excluded from a test, it is because of the Namesake Exception. In these cases, one more letter is all that is needed to spell the name of the Historical Event, greatly increasing the probability of sharing the Event in their names.

In fact, GEORGE V FREDERICK ERNEST ALBERT, the Monarch during WORLD WAR ONE, and ALBERT FREDERICK ARTHUR GEORGE VI, who served during WORLD WAR TWO, have each other's war in their names because of the similarity in the names of the wars, as well as similarities in their names. Again, ALBERT FREDERICK ARTHUR GEORGE VI has expressions for WORLD WAR TWO in his name, as he should, and because of this, he has a 70.3% chance of having expressions for WORLD WAR ONE in his name. GEORGE V FREDERICK ERNEST ALBERT has a 61.5% chance of having WORLD WAR ONE in his name. Let us look at this close similarity.

WORLD WAR ONE/TWO EXCEPTIONS

The names of WORLD WAR ONE and WORLD WAR TWO are very similar. They share two words—WORLD and WAR, and, in the third word, they share an "O." So, nine out of eleven letters are the exact same letters. When we convert the letters into numbers, they are even more similar. The third words in the two wars are ONE and TWO. The "N" or "E" in ONE is equal to 5, just as the "W" in TWO is equal to 5. This means that only the "E" in ONE and the "T" in TWO have a different numerical value. Someone with WORLD WAR ONE in their name only needs a 2 in their name to have WORLD WAR TWO. In fact, someone with WORLD WAR ONE in their name has a 61.9% probability of having WORLD WAR TWO and those with WORLD WAR TWO have a 70.3% probability of having WORLD WAR ONE. In some situations, it is 100%, which we can see with simple logic. No one can have WORLD WAR II without having WORLD WAR I.

As we know, THOMAS WOODROW WILSON is associated with WORLD WAR ONE and has two of the four expressions for the war. He, therefore, has a 61.9% probability of having one or more expressions of WORLD WAR TWO in his name. For this reason, THOMAS WOODROW WILSON is excluded from the test for WORLD WAR TWO. On the other hand, JOHN FITZGERALD KENNEDY has WORLD WAR TWO in his name for good reason but Displays WORLD WAR ONE because of the shared letters between the wars. JOHN FITZGERALD KENNEDY is excluded from WORLD WAR ONE for this reason.

WWI/WWII AND WORLD WAR I/WORLD WAR II EXCEPTIONS

As stated, any name that has a Presentation of WORLD WAR II will, with the simple exclusion of one letter or number, have a Display of WORLD WAR I. So, RICHARD MILHAUS NIXON, who served in WORLD WAR II, and BARACK HUSSEIN OBAMA II, who is the 64-Year Phenomenon for WORLD WAR II, are excluded from the tests for WORLD WAR I. Similarly, a name that has WWII in it will also have WWI. This excludes DWIGHT DAVID EISENHOWER from the test for WWI.

Similarly, WILLIAM HOWARD TAFT has a meaningful reason for having WWI in his name. He happened to have an extra "I" in his name—as in WWII—but he likely has the extra "I" because of his Presentation of THE CIVIL WAR.

SECOND WORLD WAR AND WORLD WAR ONE EXEPTIONS

British Prime Minister DAVID WILLIAM DONALD CAMERON has SECOND WORLD WAR in his name. The word SECOND has the letters of ONE in it, so CAMERON also has WORLD WAR ONE in his name. Therefore, he is an exception that is excluded from the test for Prime Ministers and WORLD WAR ONE. In addition, he cannot have WORLD WAR II in his name without also having WORLD WAR I.

THE CIVIL WAR/WORLD WAR I EXCEPTIONS

Having THE CIVIL WAR in one's name gives one a 62.1% chance of also having a Display of WORLD WAR I. This is the most likely reason for ABRAHAM LINCOLN II and RUTHERFORD BIRCHARD HAYES having WORLD WAR I in their names. Those without a Display of THE CIVIL WAR, have only a 15.3% chance of having WORLD WAR I in their names. In other words, people with THE CIVIL WAR in their name have four times the chance of having it than those who do not. For this reason, the names of ABRAHAM LINCOLN II and RUTHERFORD BIRCHARD HAYES are excluded from this test. The reader will note that RUTHERFORD BIRCHARD HAYES is also excluded for the Namesake of Veteran Exception.

AWOI EXCEPTIONS

This table demonstrates how common and how rare the four letters "A," "W," "O," and "I" are in the names of the Presidents:

LEVEL TWO: THE SEARCH FOR **AWOI** IN THE NAMES OF U.S. PRESIDENTS

	(PRESENT)	(MISSING)
GEORGE WASHINGTON	***AWOI***	
JOHN ADAMS JR	AO	WI
THOMAS JEFFERSON II	AOI	W
JAMES MADISON JR	AOI	W
JAMES MONROE	AO	WI
JOHN QUINCY ADAMS	AOI	W
ANDREW JACKSONJR	AWO	I
MARTIN VAN BUREN SR	AI	OW
WILLIAM HENRY HARRISON	***AWOI***	
JOHN TYLER JR	O	AWI
JAMES KNOX POLK	AO	WI
ZACHARY TAYLOR	AO	WI
MILLARD FILLMORE	AOI	W
FRANKLIN PIERCE SR	AI	WO
JAMES BUCHANAN JR	A	WOI
ABRAHAM LINCOLN II	AOI	W
ANDREW JOHNSON JR	AWO	I
HIRAM ULYSSES GRANT	AI	WO
RUTHERFORD BIRCHARD HAYES I	AOI	W
JAMES ABRAM GARFIELD I	AI	WO
CHESTER ALAN ARTHUR I	AI	WO
STEPHEN GROVER CLEVELAND	AO	WI
BENJAMIN HARRISON VIII	AOI	W
WILLIAM MCKINLEY JR	AWI	O
THEODORE ROOSEVELT JR	O	AWI
WILLIAM HOWARD TAFT I	------EXCLUSION FROM TEST-------	
THOMAS WOODROW WILSON	------EXCLUSION FROM TEST-------	
WARREN GAMALIEL HARDING	AWI	O
JOHN CALVIN COOLIDGE JR	AOI	W
HERBERT CLARK HOOVER I	OI	AW

LEVEL TWO: THE SEARCH FOR **AWOI** IN THE NAMES OF U.S. PRESIDENTS		
	(PRESENT)	(MISSING)
FRANKLIN DELANO ROOSEVELT SR	AOI	W
HARRY S. TRUMAN	A	WOI
DWIGHT DAVID EISENHOWER I	-------EXCLUSION FROM TEST-----------	
JOHN FITZGERALD KENNEDY SR	AOI	W
LYNDON BAINES JOHNSON	AOI	W
RICHARD MILHAUS NIXON	AIO	W
LESLIE LYNCH KING JR	I	AWO
JAMES EARL CARTER JR	A	WOI
RONALD WILSON REAGAN	--------EXCLUSION FROM TEST-----------	
GEORGE HERBERT WALKER BUSH	AWO	I
WILLIAM JEFFERSON BLYTHE III	-------EXCLUSION FROM TEST---------	
GEORGE WALKER BUSH	AWO	I
BARACK HUSSEIN OBAMA II	AOI	W
DONALD JOHN TRUMP SR	AO	WI

WOODROW WILSON, WILLIAM HOWARD TAFT, and DWIGHT DAVID EISENHOWER have WWI and/or WWII in their names, giving them a W and an I in their name. In addition, WOODROW WILSON has WORLD WAR ONE, making it more probable for him to have AWOI. WILLIAM HOWARD TAFT and RONALD WILSON REAGAN have WORLD WAR I in their names, and WILLIAM JEFFERSON BLYTHE has WORLD WAR II, so they all have a strong probability of having AWOI in their names. Therefore, they are excluded from the tests.

EXCLUSIONS FOR LENGTH OF NAME

Some leaders have especially long names. The number of letters in a name can exceed the other names in the test to the point where it can significantly increase their probability of having an Incidental Display. There are many people in history whose name would have everything in it because of the length of their name. For example, **PABLO DIEGO JOSÉ FRANCISCO DE PAULA JUAN NEPOMUCENO CRISPÍN CRISPINIANO MARÍA REMEDIOS DE LA SANTÍSIMA TRINIDAD RUIZ PICASSO** has 107 letters in his name. He likely has all the wars and events in history in his name.

APPENDIX C

THE TAFT-OBAMA-COOLIDGE-BALFOUR-ASSOCIATIONS

STRONG ASSOCIATION WITH THE HISTORICAL EVENT

I found it curious that outside of the names of the leaders with a strong involvement in a Historical Event, who had a Presentation of the Event, and the 64-Year Phenomenon who also had a Presentation, four other leaders with strong associations with—but not a direct involvement in—the actual Event, have the Event in their names.

WILLIAM HOWARD TAFT was the first somewhat unexpected but not overly surprising name I found while performing the tests. His name came up when I was examining the names of U.S. Presidents for Displays of THE CIVIL WAR. While the other Presidents with THE CIVIL WAR in their names were more directly involved in the war, Taft was strongly associated with the long aftermath of the war. Having been interested in the Presidents since childhood, I was not, as I have said, overly surprised by the finding of the Display in Taft. I knew about his racism, his involvement on the wrong side of Cuba's Negro Rebellion, and his appointment of an ex-Confederate and ex-Klansman to Chief Justice of the Supreme Court. Because of these events, I understood the Display and I considered it to be a Presentation—not an Incidental Display.

BARACK HUSSEIN OBAMA II was another President who was not directly involved in THE CIVIL WAR, but who had several strong associations with it, and he has a Display of the war in his name. This was not really surprising, because some of the events in the aftermath of THE CIVIL WAR, including Amendments to the Constitution, predicted the eventuality of an African American President.

My history consultant throughout my work—Jake Daniel—has impressed upon me that a war does not start when the belligerents declare war and begin fighting. The build-up of tension and all the contributing factors that lead up to it are also a part of the history of the war. Nor does a war end when someone surrenders. The aftermath of the physical surrender of armies is just as much a part of it. There are treaties and agreements, but these are often made with resentments, and there are often lingering or unresolved tensions.

As just mentioned, one aftermath of the success of the Union in THE CIVIL WAR, was the passing of the 13th Amendment, which abolished slavery, the 14th Amendment, which defined citizenship, and the 15th Amendment, which prohibited the denial of right to vote based on race, color or previous condition of servitude. Collectively, these three Civil War amendments were intended to give civil rights and protection to those who were formerly enslaved. One of the most positive results of the Civil War Amendments was the election of an African American President—BARACK HUSSEIN OBAMA II. Indeed, it should be no surprise that he has THE CIVIL WAR encoded in his name.

JOHN CALVIN COOLIDGE, JR was a President who was not directly involved in WORLD WAR I, but had several strong associations with it, and he has a Display of the war in his name. Coolidge was first elected Governor of Massachusetts by a very small margin. It is likely he won because of his strong support for U.S. involvement in WORLD WAR I. And he was elected Governor just one week before the war ended. As Governor, he gave every WORLD WAR I Veteran in his state $100, an amount valued at about $2,000 in today's dollars. This very likely helped him a few years later to win re-election. Another association is his vetoing a bill that would give money to the nation's WORLD WAR I Veterans. His strongest association was his authorization of the Dawes Plan after the war. The plan was designed to resolve the problem of Germany's postwar reparations.

ARTHUR JAMES BALFOUR was still another name that came to be of special interest to me. When conducting my tests, I found that he had a Covert Presentation of HOLOCAUST in his name. He was the author of the Balfour Declaration, which, in 1917, announced the United Kingdom's support for the Zionist Movement for a Jewish Homeland in Palestine. My history consultant made it clear how important this was in world history and in Jewish history. The effects of this historical document on the world cannot be underestimated. Although he was not directly involved in the HOLOCAUST, I came to see the reason the Presentation of HOLOCAUST is in his name. Historically, the only two Prime Ministers of the United Kingdom with a long friendship with the Jews have been WINSTON LEONARD CHURCHILL and ARTHUR JAMES BALFOUR.

I find it quite interesting that ALEXANDER FREDERICK DOUGLAS-HOME has DER HOLOCAUST in his name. While serving as a Member of Parliament and as a Junior Officer, he was present at the final meeting between Prime Minister ARTHUR NEVILLE CHAMBERLAIN and ADOLF HITLER. As much as it is possible this meeting had a significant impact on him, only he would have known that. The finding of DER HOLOCAUST in his name must, therefore, only be considered an Incidental Display, and, in the statistical tests, he must still be considered a failure to predict. It appears from the findings in this book that only those with a strong involvement in or, as we now see, a strong association with the Event, should be expected to have a Display of the Event in their name, which we would then call a Presentation.

APPENDIX D

THE ALTERNATE PREDICTION: THE GREAT WAR AND HERBERT HENRY ASQUITH

THE ALTERNATE PREDICTION: THE GREAT WAR AND HERBERT HENRY ASQUITH

The statistical tests in this book include tests for four similar, substitutable, and interchangeable expressions for each of the world wars. These are WORLD WAR ONE/WORLD WAR I/WWI/FIRST WORLD WAR and WORLD WAR TWO/WORLD WAR II/WWII/SECOND WORLD WAR.

When the first world war began, no one knew that there would be a second. The only mentions of WORLD WAR II were made in the same way we talk today about a hypothetical WORLD WAR III. So, there wasn't a WORLD WAR I until there was a WORLD WAR II. The four 'world war' expressions for each of the two world wars have been used universally since the beginning of WORLD WAR II.

The United Kingdom declared war on Germany on August 4, 1914. The war was known as THE GREAT WAR or WORLD WAR. A search of the names of British Prime Ministers finds that the only Prime Minister with less than twenty letters in his or her name to contain THE GREAT WAR is HERBERT HENRY ASQUITH. As he was the first Prime Minister to serve during the war, this Presentation provides supporting evidence for Claim 1 and Claim 3.

The United States entered the war much later, declaring war on Germany on April 6, 1917, thereby making it a world war. American newspapers called it THE WORLD WAR. The names of three U.S. Presidents with less than twenty letters contain THE WORLD WAR. They are THOMAS WOODROW WILSON, HERBERT CLARK HOOVER, and THEODORE ROOSEVELT. These findings provide further support for Claim 1 and Claim 3.

I chose not to include statistical tests for THE GREAT WAR in the name of the Prime Ministers of the United Kingdom or THE WORLD WAR in the names of the Presidents of the United States because these two expressions are no longer in common use and because the four 'world war' expressions have been used universally since the beginning of WORLD WAR II.

COVERT PRESENTATIONS OF **THE GREAT WAR** IN THE PRIME MINISTERS OF THE U.K.

	(PRESENT)	(MISSING)
WILLIAM PITT II	TGRATWR	HEEA
HENRY ADDINGTON	THEGREAWR	TA
WILLIAM WYNDHAM GRENVILLE	HEGREAWAR	TT
WILLIAM HENRY CAVENDISH CAVENDISH-BENTINCK	(((THE GREAT WAR)))	38 LETTERS
SPENCER PERCEVAL I	EGREAWAR	THT
ROBERT BANKS JENKINSON	TEGREAWAR	HG
GEORGE CANNING JNR	EGREAWAR	THT
FREDERICK JOHN ROBINSON	THEREATWAR	G
ARTHUR WELLESLEY	THEGREAWAR	T
CHARLES GREY II	HEGREAAR	TTW
ROBERT PEEL II	TEGREWR	HATA
HENRY WILLIAM LAMB	THEGREAWAR	T
JOHN RUSSELL II	HEREAAR	TGTWE
EDWARD GEORGE GEOFFREY SMITH-STANLEY	(((THE GREAT WAR)))	32 LETTERS
GEORGE HAMILTON-GORDON	THEGREAWR	TA
HENRY JOHN TEMPLE	THEGREAW	TAR
BENJAMIN DISRAELI	TEREAWAR	HGT
WILLIAM EWART GLADSTONE	TEGREATWAR	H
ARCHIBALD PHILIP PRIMROSE	THEGRAAR	ETW
ROBERT ARTHUR TALBOT GASCOYNE-CECIL	(((THE GREAT WAR)))	31 LETTERS
ARTHUR JAMES BALFOUR	THERATAR	GEW
HENRY CAMPBELL BANNERMAN	**THE GREAT WAR**	**22 LETTERS**
HERBERT HENRY ASQUITH	***THE GREAT WAR***	**19 LETTERS**
DAVID LLOYD GEORGE I	EGREAR	THTWA
ANDREW BONAR LAW I	TEREAWAR	HGT
STANLEY BALDWIN	TEGREATWA	HR
JAMES RAMSAY MACDONALD	EGREAA	THTWR
ARTHUR NEVILLE CHAMBERLAIN	THEREATWAR	G
WINSTON LEONARD CHURCHILL	THEGREAWAR	T
CLEMENT RICHARD ATTLEE	THEREATWAR	G
ROBERT ANTHONY EDEN	THEGREATWR	A
MAURICE HAROLD MACMILLAN	HEREAAR	TGTW
ALEXANDER FREDERICK DOUGLAS-HOME	THEGREAWAR	T
JAMES HAROLD WILSON	HEREAWAR	TGT
EDWARD RICHARD GEORGE HEATH	THEGREAWAR	T
LEONARD JAMES CALLAGHAN	HEGREAWA	TGTR
MARGARET HILDA ROBERTS THATCHER	***THE GREAT WAR***	**28 LETTERS**
JOHN ROY MAJOR	HEGRAAR	TETW
ANTHONY CHARLES LYNTON BLAIR	(((THE GREAT WAR)))	25 LETTERS
JAMES GORDON BROWN	TEGREAWAR	HT
DONALD WILLIAM DAVID CAMERON	EREAWAR	THGT
THERESA MARY BRASIER MAY	(((THE GREAT WAR)))	21 LETTERS
ALEXANDER BORIS DE PFEFFEL JOHNSON	THEGREAWAR	T

If we examine the names of all Prime Ministers of the United Kingdom, we find that three most likely have THE GREAT WAR in their names because of how many letters they have in their name.

COVERT PRESENTATIONS OF **THE GREAT WAR** IN THE PRIME MINISTERS OF THE U.K.

	(PRESENT)	(MISSING)
WILLIAM PITT II	TGRATWR	HEEA
HENRY ADDINGTON	THEGREAWR	TA
WILLIAM WYNDHAM GRENVILLE	HEGREAWAR	TT
SPENCER PERCEVAL I	EGREAWAR	THT
ROBERT BANKS JENKINSON	TEGREAWAR	HG
GEORGE CANNING JNR	EGREAWAR	THT
FREDERICK JOHN ROBINSON	THEREATWAR	G
ARTHUR WELLESLEY	THEGREAWAR	T
CHARLES GREY II	HEGREAAR	TTW
ROBERT PEEL II	TEGREWR	HATA
HENRY WILLIAM LAMB	THEGREAWAR	T
JOHN RUSSELL II	HEREAAR	TGTWE
GEORGE HAMILTON-GORDON	THEGREAWR	TA
HENRY JOHN TEMPLE	THEGREAW	TAR
BENJAMIN DISRAELI	TEREAWAR	HGT
WILLIAM EWART GLADSTONE	TEGREATWAR	H
ARCHIBALD PHILIP PRIMROSE	THEGRAAR	ETW
ARTHUR JAMES BALFOUR	THERATAR	GEW
HENRY CAMPBELL BANNERMAN	(((THE GREAT WAR)))	22 LETTERS
HERBERT HENRY ASQUITH	***THE GREAT WAR***	**19 LETTERS**
DAVID LLOYD GEORGE I	EGREAR	THTWA
ANDREW BONAR LAW I	TEREAWAR	HGT
STANLEY BALDWIN	TEGREATWA	HR
JAMES RAMSAY MACDONALD	EGREAA	THTWR
ARTHUR NEVILLE CHAMBERLAIN	THEREATWAR	G
WINSTON LEONARD CHURCHILL	THEGREAWAR	T
CLEMENT RICHARD ATTLEE	THEREATWAR	G
ROBERT ANTHONY EDEN	THEGREATWR	A
MAURICE HAROLD MACMILLAN	HEREAAR	TGTW
ALEXANDER FREDERICK DOUGLAS-HOME	THEGREAWAR	T
JAMES HAROLD WILSON	HEREAWAR	TGT
EDWARD RICHARD GEORGE HEATH	THEGREAWAR	T
LEONARD JAMES CALLAGHAN	HEGREAWA	TGTR
MARGARET HILDA ROBERTS THATCHER	***THE GREAT WAR***	**28 LETTERS** 64-YR PHEN
JOHN ROY MAJOR	HEGRAAR	TETW
ANTHONY CHARLES LYNTON BLAIR	(((THE GREAT WAR)))	25 LETTERS
JAMES GORDON BROWN	TEGREAWAR	HT
DONALD WILLIAM DAVID CAMERON	EREAWAR	THGT
THERESA MARY BRASIER MAY	(((THE GREAT WAR)))	21 LETTERS
ALEXANDER BORIS DE PFEFFEL JOHNSON	THEGREAWAR	T

If we exclude the three Prime Ministers with more than 31 letters in their name, we find five Prime Ministers have THE GREAT WAR. Two of them are correct predictions. The Prime Minister who served during THE GREAT WAR and the 64-Year Phenomenon. The other three are incorrect in that context.

COVERT PRESENTATIONS OF **THE GREAT WAR** IN THE PRIME MINISTERS WITH LESS THAN 21 LETTERS

	(PRESENT)	(MISSING)
WILLIAM PITT II	TGRATWR	HEEA
HENRY ADDINGTON	THEGREAWR	TA
SPENCER PERCEVAL I	EGREAWAR	THT
ROBERT BANKS JENKINSON	TEGREAWAR	HG
GEORGE CANNING JNR	EGREAWAR	THT
ARTHUR WELLESLEY	THEGREAWAR	T
CHARLES GREY II	HEGREAAR	TTW
ROBERT PEEL II	TEGRETWR	HAA
HENRY WILLIAM LAMB	THEGREAWAR	T
JOHN RUSSELL II	HEREAAR	TGTWE
GEORGE HAMILTON-GORDON	THEGREAWR	TA
HENRY JOHN TEMPLE	THEGREAW	TAR
BENJAMIN DISRAELI	TEREAWAR	HGT
ARTHUR JAMES BALFOUR	THERATAR	GEW
HERBERT HENRY ASQUITH	***THE GREAT WAR***	**19 LETTERS**
DAVID LLOYD GEORGE I	EGREAR	THTWA
ANDREW BONAR LAW I	TEREAWAR	HGT
STANLEY BALDWIN	TEGREATWA	HR
JAMES RAMSAY MACDONALD	EGREAA	THTWR
CLEMENT RICHARD ATTLEE	THEREATWAR	G
ROBERT ANTHONY EDEN	THEGREATWR	A
JAMES HAROLD WILSON	HEREAWAR	TGT
JOHN ROY MAJOR	HEGRAAR	TETW
JAMES GORDON BROWN	TEGREAWAR	HT

The more letters there are in a name, the greater likelihood of finding more words. Thus, the Prime Ministers in this table with a large number of letters have a greater chance of displaying THE GREAT WAR. What is very interesting to note is that if we look at the names of Prime Ministers with less than 21 letters, only HERBERT HENRY ASQUITH remains.

In all cases, the Heads of State who play a central role during the Events in this book have the Events in variations of their names with less letters than any other leader. In fact, with the exception of WINSTON LEONARD CHURCHILL, who has WORLD WAR TWO, WORLD WAR II, and DER HOLOCAUST with twenty-three letters in his name, Heads of State have their Presentations in their names with less than twenty letters. ABRAHAM LINCOLN has THE CIVIL WAR in thirteen sounds at Level One and sixteen letters at Level Three. WOODROW WILSON has WORLD WAR ONE and WWI in thirteen letters, and, as we now see, he has THE WORLD WAR in nineteen letters. FRANKLIN ROOSEVELT has WORLD WAR TWO in thirteen letters; FRANKLIN D ROOSEVELT has SECOND WORLD WAR in eighteen letters. DAVID L GEORGE I has WORLD WAR I in thirteen letters. DWIGHT EISENHOWER has WWI in sixteen letters. ADOLFUS JACOB HITLER has an Overt Presentation of DER HOLOCAUST in eighteen letters and he has a Covert Presentation in thirteen letters. And WASHINGTON has AWOl in only ten letters.

Likewise, the British Prime Minister with the least letters in his or her name and the only Prime Minister with less than twenty letters in his or her name to have THE GREAT WAR is HERBERT HENRY ASQUITH.

The Covert Presentation of THE GREAT WAR in the name of HERBERT HENRY ASQUITH provides supporting evidence for Claim 1 and Claim 3.

With this finding, we can see that Claim 1 is true in all cases—with a correlation of +1. All Heads of State who played a central role in the Event have a Superior presentation of the Event in their name.

We can also see that Claim 3 is true in all cases—with a correlation of +1.

APPENDIX E

THE 64-YEAR PHENOMENON

THE 64-YEAR PHENOMENON

During my studies of the leaders in this book, I came across what I call the 64-Year Phenomenon. The leader who serves approximately 64 years after a major turning point in a Historical Event also contains the name of the Event. This major turning point is a defining moment in the Event—one that typifies or determines all subsequent related occurrences.

If a leader is serving at the time of the 64-year anniversary of a Historical Event and is still serving on the date of the 65-year anniversary, that leader is the 64-Year Phenomenon and is expected to have the Event in his or her name. If, however, a new leader takes office during that one-year period of time between the 64-year anniversary and the 65-year anniversary, that new leader becomes the 64-Year Phenomenon and is the one who contains the Event in their name. If more than one leader takes office during that one-year period of time, it is the first of those who becomes the 64-Year Phenomenon and is the one who contains the Event in his or her name.

1. WILLIAM HARRISON served his brief term from March 4, 1841, until April 4, 1841. He was the first President to begin to serve after the 64th anniversary of the Declaration of Independence on July 4, 1776.

2. HERBERT CLARK HOOVER began his one term as President on March 4, 1929, and he served until March 4, 1933. So, during the entire year from the 64th anniversary of the end of the war (May 26, 1929) until the 65th anniversary (May 26, 1930), HERBERT CLARK HOOVER was President. He is the 64-Year Phenomenon of THE CIVIL WAR and he contains THE CIVIL WAR in his name.

3. WILLIAM JEFFERSON BLYTHE III (the birth name of Bill Clinton) began his term on January 20, 1993, and he served until January 20, 2001. The 128th anniversary (64 X 2) of the end of THE CIVIL WAR was May 26, 1993, and the 129th was May 26, 1994. He was President during that entire year.

4. RONALD WILSON REAGAN began his term on January 20, 1981, and, he served until January 20, 1989. During the years of the 64th and 65th anniversaries of WORLD WAR I, November 11, 1918, and November 11, 1919, REAGAN served as President of the United States.

5. BARACK HUSSEIN OBAMA II served as President from January 20, 2009, until January 20, 2017, covering the year between September 2, 2009, until September 2, 2010, the 64th and 65th anniversaries of the declared end of WORLD WAR II.

6. ELIZABETH II ALEXANDRA MARY WINDSOR had served as Queen of the United Kingdom beginning in 1952. If we add 64 years to 1914 (the beginning of WORLD WAR ONE) or 1918 (the end of WORLD WAR ONE) or any year in the aftermath, we get a year that Queen Elizabeth was the Monarch of the United Kingdom. She contains WORLD WAR I in her name.

7. ELIZABETH II ALEXANDRA MARY WINDSOR had remained Queen of the United Kingdom even during the 64 years after WORLD WAR TWO. She also contains WORLD WAR II in her name.

8. MARGARET HILDA ROBERTS THATCHER served as Prime Minister of the United Kingdom from 1979 until 1990, covering 64 years after 1915 through 1926.

9. DONALD WILLIAM DAVID CAMERON served as Prime Minister of the United Kingdom from May 11, 2010, until November 23, 2016. He was the first person to begin serving during the one year between the 64th and 65th anniversaries of the end of WORLD WAR II.

10. The turning point in the HOLOCAUST considered the most defining moment is when ADOLFUS JACOB HITLER became Chancellor of Germany and the Nazi party began to rule Germany. This was January 30, 1933.

HELMUT JOSEPH MICHAEL KOHL served as Chancellor of Germany from October 1, 1982, until October 27, 1998. HITLER became Chancellor on January 30, 1933, a turning point that set the HOLOCAUST in motion. Add 64 years and we get January 30, 1997. Kohl was already Chancellor on that date and remained Chancellor on the date of the 65-year anniversary—making him the 64-Year Phenomenon for the HOLOCAUST for Germany.

11. ANTHONY CHARLES LYNTON BLAIR served as the Prime Minister of the United Kingdom from May 2, 1997, to June 27, 2007. He became Prime Minister during the year that began with the 64-year anniversary of the turning point of the HOLOCAUST, and he continued beyond the 65-year anniversary. This makes him the 64-Year Phenomenon for the HOLOCAUST for the United Kingdom.

SECTION VI

STATISTICS

A STATISTICAL ANALYSIS OF THE TESTS IN THIS BOOK

A Probabilistic Quantification of Unusual Phenomena

ABSTRACT

People are attracted to events that seem unusual or that have low probability, even though unusual events occur every day. What about events we expect would have low probability, but occur with unexpected frequency under particular circumstances?

This project was conceived as providing supporting statistical measures for a recurring phenomenon identified by David Daniel. This phenomenon involves words that can be spelled using the letters (or letter-to-number translations) that comprise the names of well-known historical figures.

In this analysis, we estimate the occurrence of the phenomenon within the general population as a way to model random outcomes. Probabilities are determined to express the likelihood that observations within the historical figure populations would occur by chance. We run hypothesis tests to identify whether the historical figure measures fall outside a 95% confidence interval around the general population samples.

Due to correlation between the number of letters in a name and the existence of words within that name, we also calculate statistical measures for limited ranges of name lengths.

We expand on this approach to identify the chances of multiple phenomena being observed across independent populations, and by considering the composite populations in total.

We proceed to evaluate Mr. Daniel's contention that the observations he has made are unlikely to have been caused by chance. We will show that this is precisely the case in nearly every instance.

The analysis considers the populations of groups of Heads of State, compared to random samples of citizens from their respective countries. For Heads of State, Presentation of a Historical Event in his or her name, along with that person also having consequential involvement in the Event, is considered a Success. Also, for Heads of State, the lack of Presentation of an Event in a person's name, along with that person not having consequential involvement in the Event, is also a Success. For Heads of State, inconsistency between name Presentation and consequential Event involvement is a Failure. By definition, a citizen has no consequential involvement in any Event. Therefore, Presentation of an Event in the name of a citizen is a Failure. The absence of an Event Presentation in the name of a citizen is a Success.

The statistical test result shown on and just below Line 6, compares the citizens' proportion of a Success against the Heads of State proportion. In the case of Test 1 that follows, the Heads of State population is specifically the U.S. Presidents. Analysis of the citizens' sample yields a resulting point estimate and a 95% confidence interval.

If the proportion of a Success for Heads of State is within the confidence interval of the citizens' proportion, the text in the box will read "Fail to Reject." This means we see no significant evidence that the citizens' proportion is different from the Heads of State proportion.

If the proportion of a Success for Heads of State falls outside the confidence interval of the citizens' proportion, the text in the box will read "Reject" along with an indication of whether the Heads of State proportion exceeds ("High") or falls short of ("Low") the confidence interval of the citizen population sample. This result means we have identified significant evidence that the citizens' proportion is different from the Heads of State proportion.

Summary of Probabilities - Test 1
AWOI - US Presidents - Level 1

		American Citizens Sample	US Presidents Population
	OVERT (abbreviated event name)		
1.	Total in group	780	45
2.	Event Presentation in Name	35	2
3.	Consequential Event Participants	0	2
4.	Correct Presentation/Participation Matches (Successes)	745	45
5. (1)-(4)	Incorrect Presentation/Participation Matches (Failures)	35	0
	Group-Specific Statistics		
6. (4)/(1)	Probability of a Success	0.9551	1.0000
	95% Confidence lower bound of (6)	0.9406	**Reject (High)**
	95% Confidence upper bound of (6)	0.9697	
	Outcomes Based on Sample Distribution		
7. Pr((4);(1),(6#))	Probability of Population Number of Successes or More		0.1267
8. c((4),(3))	Number of Ways to Select Participants given Number of Successes		990
9. (7)/(8)	Random Probability of Outcome or Better		1.280E-04
10. 1/(9)	or 1 in...		7,814
11. Π(9)	Cumulative Probability		1.280E-04
12. 1/(11)	or 1 in...		7,814
			Test 1 only

In this case, the statistical test indicates "Reject (High)", meaning the proportion of successes for citizens is different than that for the Heads of State population with at least 95% certainty, and that the Heads of State proportion is greater than the citizens' proportion. This will continue to be the case for most of the other tests. An explanation will be offered in situations where this is not the case.

The probabilities on Line 9 represent the likelihood that a random sample of the citizens, of the size shown on Line 1 for the Heads of State, would result in the exact outcome or better, i.e., fewer Failures, if applicable, as shown in the Heads of State population.

Summary of Probabilities - Test 3
AWOI - UK Monarchs - Level 2

		British Citizens Sample	British Monarchs Population
	OVERT (abbreviated event name)		
1.	Total in group	541	11
2.	Event Presentation in Name	44	1
3.	Consequential Event Participants	0	1
4.	Correct Presentation/Participation Matches (Successes)	497	11
5. (1)-(4)	Incorrect Presentation/Participation Matches (Failures)	44	0
	Group-Specific Statistics		
6. (4)/(1)	Probability of a Success	0.9187	1.0000
	95% Confidence lower bound of (6)	0.8956	**Reject**
	95% Confidence upper bound of (6)	0.9417	**(High)**
	Outcomes Based on Sample Distribution		
7. Pr((4);(1),(6#))	Probability of Population Number of Successes or More		0.3933
8. c((4),(3))	Number of Ways to Select Participants given Number of Successes		11
9. (7)/(8)	Random Probability of Outcome or Better		0.0358
10. 1/(9)	or 1 in…		28
11. Π(9)	Cumulative Probability		4.576E-06
12. 1/(11)	or 1 in…		2.185E+05
			Tests 1, 3

The cumulative probability represented by the value on line 11 is for the combination of tests noted on each exhibit below line 12. Where the tests are independent, the probabilities of the individual tests are simply multiplied together. By definition, tests for two different populations (in this case, US Presidents and British Monarchs) are independent. So independence is assumed between tests 1 and 3.

Summary of Probabilities - Test 4
THE CIVIL WAR - US Presidents - Level 1

		American Citizens Sample	US Presidents Population
	COVERT (full spelling event name)		
1.	Total in group	780	41
2.	Event Presentation in Name	10	1
3.	Consequential Event Participants	0	1
4.	Correct Presentation/Participation Matches (Successes)	770	41
5. (1)-(4)	Incorrect Presentation/Participation Matches (Failures)	10	0
	Group-Specific Statistics		
6. (4)/(1)	Probability of a Success	0.9872	1.0000
	95% Confidence lower bound of (6)	0.9793	**Reject**
	95% Confidence upper bound of (6)	0.9951	**(High)**
	Outcomes Based on Sample Distribution		
7. Pr((4);(1),(6#))	Probability of Population Number of Successes or More		0.5892
8. c((4),(3))	Number of Ways to Select Participants given Number of Successes		41
9. (7)/(8)	Random Probability of Outcome or Better		0.0144
10. 1/(9)	or 1 in...		70
11. Π(9)	Cumulative Probability		6.576E-08
12. 1/(11)	or 1 in...		1.521E+07
			Tests 1, 3, 4

Since Test 1 and Test 4 both query the US Presidents, a check for independence between the two tests must also be performed.

Presentation of AWOI at Level 1 and THE CIVIL WAR at Level 1, failed to reject the null hypothesis of independence. For names presenting AWOI at Level 1, no significant difference was seen between that name presenting THE CIVIL WAR or not. Specifically, if a name presented AWOI at Level 1, that name was just 0.5% likely to present THE CIVIL WAR at Level 1. If a name did not present AWOI at Level 1, that name was just 0.6% likely to present THE CIVIL WAR at Level 1. This difference was found to be not statistically significant, resulting in a failure to reject the null hypothesis of independence at the 95% confidence level.

Exhibits showing tests for independence with statistically significant levels of dependency are presented following this section of probability summaries, beginning on page 369.

In the cases suggesting independence, the probabilities of the individual tests are again simply multiplied together. The cumulative probability shown on line 11 is the composite of tests 1, 3 and 4 with the assumption of independence.

Summary of Probabilities - Test 5
THE CIVIL WAR - US Presidents - Level 2

		American Citizens Sample	US Presidents Population
	COVERT (full spelling event name)		
1.	Total in group	780	44
2.	Event Presentation in Name	65	6
3.	Consequential Event Participants	0	6
4.	Correct Presentation/Participation Matches (Successes)	715	44
5. (1)-(4)	Incorrect Presentation/Participation Matches (Failures)	65	0
	Group-Specific Statistics		
6. (4)/(1)	Probability of a Success	0.9167	1.0000
	95% Confidence lower bound of (6)	0.8973	**Reject**
	95% Confidence upper bound of (6)	0.9361	**(High)**
	Outcomes Based on Sample Distribution		
7. Pr((4);(1),(6#))	Probability of Population Number of Successes or More		0.0217
8. c((4),(3))	Number of Ways to Select Participants given Number of Successes		7.059E+06
9. (7)/(8)	Random Probability of Outcome or Better		3.080E-09
10. 1/(9)	or 1 in...		3.247E+08
11. Π(9)	Cumulative Probability		1.409E-14
12. 1/(11)	or 1 in...		7.095E+13
			Tests 1, 3, 5

Test 5 shows the probability of THE CIVIL WAR presentation at Level 2, which is first, middle, and last names. Test 5 is an alternate view of Test 4, so we are not looking to accumulate probabilities between tests 4 and 5. However, since Test 1 and Test 5 both query the US Presidents, a check for independence between the two tests must also be performed.

Presentation of AWOI at Level 1 and THE CIVIL WAR at Level 2, again failed to reject the null hypothesis of independence. The frequency of presentation of THE CIVIL WAR in a name at Level 2 was not significantly different whether the name presented AWOI at Level 1 or not. Specifically, if a name presents AWOI at Level 1, that name is 4.0% likely to present THE CIVIL WAR at Level 2. If a name does not present AWOI at Level 1, that name is 4.6% likely to present THE CIVIL WAR at Level 2. This difference was found to be not statistically significant, resulting in a failure to reject the null hypothesis of independence at the 95% confidence level.

In this case, the cumulative probability includes Test 5 instead of Test 4. Again, independence is suggested, and the probabilities of the individual tests are simply multiplied together. The cumulative probability shown on line 11 is the composite of tests 1, 3 and 5 with the assumption of independence.

Summary of Probabilities - Test 6
THE CIVIL WAR - US Presidents - Level 3

		American Citizens Sample	US Presidents Population
	COVERT (full spelling event name)		
1.	Total in group	780	45
2.	Event Presentation in Name	73	7
3.	Consequential Event Participants	0	7
4.	Correct Presentation/Participation Matches (Successes)	707	45
5. (1)-(4)	Incorrect Presentation/Participation Matches (Failures)	73	0
	Group-Specific Statistics		
6. (4)/(1)	Probability of a Success	0.9064	1.0000
	95% Confidence lower bound of (6)	0.8860	**Reject**
	95% Confidence upper bound of (6)	0.9269	**(High)**
	Outcomes Based on Sample Distribution		
7. Pr((4);(1),(6#))	Probability of Population Number of Successes or More		0.0120
8. c((4),(3))	Number of Ways to Select Participants given Number of Successes		4.538E+07
9. (7)/(8)	Random Probability of Outcome or Better		2.647E-10
10. 1/(9)	or 1 in...		3.778E+09
11. Π(9)	Cumulative Probability		1.211E-15
12. 1/(11)	or 1 in...		8.256E+14
			Tests 1, 3, 6

Test 6 shows the probability of THE CIVIL WAR presentation at Level 3, which is first, middle, and last names plus any name suffix (e.g., Jr., Sr., II). Since Test 6 is an alternate view of Tests 4 and 5, we are not looking to accumulate probabilities between any two (or all three) of these tests. However, since Test 1 and Test 6 both query the US Presidents, a check for independence between the two tests must also be performed.

Presentation of AWOI at Level 1 and THE CIVIL WAR at Level 3, again failed to reject the null hypothesis of independence. The frequency of presentation of THE CIVIL WAR in a name at Level 3 was not significantly different whether the name presented AWOI at Level 1 or not. Specifically, if a name presents AWOI at Level 1, that name is 4.2% likely to present THE CIVIL WAR at Level 3. If a name does not present AWOI at Level 1, that name is 5.4% likely to present THE CIVIL WAR at Level 3. This difference was found to be not statistically significant, resulting in a failure to reject the null hypothesis of independence at the 95% confidence level.

In this case, the cumulative probability includes Test 6 instead of Test 4 or Test 5. Again, independence is suggested, and the probabilities of the individual tests are simply multiplied together. The cumulative probability shown on line 11 is the composite of tests 1, 3 and 6 with the assumption of independence.

Summary of Probabilities - Test 19
WORLD WAR ONE / WWI / WORLD WAR I / FIRST WORLD WAR - US Presidents - Mixed Levels

		American Citizens Sample	US Presidents Population
	COVERT / OVERT / MIXED as appropriate		
1.	Total in group	780	36
2.	Event Presentation in Name	166	7
3.	Consequential Event Participants	0	7
4.	Correct Presentation/Participation Matches (Successes)	614	36
5. (1)-(4)	Incorrect Presentation/Participation Matches (Failures)	166	0
	Group-Specific Statistics		
6. (4)/(1)	Probability of a Success	0.7872	1.0000
	95% Confidence lower bound of (6)	0.7585	**Reject**
	95% Confidence upper bound of (6)	0.8159	**(High)**
	Outcomes Based on Sample Distribution		
7. Pr((4);(1),(6#))	Probability of Population Number of Successes or More		1.814E-04
8. c((4),(3))	Number of Ways to Select Participants given Number of Successes		8.348E+06
9.	Conditional Probability of Outcome or Better		0.9024
10. 1/(9)	or 1 in…		1.11
11. Π(9)	Conditional Cumulative Probability		1.093E-15
12. 1/(11)	or 1 in…		9.148E+14
			Tests 1, 3, 6, 19

Test 19 shows the probability of World War One presentation using any of the four defined criteria. However, since Tests 1, 6, and 19 all query the US Presidents, checks for independence between them must also be performed.

Presentation of AWOI at Level 1 and World War One rejected the null hypothesis of independence. The frequency of presentation of World War One in a name was significantly different between whether the name presented AWOI at Level 1 or not. Specifically, if a name presents AWOI at Level 1, that name is 36.0% likely to present World War One. If a name does not present AWOI at Level 1, that name is 18.3% likely to present World War One. This difference was found to be statistically significant, indicating dependence with greater than 99.9% certainty.

Furthermore, presentation of THE CIVIL WAR at Level 3 and World War One also rejected the null hypothesis of independence. The frequency of presentation of World War One in a name was significantly different between whether the name presented THE CIVIL WAR at Level 3 or not. Specifically, if a name presents THE CIVIL WAR at Level 3, that name is 62.1% likely to present World War One. If a name does not present THE CIVIL WAR at Level 3, that name is 16.4% likely to present World War One. This difference was found to be statistically significant, rejecting the null hypothesis for independence, indicating dependence with greater than 99.9% certainty.

If a name presents both AWOI at Level 1 and THE CIVIL WAR at Level 3, that name is 90.2% likely to present World War One. If a name does not present both AWOI at Level 1 and THE CIVIL WAR at Level 3, that name is 18.7% likely to present World War One. This difference was found to be statistically significant, indicating dependence with greater than 99.9% certainty.

Due to rejection of the null hypotheses for independence, a conditional probability is appropriate here, indicated on line 9. The conditional cumulative probability on line 11 incorporates this value.

Exhibits documenting the tests for independence that show dependency with at least 95% confidence follow this section of probability summaries on page 369. An exhibit showing the test for independence of Tests 1 and 3, versus Test 19, is the first to be shown. Tests for independence were generated from a sample of 30,000 random names representing the general population.

Summary of Probabilities - Test 32
WORLD WAR TWO / WWII / WORLD WAR II / SECOND WORLD WAR - US Presidents - Mixed Levels

		American Citizens Sample	US Presidents Population
	COVERT / OVERT / MIXED as appropriate		
1.	Total in group	780	38
2.	Event Presentation in Name	107	7
3.	Consequential Event Participants	0	6
4.	Correct Presentation/Participation Matches (Successes)	673	37
5. (1)-(4)	Incorrect Presentation/Participation Matches (Failures)	107	1
	Group-Specific Statistics		
6. (4)/(1)	Probability of a Success	0.8628	0.9737
	95% Confidence lower bound of (6)	0.8387	**Reject**
	95% Confidence upper bound of (6)	0.8870	**(High)**
	Outcomes Based on Sample Distribution		
7. Pr((4);(1),(6#))	Probability of Population Number of Successes or More		0.0259
8. c((4),(3))	Number of Ways to Select Participants given Number of Successes		2.325E+06
9.	Conditional Probability of Outcome or Better		0.5502
10. 1/(9)	or 1 in...		1.818
11. Π(9)	Conditional Cumulative Probability		6.014E-16
12. 1/(11)	or 1 in...		1.663E+15
			Tests 1, 3, 6, 19, 32

Test 32 shows the probability of World War Two presentation using any of the four defined criteria. However, since Tests 1, 6, 19, and 32 all query the US Presidents, checks for independence between them must also be performed.

Presentation of AWOI at Level 1 and World War Two rejected the null hypothesis of independence. The frequency of presentation of World War Two in a name was significantly different between whether the name presented AWOI at Level 1 or not. Specifically, if a name presents AWOI at Level 1, that name is 18.1% likely to present World War Two. If a name does not present AWOI at Level 1, that name is 10.5% likely to present World War Two. This difference was found to be statistically significant, indicating dependence with greater than 99.9% certainty.

Furthermore, presentation of THE CIVIL WAR at Level 3 and World War Two also rejected the null hypothesis of independence. The frequency of presentation of World War Two in a name was significantly different between whether the name presented THE CIVIL WAR at Level 3 or not. Specifically, if a name presents THE CIVIL WAR at Level 3, that name is 33.6% likely to present World War Two. If a name does not present THE CIVIL WAR at Level 3, that name is

9.5% likely to present World War Two. This difference was found to be statistically significant, indicating dependence with greater than 99.9% certainty.

Presentation of World War One and World War Two also rejected the null hypothesis of independence. The frequency of presentation of World War Two in a name was significantly different between whether the name presented World War One or not. Specifically, if a name presents World War One, that name is 55.0% likely to present World War Two. If a name does not present World War One, that name is 0.5% likely to present World War Two. This difference was found to be statistically significant, indicating dependence with greater than 99.9% certainty.

If a name presents all of AWOI at Level 1, THE CIVIL WAR at Level 3, and World War One, that name is 43.2% likely to present World War Two. If a name does not present all of AWOI at Level 1, THE CIVIL WAR at Level 3, and World War One, that name is 10.8% likely to present World War Two. This difference was found to be statistically significant, indicating dependence with greater than 99.9% certainty.

Due to rejection of the null hypotheses for independence, a conditional probability is appropriate here, indicated on line 9. The conditional cumulative probability on line 11 incorporates this value.

An exhibit showing the test for independence of Tests 1, 6, and 19, versus Test 32, is presented following this section of probability summaries on page 369.

Summary of Probabilities - Test 37
WORLD WAR ONE / WWI / WORLD WAR I / FIRST WORLD WAR - UK Prime Ministers - Mixed Levels
<= 30 LETTERS

			British Citizens Sample	UK Prime Ministers Population
	COVERT / OVERT / MIXED as appropriate			
1.		Total in group	541	33
2.		Event Presentation in Name	78	6
3.		Consequential Event Participants	0	6
4.		Correct Presentation/Participation Matches (Successes)	463	31
5.	(1)-(4)	Incorrect Presentation/Participation Matches (Failures)	78	2
		Group-Specific Statistics		
6.	(4)/(1)	Probability of a Success	0.8558	0.9394
		95% Confidence lower bound of (6)	0.8262	**Reject**
		95% Confidence upper bound of (6)	0.8854	**(High)**
		Outcomes Based on Sample Distribution		
7.	Pr((4);(1),(6#))	Probability of Population Number of Successes or More		0.1265
8.	c((4),(3))	Number of Ways to Select Participants given Number of Successes		7.363E+05
9.	(7)/(8)	Random Probability of Outcome or Better		1.718E-07
10.	1/(9)	or 1 in…		5.822E+06
11.		Cumulative Probability		1.033E-22
12.	1/(11)	or 1 in…		9.680E+21
				Tests 1, 3, 6, 19, 32, 37

Test 37 shows the results for the presentation of World War One in a name using any of the four defined criteria for the British Prime Minister names with 30 or fewer letters. Since this is a test for a population not yet considered, it is independent of the previous tests. So the cumulative probability here is simply the product of the probability of this test multiplied by the probability of the combination of tests 1, 3, 6, 19, and 32.

Summary of Probabilities - Test 42
WORLD WAR TWO / WWII / WORLD WAR II / SECOND WORLD WAR - UK PMs - Mixed Levels
<= 30 LETTERS

			British Citizens Sample	UK Prime Ministers Population
		COVERT / OVERT / MIXED as appropriate		
1.		Total in group	541	34
2.		Event Presentation in Name	52	3
3.		Consequential Event Participants	0	2
4.		Correct Presentation/Participation Matches (Successes)	489	33
5.	(1)-(4)	Incorrect Presentation/Participation Matches (Failures)	52	1
		Group-Specific Statistics		
6.	(4)/(1)	Probability of a Success	0.9039	0.9706
		95% Confidence lower bound of (6)	0.8790	Reject
		95% Confidence upper bound of (6)	0.9287	(High)
		Outcomes Based on Sample Distribution		
7.	Pr((4);(1),(6#))	Probability of Population Number of Successes or More		0.1486
8.	c((4),(3))	Number of Ways to Select Participants given Number of Successes		528
9.		Conditional Probability of Outcome or Better		0.5500
10.	1/(9)	or 1 in…		2
11.	Π(9)	Conditional Cumulative Probability		5.682E-23
12.	1/(11)	or 1 in…		1.760E+22

Tests 1, 3, 6, 19, 32, 37, 42

Test 42 shows the probability of World War Two presentation using any of the four defined criteria for the British Prime Minister names with 30 or fewer letters, but since Tests 37 and 42 both query the UK PMs, a check for independence between them must also be performed.

Presentation of World War One and World War Two rejected the null hypothesis of independence. The frequency of presentation of World War Two in a name was significantly different between whether the name presented World War One or not. Specifically, if a name presents World War One, that name is 55.0% likely to present World War Two. If a name does not present World War One, that name is 0.5% likely to present World War Two. This difference was found to be statistically significant, indicating dependence with greater than 99.9% certainty.

Due to rejection of the null hypothesis for independence, a conditional probability is appropriate here, indicated on line 9. The conditional cumulative probability on line 11 incorporates this value.

An exhibit showing the test for independence of Test 37 versus Test 42 is presented following this section of probability summaries on page 369.

Summary of Probabilities - Test 47
WORLD WAR ONE / WWI / WORLD WAR I / FIRST WORLD WAR - UK Monarchs - Mixed Levels
<= 30 LETTERS

		British Citizens Sample	British Monarchs Population
	COVERT / OVERT / MIXED as appropriate		
1.	Total in group	541	8
2.	Event Presentation in Name	78	3
3.	Consequential Event Participants	0	2
4.	Correct Presentation/Participation Matches (Successes)	463	7
5. (1)-(4)	Incorrect Presentation/Participation Matches (Failures)	78	1
	Group-Specific Statistics		
6. (4)/(1)	Probability of a Success	0.8558	0.8750
	95% Confidence lower bound of (6)	0.8262	**Fail to**
	95% Confidence upper bound of (6)	0.8854	**Reject**
	Outcomes Based on Sample Distribution		
7. Pr((4);(1),(6#))	Probability of Population Number of Successes or More		0.6756
8. c((4),(3))	Number of Ways to Select Participants given Number of Successes		21
9.	Conditional Probability of Outcome or Better		0.3979
10. 1/(9)	or 1 in...		3
11. Π(9)	Conditional Cumulative Probability		2.261E-23
12. 1/(11)	or 1 in...		4.423E+22
			Tests 1, 3, 6, 19, 32, 37, 42, 47

Test 47 shows the probability of World War One presentation using any of the four defined criteria for the UK Monarch names with 30 or fewer letters, but since Tests 3 and 47 both query the UK Monarchs, a check for independence between the two tests must also be performed.

Presentation of AWOI at Level 2 and World War One rejected the null hypothesis of independence for names with 30 letters or less. The frequency of presentation of World War One in a name was significantly different between whether the name presented AWOI at Level 2 or not. Specifically, if a name presents AWOI at Level 2, that name is 40.6% likely to present World War One. If a name does not present AWOI at Level 2, that name is 17.5% likely to present World War One. This difference was found to be statistically significant, indicating dependence with greater than 99.9% certainty.

Due to rejection of the null hypothesis for independence, a conditional probability is appropriate here, indicated on line 9. The conditional cumulative probability on line 11 incorporates this value.

An exhibit showing the test for independence of Test 3 versus Test 47 is presented following this section of probability summaries on page 369.

Summary of Probabilities - Test 52
WORLD WAR TWO / WWII / WORLD WAR II / SECOND WORLD WAR - UK Monarchs - Mixed Levels
<= 30 LETTERS

		British Citizens Sample	British Monarchs Population
	COVERT / OVERT / MIXED as appropriate		
1.	Total in group	541	8
2.	Event Presentation in Name	52	3
3.	Consequential Event Participants	0	2
4.	Correct Presentation/Participation Matches (Successes)	489	7
5. (1)-(4)	Incorrect Presentation/Participation Matches (Failures)	52	1
	Group-Specific Statistics		
6. (4)/(1)	Probability of a Success	0.9039	0.8750
	95% Confidence lower bound of (6)	0.8790	**Reject (Low)**
	95% Confidence upper bound of (6)	0.9287	
	Outcomes Based on Sample Distribution		
7. Pr((4);(1),(6#))	Probability of Population Number of Successes or More		0.8246
8. c((4),(3))	Number of Ways to Select Participants given Number of Successes		21
9.	Conditional Probability of Outcome or Better		0.5534
10. 1/(9)	or 1 in…		2
11. Π(9)	Conditional Cumulative Probability		1.251E-23
12. 1/(11)	or 1 in…		7.993E+22

Tests 1, 3, 6, 19, 32, 37, 42, 47, 52

Test 52 shows the probability of World War Two presentation using any of the four defined criteria for the UK Monarch names with 30 or fewer letters. However, since Tests 3, 47, and 52 all query the UK Monarchs, checks for independence between them must also be performed.

Presentation of AWOI at Level 2 and World War Two rejected the null hypothesis of independence for names with 30 letters or less. The frequency of presentation of World War Two in a name was significantly different between whether the name presented AWOI at Level 2 or not. Specifically, if a name presents AWOI at Level 2, that name is 23.0% likely to present World War Two. If a name does not present AWOI at Level 2, that name is 10.1% likely to present World War Two. This difference was found to be statistically significant, indicating dependence with greater than 99.9% certainty.

Presentation of World War One and World War Two rejected the null hypothesis of independence for names with 30 letters or less. The frequency of presentation of World War Two in a name was significantly different between whether the name presented World War One or not. Specifically, if a name presents World War One, that name is 55.0% likely to present World War Two. If a name does not present World War One, that name is 0.5% likely to present

World War Two. This difference was found to be statistically significant, indicating dependence with greater than 99.9% certainty.

If a name presents both AWOl and World War One, that name is 55.5% likely to present World War Two. If a name does not present both AWOl and World War One, that name is 9.7% likely to present World War Two. This difference was found to be statistically significant, rejecting the null hypothesis for independence, indicating dependence with greater than 99.9% certainty.

Due to rejection of the null hypotheses for independence, a conditional probability is appropriate here, indicated on line 9. The conditional cumulative probability on line 11 incorporates this value.

An exhibit showing the test for independence of Tests 3 and 47, versus Test 52, is presented following this section of probability summaries on page 370.

Summary of Probabilities - Test 53
HOLOCAUST - German Chancellors - Level 2
<= 33 LETTERS

		German Citizens Sample	German Chancellors Population
	COVERT (full spelling event name)		
1.	Total in group	1,018	32
2.	Event Presentation in Name	94	3
3.	Consequential Event Participants	0	3
4.	Correct Presentation/Participation Matches (Successes)	924	32
5. (1)-(4)	Incorrect Presentation/Participation Matches (Failures)	94	0
	Group-Specific Statistics		
6. (4)/(1)	Probability of a Success	0.9077	1.0000
	95% Confidence lower bound of (6)	0.8899	**Reject**
	95% Confidence upper bound of (6)	0.9254	**(High)**
	Outcomes Based on Sample Distribution		
7. Pr((4);(1),(6#))	Probability of Population Number of Successes or More		0.0450
8. c((4),(3))	Number of Ways to Select Participants given Number of Successes		4,960
9. (7)/(8)	Random Probability of Outcome or Better		9.080E-06
10. 1/(9)	or 1 in...		110,130
11.	Cumulative Probability		1.136E-28
12. 1/(11)	or 1 in...		8.803E+27
			Tests 1, 3, 6, 19, 32, 37, 42, 47, 52, 53

Test 53 shows the results for the COVERT presentation of HOLOCAUST at Level 2, for German Chancellor names with 33 or fewer letters. Since this is a test for a population not yet considered, it is independent of the previous tests. So, the cumulative probability here is simply the product of the probability of this test multiplied by the probability of the combination of tests 1, 3, 6, 19, 32, 37, 42, 47, and 52.

Summary of Probabilities - Test 54
HOLOCAUST - German Chancellors - Level 2
<= 33 LETTERS

		German Citizens Sample	German Chancellors Population
	OVERT (full spelling event name)		
1.	Total in group	1,018	32
2.	Event Presentation in Name	10	2
3.	Consequential Event Participants	0	2
4.	Correct Presentation/Participation Matches (Successes)	1,008	32
5. (1)-(4)	Incorrect Presentation/Participation Matches (Failures)	10	0
	Group-Specific Statistics		
6. (4)/(1)	Probability of a Success	0.9902	1.0000
	95% Confidence lower bound of (6)	0.9841	**Reject**
	95% Confidence upper bound of (6)	0.9962	**(High)**
	Outcomes Based on Sample Distribution		
7. Pr((4);(1),(6#))	Probability of Population Number of Successes or More		0.7291
8. c((4),(3))	Number of Ways to Select Participants given Number of Successes		496
9. (7)/(8)	Random Probability of Outcome or Better		0.0015
10. 1/(9)	or 1 in...		680
11.	Cumulative Probability		1.839E-26
12. 1/(11)	or 1 in...		5.437E+25

Tests 1, 3, 6, 19, 32, 37, 42, 47, 52, 54

Test 54 shows results for the OVERT presentation of HOLOCAUST at Level 2, for German Chancellor names with 33 or fewer letters. Test 53 showed the results with COVERT presentation. Since test 54 is an alternate view of test 53, we are not looking to accumulate probabilities between these two tests. In this case, the cumulative probability includes test 54 instead of test 53. Again, independence is assumed between test 54 and the preceding tests.

Summary of Probabilities - Test 55
DER HOLOCAUST - German Chancellors - Level 1

		German Citizens Sample	German Chancellors Population
	COVERT (full spelling event name)		
1.	Total in group	1,070	37
2.	Event Presentation in Name	2	1
3.	Consequential Event Participants	0	1
4.	Correct Presentation/Participation Matches (Successes)	1,068	37
5. (1)-(4)	Incorrect Presentation/Participation Matches (Failures)	2	0
	Group-Specific Statistics		
6. (4)/(1)	Probability of a Success	0.9981	1.0000
	95% Confidence lower bound of (6)	0.9955	Unable to Perform Test
	95% Confidence upper bound of (6)	1.0007	
	Outcomes Based on Sample Distribution		
7. Pr((4);(1),(6#))	Probability of Population Number of Successes or More		1.0000
8. c((4),(3))	Number of Ways to Select Participants given Number of Successes		37
9. (7)/(8)	Random Probability of Outcome or Better		1.0000
10. 1/(9)	or 1 in...		1
11.	Cumulative Probability		1.251E-23
12. 1/(11)	or 1 in...		7.993E+22

Tests 1, 3, 6, 19, 32, 37, 42, 47, 52

Test 55 shows results for the COVERT presentation of DER HOLOCAUST for German Chancellors at Level 1, first and last names only.

This test shows an "Unable to Perform Test" outcome. Too few event presentations in names were identified in the citizens' sample for this test to be statistically valid. Any random sample of 37 citizens would almost certainly provide 37 successes, thus a 100% probability is shown on lines 7 and 9.

Furthermore, too few presentations were shown in even the 30,000-name list to be used for a formal test of independence. This prevents any change in the cumulative probability to be determined.

The cumulative probability shown here is unchanged from that shown on test 52.

Summary of Probabilities - Test 56
DER HOLOCAUST - German Chancellors - Level 2
<= 33 LETTERS

			German Citizens Sample	German Chancellors Population
		COVERT (full spelling event name)		
1.		Total in group	1,018	32
2.		Event Presentation in Name	79	2
3.		Consequential Event Participants	0	2
4.		Correct Presentation/Participation Matches (Successes)	939	32
5.	(1)-(4)	Incorrect Presentation/Participation Matches (Failures)	79	0
		Group-Specific Statistics		
6.	(4)/(1)	Probability of a Success	0.9224	1.0000
		95% Confidence lower bound of (6)	0.9060	**Reject**
		95% Confidence upper bound of (6)	0.9388	**(High)**
		Outcomes Based on Sample Distribution		
7.	Pr((4);(1),(6#))	Probability of Population Number of Successes or More		0.0754
8.	c((4),(3))	Number of Ways to Select Participants given Number of Successes		496
9.	(7)/(8)	Random Probability of Outcome or Better		1.520E-04
10.	1/(9)	or 1 in…		6,578
11.		Cumulative Probability		1.902E-27
12.	1/(11)	or 1 in…		5.258E+26

Tests 1, 3, 6, 19, 32, 37, 42, 47, 52, 56

Test 56 shows results for the COVERT presentation of DER HOLOCAUST for German Chancellors at Level 2, for only names with 33 or fewer letters. Since test 56 is an alternate view of tests 53 through 55, we are not looking to accumulate probabilities between any of these tests. In this case, the cumulative probability includes test 56 instead of any of tests 53 through 55. Again, independence is assumed between test 56 and the preceding tests.

Summary of Probabilities - Test 57
DER HOLOCAUST - German Chancellors - Level 2

		German Citizens Sample	German Chancellors Population
	OVERT (full spelling event name)		
1.	Total in group	1,070	37
2.	Event Presentation in Name	11	1
3.	Consequential Event Participants	0	1
4.	Correct Presentation/Participation Matches (Successes)	1,059	37
5. (1)-(4)	Incorrect Presentation/Participation Matches (Failures)	11	0
	Group-Specific Statistics		
6. (4)/(1)	Probability of a Success	0.9897	1.0000
	95% Confidence lower bound of (6)	0.9837	**Reject**
	95% Confidence upper bound of (6)	0.9958	**(High)**
	Outcomes Based on Sample Distribution		
7. Pr((4);(1),(6#))	Probability of Population Number of Successes or More		0.6823
8. c((4),(3))	Number of Ways to Select Participants given Number of Successes		37
9. (7)/(8)	Random Probability of Outcome or Better		0.0184
10. 1/(9)	or 1 in…		54
11.	Cumulative Probability		2.307E-25
12. 1/(11)	or 1 in…		4.335E+24

Tests 1, 3, 6, 19, 32, 37, 42, 47, 52, 57

Test 57 shows results for the OVERT presentation of DER HOLOCAUST at Level 2 for German Chancellors. Since test 57 is an alternate view of tests 53 through 56, we are not looking to accumulate probabilities between any of these tests. In this case, the cumulative probability includes test 57 instead of any of tests 53 through 56. Again, independence is assumed between test 57 and the preceding tests.

Summary of Probabilities - Test 58
HOLOCAUST - UK Prime Ministers - Level 2
>= 11 and <= 30 LETTERS

		British Citizens Sample	UK Prime Ministers Population
	COVERT (full spelling event name)		
1.	Total in group	460	40
2.	Event Presentation in Name	22	4
3.	Consequential Event Participants	0	3
4.	Correct Presentation/Participation Matches (Successes)	438	39
5. (1)-(4)	Incorrect Presentation/Participation Matches (Failures)	22	1
	Group-Specific Statistics		
6. (4)/(1)	Probability of a Success	0.9522	0.9750
	95% Confidence lower bound of (6)	0.9327	**Reject**
	95% Confidence upper bound of (6)	0.9717	**(High)**
	Outcomes Based on Sample Distribution		
7. Pr((4);(1),(6#))	Probability of Population Number of Successes or More		0.4237
8. c((4),(3))	Number of Ways to Select Participants given Number of Successes		9,139
9.	Conditional Probability of Outcome or Better		0.0388
10. 1/(9)	or 1 in...		26
11. Π(9)	Conditional Cumulative Probability		4.413E-30
12. 1/(11)	or 1 in...		2.266E+29

Tests 1, 3, 6, 19, 32, 37, 42, 47, 52, 53, 58

Test 58 shows the results for the COVERT presentation of HOLOCAUST at Level 2 for UK Prime Minister names with 11 or more and 30 or fewer letters.

This is the first test to show a "Fail to Reject" outcome. Insufficient evidence was observed to say that the probability of a Success for citizens is different from the UK Prime Ministers population proportion. In a sample of 48 citizens, an outcome matching the UK Prime Ministers population proportion would not be unusual. Interestingly, the only "Fail to Reject" outcomes occur within the DER HOLOCAUST tests.

In addition, since Tests 37, 42 and 58 all query the UK Prime Ministers, a check for independence between them must also be performed.

Presentation of World War One and HOLOCAUST rejected the null hypothesis of independence for names with 11 or more and 30 or fewer letters. The frequency of presentation of HOLOCAUST in a name was significantly different between whether the name presented World War One or not. Specifically, if a name presents World War One, that name is 3.0% likely to present HOLOCAUST. If a name does not present World War One, that name is 1.6% likely to present HOLOCAUST. This difference was found to be statistically significant, indicating dependence with greater than 99.9% certainty.

Furthermore, presentation of World War Two and HOLOCAUST rejected the null hypothesis of independence for names with 11 or more and 30 or fewer letters. The frequency of presentation of HOLOCAUST in a name was significantly different between whether the name presented World War Two or not. Specifically, if a name presents World War Two, that name is 3.9% likely to present HOLOCAUST. If a name does not present World War Two, that name is 1.6% likely to present HOLOCAUST. This difference was found to be statistically significant, indicating dependence with greater than 99.9% certainty.

If a name presents both World War One and World War Two, that name is 3.8% likely to present HOLOCAUST. If a name does not present both World War One and World War Two, that name is 1.6% likely to present HOLOCAUST. This difference was found to be statistically significant, rejecting the null hypothesis for independence, indicating dependence with greater than 99.9% certainty.

Due to rejection of the null hypotheses for independence, a conditional probability is appropriate here, indicated on line 9. The conditional cumulative probability on line 11 incorporates this value.

An exhibit showing the test for independence of Tests 37 and 42, versus Test 58, is presented following this section of probability summaries on page 370.

Summary of Probabilities - Test 61
DER HOLOCAUST - UK Prime Ministers - Level 2
>= 13 and <= 30 LETTERS

		British Citizens Sample	UK Prime Ministers Population
	COVERT (full spelling event name)		
1.	Total in group	362	39
2.	Event Presentation in Name	12	3
3.	Consequential Event Participants	0	2
4.	Correct Presentation/Participation Matches (Successes)	350	38
5. (1)-(4)	Incorrect Presentation/Participation Matches (Failures)	12	1
	Group-Specific Statistics		
6. (4)/(1)	Probability of a Success	0.9669	0.9744
	95% Confidence lower bound of (6)	0.9484	**Fail to**
	95% Confidence upper bound of (6)	0.9853	**Reject**
	Outcomes Based on Sample Distribution		
7. Pr((4);(1),(6#))	Probability of Population Number of Successes or More		0.6276
8. c((4),(3))	Number of Ways to Select Participants given Number of Successes		703
9.	Conditional Probability of Outcome or Better		0.0388
10. 1/(9)	or 1 in…		26
11. Π(9)	Conditional Cumulative Probability		4.413E-30
12. 1/(11)	or 1 in…		2.266E+29

Tests 1, 3, 6, 19, 32, 37, 42, 47, 52, 53, 61

Test 61 shows the results for the COVERT presentation of DER HOLOCAUST at Level 2 for UK Prime Minister names with 13 or more and 30 or fewer letters.

This test shows a "Fail to Reject" outcome. Insufficient evidence was observed to say that the probability of a Success for citizens is different from the UK Prime Ministers population proportion. In a sample of 41 citizens, an outcome matching the UK Prime Ministers population proportion would not be unusual.

In addition, since Tests 37, 42 and 61 all query the UK Prime Ministers, a check for independence between them must also be performed.

Presentation of World War One and DER HOLOCAUST rejected the null hypothesis of independence for names with 13 or more and 30 or fewer letters. The frequency of presentation of DER HOLOCAUST in a name was significantly different between whether the name presented World War One or not. Specifically, if a name presents World War One, that name is 3.0% likely to present DER HOLOCAUST. If a name does not present World War One, that name is 0.8% likely to present DER HOLOCAUST. This difference was found to be statistically significant, rejecting the null hypothesis for independence, indicating dependence with greater than 99.9% certainty.

Furthermore, presentation of World War Two and DER HOLOCAUST rejected the null hypothesis of independence for names with 11 or more and 30 or fewer letters. The frequency of presentation of DER HOLOCAUST in a name was significantly different between whether the name presented World War Two or not. Specifically, if a name presents World War Two, that name is 3.9% likely to present DER HOLOCAUST. If a name does not present World War Two, that name is 1.0% likely to present DER HOLOCAUST. This difference was found to be statistically significant, indicating dependence with greater than 99.9% certainty.

If a name presents both World War One and World War Two, that name is 3.8% likely to present DER HOLOCAUST. If a name does not present both World War One and World War Two, that name is 1.0% likely to present DER HOLOCAUST. This difference was found to be statistically significant, rejecting the null hypothesis for independence, indicating dependence with greater than 99.9% certainty.

Since test 61 is an alternate view of test 58, we are not looking to accumulate probabilities between these two tests. Due to rejection of the null hypotheses for independence between this and earlier tests, a conditional probability is appropriate here, indicated on line 9. The conditional cumulative probability on line 11 incorporates this value.

An exhibit showing the test for independence of Tests 37 and 42, versus Test 61, is presented following this section of probability summaries on page 370.

Summary of Probabilities - Test 62
DER HOLOCAUST - UK Prime Ministers - Level 2

		British Citizens Sample	UK Prime Ministers Population
	OVERT (full spelling event name)		
1.	Total in group	541	43
2.	Event Presentation in Name	0	1
3.	Consequential Event Participants	0	1
4.	Correct Presentation/Participation Matches (Successes)	541	43
5. (1)-(4)	Incorrect Presentation/Participation Matches (Failures)	0	0
	Group-Specific Statistics		
6. (4)/(1)	Probability of a Success	1.0000	1.0000
	95% Confidence lower bound of (6)	1.0000	**Unable to Perform Test**
	95% Confidence upper bound of (6)	1.0000	
	Outcomes Based on Sample Distribution		
7. Pr((4);(1),(6#))	Probability of Population Number of Successes or More		1.0000
8. c((4),(3))	Number of Ways to Select Participants given Number of Successes		43
9.	Conditional Probability of Outcome or Better		1.0000
10. 1/(9)	or 1 in…		1
11. Π(9)	Conditional Cumulative Probability		1.136E-28
12. 1/(11)	or 1 in…		8.803E+27
			Tests 1, 3, 6, 19, 32, 37, 42, 47, 52, 53

Test 62 shows results for the OVERT presentation of DER HOLOCAUST at Level 2 for UK Prime Ministers.

This test shows an "Unable to Perform Test" outcome. Too few event presentations were identified in the citizens' population sample for this test to be statistically valid. Any random sample of 54 citizens would almost certainly provide 54 successes, thus a 100% probability is shown on lines 7 and 9.

Furthermore, too few presentations were shown in even the 30,000-name list to be used for a formal test of independence. This prevents any change in the cumulative probability to be determined.

The cumulative probability shown here is unchanged from that shown on test 53.

Summary of Probabilities - Test 63
HOLOCAUST - UK Monarchs - Level 2

			British Citizens Sample	UK Monarchs Population
		COVERT (full spelling event name)		
1.		Total in group	541	12
2.		Event Presentation in Name	22	1
3.		Consequential Event Participants	0	1
4.		Correct Presentation/Participation Matches (Successes)	519	12
5.	(1)-(4)	Incorrect Presentation/Participation Matches (Failures)	22	0
		Group-Specific Statistics		
6.	(4)/(1)	Probability of a Success	0.9593	1.0000
		95% Confidence lower bound of (6)	0.9427	Reject
		95% Confidence upper bound of (6)	0.9760	(High)
		Outcomes Based on Sample Distribution		
7.	Pr((4);(1),(6#))	Probability of Population Number of Successes or More		0.6076
8.	c((4),(3))	Number of Ways to Select Participants given Number of Successes		12
9.		Conditional Probability of Outcome or Better		0.0402
10.	1/(9)	or 1 in...		25
11.	Π(9)	Conditional Cumulative Probability		1.775E-31
12.	1/(11)	or 1 in...		5.635E+30

Tests 1, 3, 6, 19, 32, 37, 42, 47, 52, 53, 58, 63

Test 63 shows the results for the presentation of HOLOCAUST in the name of a UK Monarch. However, since Tests 3, 47, 52, and 63 all query the UK Monarchs, a check for independence between them must also be performed.

Presentation of AWOI and HOLOCAUST rejected the null hypothesis of independence. The frequency of presentation of HOLOCAUST in a name was significantly different between whether the name presented AWOI or not. Specifically, if a name presents AWOI, that name is 2.5% likely to present HOLOCAUST. If a name does not present AWOI, that name is 1.7% likely to present HOLOCAUST. This difference was found to be statistically significant, indicating dependence with greater than 99.9% certainty.

Presentation of World War One and HOLOCAUST rejected the null hypothesis of independence. The frequency of presentation of HOLOCAUST in a name was significantly different between whether the name presents World War One or not. Specifically, if a name presents World War One, that name is 3.0% likely to present HOLOCAUST. If a name does not present World War One, that name is 1.4% likely to present HOLOCAUST. This difference was found to be statistically significant, indicating dependence with greater than 99.9% certainty.

Furthermore, presentation of World War Two and HOLOCAUST rejected the null hypothesis of independence. The frequency of presentation of HOLOCAUST in a name was significantly different between whether the name presented World War Two or not. Specifically, if a name presents World War Two, that name is 3.9% likely to present HOLOCAUST. If a name does not present World War Two, that name is 1.4% likely to present HOLOCAUST. This difference was found to be statistically significant, indicating dependence with greater than 99.9% certainty.

If a name presents all of AWOI, World War One, and World War Two, that name is 3.9% likely to present HOLOCAUST. If a name does not present all of AWOI, World War One, and World War Two, that name is 1.7% likely to present HOLOCAUST. This difference was found to be statistically significant, rejecting the null hypothesis for independence, indicating dependence with greater than 99.9% certainty.

Due to rejection of the null hypotheses for independence between this and earlier tests, a conditional probability is appropriate here, indicated on line 9. The conditional cumulative probability on line 11 incorporates this value.

An exhibit showing the test for independence of Tests 3, 47, and 52, versus Test 63, is presented following this section of probability summaries on page 371.

Summary of Probabilities - Test 64
DER HOLOCAUST - UK Monarchs - Level 2

		British Citizens Sample	UK Monarchs Population
	COVERT (full spelling event name)		
1.	Total in group	541	12
2.	Event Presentation in Name	12	1
3.	Consequential Event Participants	0	1
4.	Correct Presentation/Participation Matches (Successes)	529	12
5. (1)-(4)	Incorrect Presentation/Participation Matches (Failures)	12	0
	Group-Specific Statistics		
6. (4)/(1)	Probability of a Success	0.9778	1.0000
	95% Confidence lower bound of (6)	0.9654	Reject
	95% Confidence upper bound of (6)	0.9902	(High)
	Outcomes Based on Sample Distribution		
7. Pr((4);(1),(6#))	Probability of Population Number of Successes or More		0.7640
8. c((4),(3))	Number of Ways to Select Participants given Number of Successes		12
9.	Conditional Probability of Outcome or Better		0.0389
10. 1/(9)	or 1 in...		26
11. Π(9)	Conditional Cumulative Probability		1.715E-31
12. 1/(11)	or 1 in...		5.830E+30

Tests 1, 3, 6, 19, 32, 37, 42, 47, 52, 53, 58, 64

Test 64 shows the results for the presentation of DER HOLOCAUST in the name of a UK Monarch.

Since Tests 3, 47, 52, and 64 all query the UK Monarchs, a check for independence between them must also be performed. Results of the tests for independence were mixed between this and earlier tests.

Presentation of AWOI and DER HOLOCAUST failed to reject the null hypothesis of independence. The frequency of presentation of DER HOLOCAUST in a name was not significantly different between whether the name presented AWOI or not. Specifically, if a name presents AWOI, that name is 1.5% likely to present DER HOLOCAUST. If a name does not present AWOI, that name is 1.0% likely to present DER HOLOCAUST. This difference was found to be not statistically significant, resulting in a failure to reject the null hypothesis of independence at the 95% confidence level.

Presentation of World War One and DER HOLOCAUST rejected the null hypothesis of independence. The frequency of presentation of DER HOLOCAUST in a name was significantly different between whether the name presents World War One or not. Specifically, if a name presents World War One, that name is 3.0% likely to present DER HOLOCAUST. If a name does not present World War One, that name is 0.6% likely to present DER HOLOCAUST. This difference was found to be statistically significant, indicating dependence with greater than 99.9% certainty.

Furthermore, presentation of World War Two and DER HOLOCAUST rejected the null hypothesis of independence. The frequency of presentation of DER HOLOCAUST in a name was significantly different between whether the name presented World War Two or not. Specifically, if a name presents World War Two, that name is 3.9% likely to present DER HOLOCAUST. If a name does not present World War Two, that name is 0.7% likely to present DER HOLOCAUST. This difference was found to be statistically significant, indicating dependence with greater than 99.9% certainty.

If a name presents all of AWOI, World War One, and World War Two, that name is 3.9% likely to present DER HOLOCAUST. If a name does not present all of AWOI, World War One, and World War Two, that name is 1.0% likely to present DER HOLOCAUST. This difference was found to be statistically significant, rejecting the null hypothesis for independence, indicating dependence with greater than 99.9% certainty.

Due to rejection of the null hypotheses for independence between this and earlier tests, a conditional probability is appropriate here, indicated on line 9. The conditional cumulative probability on line 11 incorporates this value.

An exhibit showing the test for independence of Tests 3, 47, and 52, versus Test 64, is presented following this section of probability summaries on page 371.

Independence Tests that showed statistically significant levels of dependence

WWI Mixed Levels (Test 19) versus AWOI Level 1 (Test 1) and THECIVILWAR Level 3 (Test 6)

		test 1 Yes	test 1 No	
test 19	Yes	347	5,304	**5,651**
	No	618	23,731	**24,349**
		965	**29,035**	**30,000**
		36.0%	18.3%	
		p-value:	1.7E-43	

		test 6 Yes	test 6 No	
test 19	Yes	1,002	4,649	**5,651**
	No	611	23,738	**24,349**
		1,613	**28,387**	**30,000**
		62.1%	16.4%	
		p-value:	0 *	

		tests 1 AND 6 Yes	tests 1 AND 6 No	
test 19	Yes	37	5,614	**5,651**
	No	4	24,345	**24,349**
		41	**29,959**	**30,000**
		90.2%	18.7%	
		p-value:	0 *	

WWII Mixed Levels (Tests 32/42) versus AWOI Level 1 (Test 1) THECIVILWAR Level 3 (Test 6) and WWI Mixed Levels (Test 19/37)

		test 1 Yes	test 1 No	
tests 32/42	Yes	175	3,063	**3,238**
	No	790	25,972	**26,762**
		965	**29,035**	**30,000**
		18.1%	10.5%	
		p-value:	8E-14	

		test 6 Yes	test 6 No	
tests 32/42	Yes	542	2,696	**3,238**
	No	1,071	25,691	**26,762**
		1,613	**28,387**	**30,000**
		33.6%	9.5%	
		p-value:	3E-202	

		tests 19/37 Yes	tests 19/37 No	
tests 32/42	Yes	3,107	131	**3,238**
	No	2,544	24,218	**26,762**
		5,651	**24,349**	**30,000**
		55.0%	0.5%	
		p-value:	0 *	

		tests 1, 6, and 19/37 Yes	tests 1, 6, and 19/37 No	
tests 32/42	Yes	16	3,222	**3,238**
	No	21	26,741	**26,762**
		37	**29,963**	**30,000**
		43.2%	10.8%	
		p-value:	2E-10	

AWOI Level 2 (Test 3) versus WWI Mixed Levels (Test 47)

		test 3 Yes	test 3 No	
test 47	Yes	688	4,961	**5,649**
	No	1,006	23,340	**24,346**
		1,694	**28,301**	**30,000**
		40.6%	17.5%	
		p-value:	3E-123	

		test 3		
		Yes	No	
	test 52 Yes	390	2,848	**3,238**
	No	1,304	25,458	**26,762**
		1,694	**28,306**	**30,000**

WWII Mixed Levels (Test 52)
versus
AWOI Level 2 (Test 3) and
WWI Mixed Levels (Test 47)

23.0%   10.1%
p-value: 1.1E-62

		test 47		
		Yes	No	
	test 52 Yes	3,107	131	**3,238**
	No	2,544	24,218	**26,762**
		5,651	**24,349**	**30,000**

55.0%   0.5%
p-value: 0 *

		tests 3 AND 47		
		Yes	No	
	test 52 Yes	382	2,856	**3,238**
	No	306	26,456	**26,762**
		688	**29,312**	**30,000**

55.5%   9.7%
p-value: 0 *

---

		tests 19/37		
		Yes	No	
	test 58 Yes	169	341	**510**
	No	5,482	21,155	**26,637**
		5,651	**21,496**	**27,147**

HOLOCAUST Level 2 (Test 58)
versus
WWI Mixed Levels (Test 19/37) and
WWII Mixed Levels (Tests 32/42)

3.0%   1.6%
p-value: 4.6E-12

		tests 32/42		
		Yes	No	
	test 58 Yes	125	385	**510**
	No	3,113	23,524	**26,637**
		3,238	**23,909**	**27,147**

3.9%   1.6%
p-value: 8.7E-19

		tests 19/37 AND 32/42		
		Yes	No	
	test 58 Yes	117	393	**510**
	No	2,986	23,651	**26,637**
		3,103	**24,044**	**27,147**

3.8%   1.6%
p-value: 1.6E-16

---

		tests 19/37		
		Yes	No	
	test 61 Yes	169	139	**308**
	No	5,482	16,665	**22,147**
		5,651	**16,804**	**22,455**

DERHOLOCAUST Level 2 (Test 61)
versus
WWI Mixed Levels (Test 19/37) and
WWII Mixed Levels (Tests 32/42)

3.0%   0.8%
p-value: 1.1E-33

		tests 32/42		
		Yes	No	
	test 61 Yes	125	183	**308**
	No	3,113	19,034	**22,147**
		3,238	**19,217**	**22,455**

3.9%   1.0%
p-value: 1.5E-39

		tests 19/37 AND 32/42		
		Yes	No	
	test 61 Yes	117	191	**308**
	No	2,956	19,191	**22,147**
		3,073	**19,382**	**22,455**

3.8%   1.0%
p-value: 7.9E-36

HOLOCAUST Level 2 (Test 63) versus AWOI Level 2 (Test 3), WWI Mixed Levels (Test 47) and WWII Mixed Levels (Test 52)

		test 3		
		Yes	No	
test 63	Yes	42	469	**511**
	No	1,653	27,836	**29,489**
		1,695	**28,305**	**30,000**
		2.5%	1.7%	
			p-value:	2.9E-31

		test 47		
		Yes	No	
test 63	Yes	169	342	**511**
	No	5,480	24,009	**29,489**
		5,649	**24,351**	**30,000**
		3.0%	1.4%	
			p-value:	1.7E-31

		test 52		
		Yes	No	
test 63	Yes	125	386	**511**
	No	3,111	26,378	**29,489**
		3,236	**26,764**	**30,000**
		3.9%	1.4%	
			p-value:	9.3E-37

		tests 3, 47, AND 52		
		Yes	No	
test 63	Yes	15	496	**511**
	No	367	29,122	**29,489**
		382	**29,618**	**30,000**
		3.9%	1.7%	
			p-value:	1.4E-31

DERHOLOCAUST Level 2 (Test 64) versus AWOI Level 2 (Test 3), WWI Mixed Levels (Test 47) and WWII Mixed Levels (Test 52)

		test 3		
		Yes	No	
test 64	Yes	25	283	**308**
	No	1,670	28,022	**29,692**
		1,695	**28,305**	**30,000**
		1.5%	1.0%	
			p-value:	0.05945

		test 47		
		Yes	No	
test 64	Yes	169	139	**308**
	No	5,480	24,212	**29,692**
		5,649	**24,351**	**30,000**
		3.0%	0.6%	
			p-value:	1.8E-59

		test 52		
		Yes	No	
test 64	Yes	125	183	**308**
	No	3,111	26,581	**29,692**
		3,236	**26,764**	**30,000**
		3.9%	0.7%	
			p-value:	2.1E-64

		tests 3, 47, AND 52		
		Yes	No	
test 64	Yes	15	293	**308**
	No	367	29,325	**29,692**
		382	**29,618**	**30,000**
		3.9%	1.0%	
			p-value:	1.5E-05

* While not absolutely zero, these values are infinitesimly small.

Name Length	Count	WWI	Presentation	WWII	Presentation
4	1	-	0%	-	0%
5	3	-	0%	-	0%
6	19	-	0%	-	0%
7	67	-	0%	-	0%
8	320	-	0%	-	0%
9	833	1	0%	-	0%
10	1,605	12	1%	2	0%
11	2,099	42	2%	5	0%
12	2,593	109	4%	25	1%
13	2,510	153	6%	39	2%
14	2,414	231	10%	75	3%
15	2,350	327	14%	118	5%
16	2,730	478	18%	215	8%
17	2,830	659	23%	331	12%
18	2,744	796	29%	436	16%
19	2,341	765	33%	480	21%
20	1,716	655	38%	440	26%
21	1,175	545	46%	389	33%
22	696	323	46%	242	35%
23	406	217	53%	175	43%
24	229	142	62%	112	49%
25	136	81	60%	59	43%
26	72	52	72%	40	56%
27	52	29	56%	26	50%
28	25	15	60%	12	48%
29	21	15	71%	13	62%
30	8	2	25%	2	25%
31	3	1	33%	1	33%
32	1	-	0%	-	0%
33	1	1	100%	1	100%

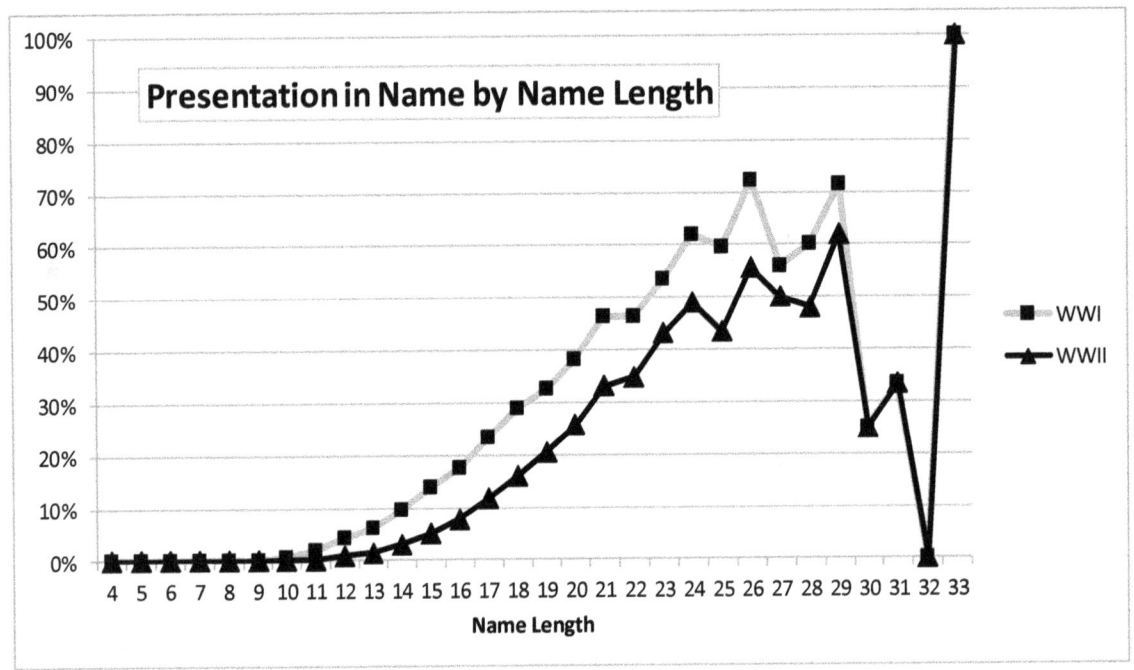